Critical Acclaim for **Best Dives' Snorkeling Adventures**

"From Hawaii's Molokini crater to the Bahamas Pelican Cays Land & Sea Park, **Best Dives' Snorkeling Adventures** *details the best places to see underwater life without strapping on a scuba tank..."*
Elaine Glusac, *American Way Magazine*

"Pack this one in your dive bag. . .Every chapter is packed with clear, factual information on everything from snorkeling sites to travel planning.
Brenda Fine, *Travel Holiday Magazine*

"...opens a new world of adventure to anyone with a mask and snorkel."
Pat Reilly, *Commerce Magazine*

" . . .We'd found getting a comprehensive and honest guide to the best [snorkeling] sites akin to searching for pirate's treasure—that is, until now. This terrific book will be packed along with our gear for all of our future snorkeling adventures."
Echo and Kevin Garett, *The Caribbean for Dummies (IDG Books)*

"A terrific vacation planner! Don't leave home without it."
Ken Liggett, Underwater Sports of NJ

"It's super!. . .a great reference and we love it."
Splash Dive-Travel Newsletter

" . .Clear, concise and extraordinarily informative. . .essential for the serious or beginning snorkeler"
Elizabeth Krystyniak, Travel Network

PhotoGraphics Publishing

23 Cool Water Court
Palm Coast, Florida 32137

Website: www.gobestdives.com
Orders: www.bookch.com
1-386-246-3672, fax 1-386-445-7365
Orders 1-800-431-1579 www.bookch.com

ISBN 0-9643844-4-2

3rd Edition © 2004 Joyce Huber, Jon Huber, Claudia Sammartino

Every effort has been made to ensure that information in this book is correct, but the publisher and authors do not assume, and hereby disclaim, any liability to any party for loss or damage caused by errors, omission, misleading information or potential problems caused by information in this guide, even if these are a result of negligence, accident or any other cause.

Cover and Back Cover Photos

Front cover photo Grand Bahama © 2004 Stephen Frink
Back cover Photos:
Top: Grand Bahama, Alexa Frink swimming with Dolphin
   ©2004 Stephen Frink
Sally Lightfoot Crab © 2004 Marc Bernardi, Aquatic Encounters
Sea Lion © 2004 Marc Bernardi, Aquatic Encounters
Xcaret Tour Bus, courtesy of Xcaret, Mexico Tourism

Map Illustrations © 2004 Joyce Huber

Best Dives'
Snorkeling
Adventures

3rd Edition

Joyce Huber, Jon Huber & Claudia Sammartino

Starfish Ratings

Snorkeling sites throughout the guide have been rated with from one to five starfish by prominent guides of each destination.

☆☆☆☆☆ Five Starfish

Best of the best for snorkeling — best marine life, best visibility and water clarity under normal weather conditions, best shipwreck or reef dive

☆☆☆☆ Four Starfish

Fantastic dive. Outstanding for marine life or visual interest

☆☆☆ Three Starfish

Superb dive. Excellent visibility and marine life or wreck

☆☆ Two Starfish

Good Dive. Interesting fish and plant life or corals; good visibility

☆ One Starfish

Pleasant dive. Something special

Table of Contents

Snorkeling, Swimming and Free Diving Basics · · · · · · · · · · 1

Do's and Don'ts · 5
Underwater Photography · · · · · · · · · · · · · · · · · · 6

Adventure Destinations
Aruba · 7
Bahamas · 13
Barbados · 39
Belize · 43
Bermuda · 54
Bonaire · 63
British Virgin Islands · · · · · · · · · · · · · · · · · · · 72
Cayman Islands · 83
Cozumel and the Yucatan · · · · · · · · · · · · · · · · · 97
Curaçao · 105
Dominica · 110
Florida Keys · 114
Florida Springs · 133
Guadeloupe · 137
Hawaii · 141
Honduras, The Bay Islands · · · · · · · · · · · · · · · · 155
Puerto Rico · 161
Saba · 165
St. Eustatius · 173
St. Lucia · 177
Turks & Caicos · 180
United States Virgin Islands · · · · · · · · · · · · · · · · 189

Extreme Adventure Destinations
Australia · 202
Galapagos · 206

Helpful Information
Sharks · 213
First Aid for Sea Stings and Coral Cuts · · · · · · · · · · 215

Acknowledgments

The authors wish to thank all of *Best Dives' Snorkeling Adventures'* contributors, correspondents, photographers and researchers for their effort and enthusiasm in preparing this guide.

Special thanks to Marc Bernardi, Aquatic Encounters; Maria Shaw, Christopher Lofting, Anita, Ken, Amanda and Neil Liggett; Richard Ockelman; Mina and Bill Heuslein; Grant St. Claire, JoAnn and Jonathan Pannaman, Alvin Jackson, Joe Giacinto, Mark Padover, Rick Sammon, Myrna Bush, Karen and Dennis Sabo, Mike Emmanuel, Lucy Portlock, Michael Young, Efra Figueroa, James Abbott, James and Nadia Spencer, Joan Bourque, Michelle Pugh, Francois Fournier, John Mazurowski and Catherine Van Kampen, BVI Tourism.

Author's Note

Snorkelers of all ages, interests and athletic abilities helped create *Best Dives' Snorkeling Adventures*. With their help, this guide includes something for *everyone, from protected lagoons with easy beach entry to open-water adventures and offbeat destinations.*

Destination chapters cover the top snorkeling spots in the Bahamas, Caribbean, Florida, Hawaii, Turks and Caicos Islands, Galapagos Islands and Australia. If we missed your favorite spot and you wish to share it with other in the next edition, e-mail us at bestdives@aol.com or write to the publisher's address on the back cover.

Visit our website www.gobestdives.com for additional products, travel specials and snorkeling information.

Snorkel Swimming and Free Diving

The Basics

Anyone in average health who can swim, don a mask and peer beneath the waters surface can easily master snorkeling. Its low-impact aerobic and a great way to keep fit. Once considered a macho endeavor, it has evolved into a family affair with fish-watching and photography the main focus.

Everyone finds his or her own skill level and degree of interest. Some relish floating on the surface (snorkel-swimming) while others work at being able to dive 30 feet or more below the surface (free diving or breath-hold diving). Some prefer beach locations, others enjoy exploring from a boat.

Like any sport, the more you do it, the better you get at it. One salty, Florida Keys dive boat captain, growing impatient with two scuba divers who were lingering over a wreck below, surprised the pair by snorkeling down 50 ft and tapping one on the shoulder, a reminder to surface.

Sightseeing Tours

A great variety of snorkeling trips and activities are offered throughout the tropics. Choices vary from sail-snorkel trips on shallow-draft catamarans or trimarans, glass-bottom-boat tours, snorkel-with-dolphins tours, snorkel-shelling tours, snorkel-picnic excursions, sunset-snorkel sails, snorkel-ship wreck-archaeological tours, snorkel-kayaking trips and learn-to-sail- and-snorkel vacations. One south Florida boat captain offers marriage ceremonies (with champagne and caviar included) while snorkeling. with your choice of wild dolphins or reef fish. Variations on the sport such as snuba, offered on St. John, USVI and a few other spots, offers a cross between scuba and snorkeling; or helmet diving, popular in Bermuda and the Bahamas, with surface-supplied air that fills a helmet worn while you walk the ocean floor.

Marked underwater trails have been popping up in the USVI, Bahamas, Bermuda and Turks and Caicos. These are reef areas marked with signs identifying corals and other marine life.

Portions of this chapter are excerpted with permission from Scubapro's *Snorkel Swimming and Breath Hold Diving* or *Snorkeling*.

Equipment

The best place to buy snorkeling equipment is at your local dive shop or specialty retailer. Many resorts and cruise ships will loan or rent you gear and very often it is of good quality. But rental rates can soar as high as $30 per hour for a mask and snorkel. Or, loan-out equipment may be worn or unavailable in your size. This is especially true for children. In comparison to the frustration you may encounter by renting, the cost of purchase is minimal. The basic equipment is a face mask and a snorkel. Fins and a safety vest are a good idea for all but ultra-shallow shoreline snorkeling.

Masks

Snorkelers who wear eyeglasses can select from masks that hold optically corrected lenses or specially ground face plates. Contact lenses may be worn with any non-prescription face masks although you risk losing them to the sea. Swimmer's goggles should *never* be used for breath-hold diving. Your nose must be included inside the air space to equalize pressure.

Snorkeling guide, Anita Liggett
Photo © 2004 Jon Huber

Ill-fitting, poor quality masks often leak or rip and can quickly sour you on the sport. To check for a proper fit hold the mask on your face just by inhaling without using the strap. Brush stray hair from your face. A mask that fits properly will not leak air or fall off. Most important, it should feel comfortable. Do not buy a mask that you cannot try on in the store. If you buy mail-order make sure you can return it, if desired.

If you wear a mustache, expect difficulty in getting a good seal. If shaving is out of the question, try a bit of Vaseline or suntan lotion on your face around the area where the mask seals. Some masks feature purge valves which allow you to easily clear them of water and others have nose-gripping devices to assist in equalizing pressure in your ears should you choose to dive down for a closer look. Whether to buy an oval or rectangular mask, one with three viewing ports or just a front plate is a matter of personal preference and comfort. Human faces come in a variety of shapes and sizes and, fortunately, so do masks. Be sure to try on several before you select.

Snorkels

Snorkels should be well fitting too. The mouthpiece should be easy to grip and fit comfortably. The size of the barrel should be commensurate with the size of the diver. Some top-of-the-line snorkels are equipped with a purge valve which is intended to help you clear water from the snorkel. These are more costly than the standard non-purge snorkels. To some divers these are considered a fad and to others a valued invention. Either will work. We prefer simple j-shaped snorkels because they are less fragile to transport. Oceanic's dry snorkels, available in dive shops, are terrific for beginners.

Masks and snorkels are made of rubber or silicone. It is important that you purchase both mask and snorkel of the same material or the rubber will discolor the silicone over time. Silicone has a softer feel and is more comfortable for prolonged use. The new colorful designer masks, fins and snorkels are a mix of thermoplastics and silicone. The choice is a matter of budget, comfort and personal preference. Rubber is less expensive and still the choice of many divers. Hypo-allergenic silicone is available for sensitive gums. Mouthpieces can be molded to fit your teeth for ultimate fit and comfort. Average cost for a good quality mask is $70, a snorkel, $25. Decent fins range from $40 to more than $100. If you cant find a dive shop, mail-order companies such as Performance Diver or L. L. Bean sell masks, fins and snorkels. Most of the ultra-cheap masks and snorkels sold in pool-supply stores or beach shops are not suitable for extended use in the ocean.

Fins

Swim fins increase swimming efficiency so much that arm strokes can be completely eliminated. Like a good mask and snorkel, quality fins will last many years. A proper fit is critical since poorly fitting fins will soon raise blisters and chafe your skin. Good dive retailers are trained to help you select the right sized fins. Flexible foot pocket fins which slip on like shoes are preferred for snorkeling. Those with very stiff, long blades will give you added speed and thrust and a good workout, but they require strong leg muscles. If you snorkel in cold water consider open back fins which are worn with a wet suit boot.

Anti-Fog Solutions

We hear from many folks that their masks fogged up and they couldn't see a thing. In fact, unless you use an anti-fog compound, condensation of exhaled moisture from your nose or evaporation from the skin will fog your face mask. To prevent this, first scour the inside of the glass plate with toothpaste(we like Colgate). Then, before each dive moisten the face plate with anti-fog compounds. In a pinch you can rub saliva on the faceplate, but you'll find the commercial products, available in dive shops, far superior.

Snorkeling Lessons

An hour in a pool with a pro will teach you all you need to learn about snorkel swimming. Most dive shops offer lessons. You may also want to pick up a copy

Stinging Corals and Marine Animals

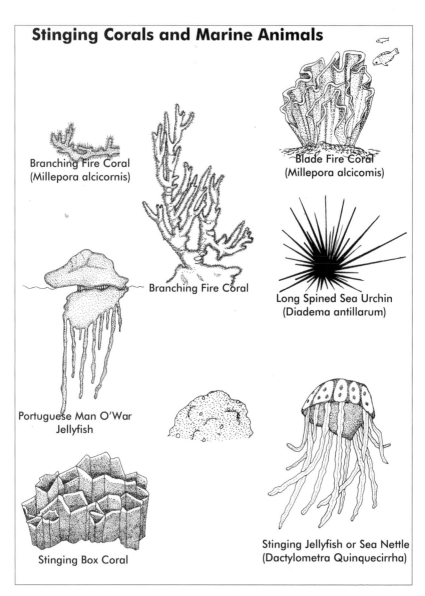

Branching Fire Coral
(Millepora alcicornis)

Blade Fire Coral
(Millepora alcicomis)

Branching Fire Coral

Long Spined Sea Urchin
(Diadema antillarum)

Portuguese Man O'War
Jellyfish

Stinging Jellyfish or Sea Nettle
(Dactylometra Quinquecirrha)

Stinging Box Coral

of Scubapro's *Snorkel Swimming and Breath Hold Diving or Snorkeling*, available in dive shops, or Snorkeling for Kids of All Ages, which can be ordered from NAUI, P.O. Box 14650, Montclair, CA 91763.

Dos and Don'ts

This chapter cannot cover every possible risk, but you may be assured that few snorkel swimmers ever have serious problems. Common sense and the basic rule of *look but don't touch* will take care of most worries.

We recommend that first-time snorkelers sign up for a guided tour with a pro-dive instructor. In addition the following may be helpful: * Never dive alone. *Always dive with a dependable buddy. *Snorkel during daylight hours only. *Check the local water conditions, tides and current. Attempts to swim against currents that exceed one knot will produce severe fatigue. Most resort area dive tour operators are familiar with local sea conditions and can offer suggestions on favorable spots.

When anchored in open water, trail a buoyed safety line at least 100 ft long over the stern of the boat. Avoid snorkeling in shipping lanes or heavy traffic areas. Be sure to display a divers flag to alert other boaters to stay clear of your area. Until you know what you're doing avoid handling marine life and corals. Coral skeletons are often razor sharp and can inflict deep painful wounds.

Galapagos Seahorse
Photo © Marc Bernardi,
Aquatic Encounters

Touching or sitting on corals is outlawed in many marine sanctuaries. Fire coral will give you a painful sting, as will jellyfish or sea urchins, when touched. Never poke your hand into holes, caves or crevices; toothy moray eels and some poisonous fish camouflage themselves and hide in coral and holes. Some venomous creatures to watch out for are the stonefish, the lionfish, the cone shell (Pacific), the Portuguese Man-O-War and the fireworm.

Avoid snorkeling in shallow surges especially over coral or rocks, since you can easily be tossed onto them by an incoming wave. Avoid wearing shiny dangling jewelry. Although exploring a kelp garden, shipwreck or coral reef is fascinating, you can enlarge your underwater outlook by learning about marine life. Once you are able to distinguish the good guys from the no-touch-ems you'll have fun hand feeding many species of fish. To get in the proper frame of mind pick up a waterproof pictorial fish book or laminated fish I.D. card. These are available dive shops or at www.gobestdives.com.

Sunburn

Sunburn is often the biggest villain the snorkeler has to contend with. A thin layer of water covering your back will make you feel deceptively cool but offer no protection from the suns harmful rays, you can be painfully burned on days when the sun is not visible. Snorkelers should wear long pants and a long-sleeved shirt or a long-sleeved lycra wetskin. At the very least wear a tee shirt. Seek out tour boats with canopies.

Precautions: Avoid exposure when taking medicines that increase sun sensitivity. Use sun block lotion with a protection factor of at least 15, wear sunglasses that block UV rays, select hats with a wide brim. Wear protective clothing of fabrics made to block the suns UV rays.

Underwater Photography

Most dive shops rent video and still cameras, some digital, usually equipped with built-in flash. For best results, shoot when the sun is high in the sky, with the hours between 10 am and 2 pm ideal. Try getting dramatic angles by diving down and angling the camera slightly up. We recommend keeping the camera attached to your wrist with a string or strap. Get in close (three ft.) for diver portraits. The more distance you allow between you and your subject the more free floating particles or snow is illuminated by your flash. Be careful not to stir up silty or sandy bottoms.

Getting cooperative fish to pose for your pictures is easy; just bring along some dried aquarium fish food or bread crumbs and sprinkle some where you want fish. Avoid carrying bloody bait fish which might attract hungry sharks. Tapping on rocks attracts fish too.

Cruises and Package Tours

Oceanic Society Expeditions feature educational snorkeling vacations to several destinations ☎ 800-326-7491 or 415-441-1106, fax 415-474-3395.

Caradonna Caribbean Tours features air/hotel packages from the U.S.. Snorkeling tours are available for some destinations ☎ 800-328-2288. E-mail: sales@caradonna.com. Website: caradonna. com.

Landfall Productions offers hassle-free, money-saving tours to most areas. ☎ 800-525-3833. Website: www.landfallproductions.com.

Neal Watsons Undersea Adventures serves the Bahamas, Bonaire, Dominican Republic, St. Lucia and Mexico. ☎ 1-800-327-8150 . E-mail: nealwatson@aol.com. Website: www.nealwatson.com.

PADI Travel Network offers special rates to destinations in this guide and worldwide. Specify that you are a snorkeler. ☎ 1-800-729-7234. E-mail: ptn1@padi.com. Website: www.padi.com.

Tropical Adventures books dive tours to the Caribbean, Cozumel and exotic destinations. ☎ 1-800-247-3483 fax 206-441-5431.

Aruba

If return visitors are the best testimony to an island's popularity, Aruba wins top prize. Each day the island's local paper fronts a group photo of ten-time returnees.

Lying well outside the hurricane belt, Aruba is a popular choice for snorkeling year round. Very low humidity and an average annual rainfall of only 20 inches eliminates freshwater runoff on the reefs—hence dependably good visibility. Easy to reach, this popular island sits just 18 miles from Venezuela's coast. And, at 20 miles long and six miles wide, it's easy to explore, both above and below the sea. Resorts and most tourist activity centers are located along its western (leeward) coast—minutes from popular reefs and wrecks. The shops and sights of the capital, Oranjestad, are nearby too.

Coral beds fringe the shore—many close enough to swim to—but attempting to find the channels and cuts through the extreme shallow reefs may be futile without a local guide. Thus, access to Aruba's best snorkeling sites is easiest by joining a snorkeling cruise that may be booked through the hotel desks or dive shops listed in this chapter.

If you opt for beach snorkeling, note that all of Aruba's beaches are open to the public except for a narrow strip (directly behind the private homes) that is

Snorkeling Sites

1. Arashi Marine Park
2. Wreck of the *Antilla*
3. Malmok
4. Harbour Reef
5. Barcadera Reef
6. Mike Reef
7. Mangel Halto Reef
8. Isla de Oro Reef

off limits. Homeowners have a sign marking where their back yard ends and the public beach begins.

Best Snorkeling Sites of Aruba

The best beach snorkeling from the mainland is off Malmok. Get there by driving north from Palm Beach along L.G. Smith Boulevard, the main coast road. There is usually a snorkeling boat moored offshore which makes it easy to spot, or, if you look straight out to sea, you'll spot the top of the *Antilla*. Park anywhere and walk down to the beach. Swim out from the shore about 10 ft to the rocks where you'll find hordes of small reef fish. Beware the spiny urchins hiding in the rocks. Always calm. Good for children.

☆☆ **Arashi**, a rocky reef offshore to the lighthouse at the northwest corner of the island, delights novice divers and snorkelers with throngs of juvenile fish, elkhorn and brain corals. Visibility is always 60 ft or better. Depths range from the shallows to 40 ft. Nice! Seas are calm with an occasional light surge. Boat access. Good for novice snorkelers.

☆☆ **Arashi Airplanes** denotes a twin-engine Beech- craft at 35 ft and a Lockheed Lodestar at 60 ft—both pur- posely scuttled to create an artificial reef. Visibility is good enough to see the Beechcraft from the surface. Both wrecks are broken up. Small fish inhabit the fuselages. Boat access.

☆☆☆☆☆ Just south of Blue Reef sits one of Aruba's most unusual sights and most popular dives, the wreck of the 400-ft, German freighter, **Antilla.** The ship was scuttled when new in 1940, when Germany invaded Holland.

Locally referred to as the "ghost ship," it is covered by tube sponges and brilliant orange cup corals. Her twisted, rusting steelwork extends upward from the main section to above the surface. The remains of the hull are home to angelfish, moray eels and throngs of silversides. Schools of yellowtail and sergeant majors sway with the gentle current. The wreck lies about a mile offshore, north of Palm Beach in 60 ft of water. Visibility is between 50 and 70 ft. Snorkelers can enjoy the wreck from the usually-calm surface or try free diving around the upper sections of the wreck.

☆☆ **Barcadera Reef,** four miles south of Oranjestad, ranges from 20 to 90 ft. Excellent for snorkelers, the reef supports dense stands of elk horn and staghorn corals, plate and finger corals, home to blue chromis, protective damselfish, wrasses, scorpion fish, blue and stoplight parrot fish and French angels. The reef lies 600 yards from the shoreline at Bacadera Harbor. Join a boat tour for this site, corals are too dense for shore access.

☆☆☆ **Mangel Halto** ("tall mangrove"), three-fourths of a mile south of Barcadera Harbor, can be reached by swimming out from the Mangel Halto Beach for 120 yards, but it's easier from a boat. The reef slopes from 15 ft to ledges and ridges at depth. Fish life includes copper sweepers, grunts, sergeant majors, and butterfly fish.

DePalm Island

First-time snorkelers (of all heights) will find waist-high snorkeling outside of DePalm Island, located one-quarter

Arashi Airplane wreck
Copyright 2004 Jon Huber

mile offshore from Aruba's Water & Electricity Plant—four miles south of Oranjestad along L.G. Smith Boulevard. A ferry to DePalm leaves the mainland every half-hour.

Snorkelers are immediately greeted by a dozen or more two-ft blue parrot fish looking for a handout. These fish meet you at the dock stairs and will leap up out of the water to eat offerings of bread or whatever munchies you tote. Feed with caution, they have sharp teeth!

More adventurous snorkelers swim out about 30 yards to find a dense coral reef, which gets more interesting the further out you swim. The reef supports an abundance of fish—blue tangs, blue and stoplight parrot fish, triggerfish, sergeant majors, yellowtail and grunts. Snorkeling depths run four ft to 15 ft.

Facilities on DePalm Island include an open-air bar and grill, showers, changing facilities and an equipment rental shack. The bar sells fish food for a small fee.

Sonesta Island

Sonesta Island, a watersports outpost owned by Sonesta Resorts at Seaport Village, is reached by a short shuttle boat ride. Guests of the Sonesta may use the island for free. Others pay $50 for the day, which includes the shuttle to and from the resort, lunch, and one cocktail.

Coupons for the island are sold in the Sonesta lobby. Snorkeling gear, rented on the island by Red Sail Sports (☎ (011) 297-586-1603) costs $10 for

a day's use (with a credit card guarantee as deposit). Island facilities include a dive shop, beach restaurant, air-conditioned fitness center. Three separate beaches cater to families or adults (topless), with a special cove for honeymooners, divers, and snorkelers.

☆☆☆ **South Airplanes**, just beyond the breakwater of the Sonesta Island main beach, is the site of two vintage twin- engine, aircraft wrecks — a Beechcraft 18 and a Convair 400, both unclaimed drug runners.

Snorkelers can see the Beechcraft, which sits in 15 ft of water, from the surface. Normally calm with one to two foot swells and a mild current.

☆ **The Barge**, in 12 ft of water lying about 100 yards off Sonesta Islands main beach, makes a fun snorkeling spot. Crowds of fish swarm the wreckage. Usually calm with a one- to two-ft swell and light current. Check with the dive shop for current conditions. Swimming and snorkeling outside the protected lagoon is not recommended for small children.

Aruba Snorkeling Tours

Most snorkeling tours include use of gear. Sail-snorkel cruises are offered by **DePalm Tours**, ☎ 582-4400/4545, Web: www.depalm.com; **Red Sail Sports** ☎ 586-1603, Web: www.redsail aruba.com; Pelican Tours ☎ 587-2302. www.pelican-aruba.com; **Mi Dushi** ☎ 586-2010. Website: www.midushi. com; and **Wave Dancer,** ☎ 297-582-5520. Website: www .arubawave dancer.com.

Red Sail and Pelican are full-service shops. Pelican is located on Palm Beach behind the Holiday Inn and offers gear rentals and sail-snorkeling tours.

© 2004 Jon Huber

Red Sail Sports four catamarans set sail for morning snorkeling, sunset and dinner cruises. Red Sail is on the beach between the Americana Aruba Beach Resort and the Hyatt. They are also on Sonesta Island and have a shop in Seaport Village.

Where to Stay on Aruba

Aruba's resorts fall into two main areas—high rise and low rise. The low-rise hotels are near town and the Seaport Village, a mall packed with beautiful shops and trendy waterfront restaurants. The high-rise resorts to the north are nearer to Malmok and the lighthouse. Most offer money-saving meal packages with vouchers that allow you to dine at other restaurants.

For a full list of accommodations on Aruba, contact the Aruba Tourism Authority, 1000 Harbor Boulevard, Ground Level, Weehawken, NJ 07086, ☎ 800-862-7822, 1-201-330-0800. E-mail: ata.newjersey@aruba.com Website: www.aruba.com, or Aruba Tourism Authority, P.O. Box 1015, L.G. Smith Blvd. 172, Eagle, Aruba, ☎ 800-TO-ARUBA; (011) 297-582-3777, Fax (011) 297-583-4702.

Bucuti Beach Resort, in the low-rise section, features a beautiful beach, 63 comfortable guest rooms, unique pirate-style restaurant, pool, on-site car rental and activity desk. ☎ 800-344-1212, (011) 297-583-1100, fax (011) 297-582-5272. E-mail: bucuti@setarnet.aw. Website: www.bucuti.com

Best Western Manchebo Beach Hotel, adjacent to the Bucuti Beach Resort, offers 72 clean, modern rooms, a beautiful beach, restaurant, cable TV, phones, safes and fridges. ☎ 800-223-1108, (011) 297-582-3444. E-mail: info@manchebo.com. Website: www.manchebo.com.

Holiday Inn Aruba Beach Resort & Casino, in the high-rise Palm Beach area, offers 600 guest rooms, four restaurants, palm-lined beach and all amenities. Adjacent Pelican Watersports has a huge catamaran that takes off for all the best snorkeling spots from the Holiday Inn docks. E-mail: reservations@sunspree-aruba.com. Website: www.sunspree-aruba.com. ☎ 800-HOLIDAY, (011) 297-586-3600.

Aruba Sonesta Beach Resort, a stunning 556-room hotel at Seaport village, sits amidst 120 shops, restaurants, casinos, cafes and entertainment facilities. A free- to-guests shuttle boat departs the hotel lobby for Sonesta Island Watersports Center. ☎ 800-SONESTA.

Additional Information:

In the U.S.: Aruba Tourism Authority, 1000 Harbor Boulevard, Ground Level, Weehawken, NJ 07086, ☎ 800-862-7822,

1-201-330-0800, fax 201-330-8757. E-mail: ata.newjersey@aruba.com Website: www.aruba.com. In Aruba: Aruba Tourism Authority, P.O. Box 1015, L.G. Smith Blvd. 172, Eagle, Aruba, ☎ 800-TO-ARUBA; (011) 297-582-3777, Fax (011) 297-583-4702.

Photo © Jean Michel Cousteau's Out Islands Snorkeling Adventures

Bahamas

Scattered across the Tropic of Cancer between Florida and Cuba, the Bahamas offer expert and novice snorkelers virtually every type of underwater adventure imaginable from dives on finely structured coral reefs to sunken galleons, underwater movie sets, submerged freighters, trains, barges and some of the best shallow, snorkeling gardens in the world. Subsea walls and cuts between and around the islands form a bustling highway for turtles, dolphins, mantas and migrating whales.

The islands top two extensive barrier reefs the Little and Great Bahama Banks. Nourished by the Gulf Stream to the west and the Antilles Current from the southeast, these extensive banks create a diverse marine habitat. Thriving coral communities, in turn, support every imaginable tropical fish and marine invertebrate including the largest population of spiny lobster in the world and the native Nassau grouper.

Three general vacation areas offer their own special delights—New Providence Island with submerged movie sets, and dazzling casinos; Grand Bahama Island, with Freeport, the second largest city, and the Under Water Explorers Society (UNEXSO); and the Family Islands, also called the Out Islands, with tranquil settings, silky beaches, miles of unexplored reefs, Robinson-Crusoe-style hideaways and village-type resorts. The Out Islands also offer outstanding beach-entry snorkeling sites.

Traditionally the Bahamas high season, from mid December through mid April, offers the best weather and sea conditions for snorkeling. Its second season encompasses the rest of the year and is known as Goombay Summer, a period when hotel rates may drop as much as 50 percent.

May through mid November brings frequent showers and a chance of hurricanes with heaviest rainfall during June, July and October, though showers are often brief. Some resorts close down from September till mid November.

NEW PROVIDENCE ISLAND

New Providence Island, home to Nassau, the Bahamas capital is also the locale for two world-class resort areas—Cable Beach and Paradise Island. Reefs surrounding the island have been used as sub-sea settings for Disney's *20,000 Leagues Beneath the Sea, Splash, Cocoon*, and the James Bond thrillers, *Thunderball, Never Say Never, For Your Eyes Only*, and *Jaws IV*. Shallow reefs and wrecks entertain thousands of snorkelers each year.

Best Snorkeling Sites of New Providence

All New Providence reefs and wrecks are boat access. Dive shops cater to scuba divers, but will take snorkelers along if space is available.

☆☆☆ **Thunderball Reef**, named for the James Bond film, is a beautiful shallow reef on the north coast of New Providence, a short boat ride from Athol Island. Visibility is exceptional and photo opportunities abound with surrounding clusters of pastel tube sponges, branching gorgonians, feather corals, pink-tipped anemones, brain, staghorn, and elkhorn corals. Friendly grouper and French angels determined to find a handout will follow you around. Spiny lobsters and small critters hide in the crevices. Sea conditions are usually calm with little or no current. Depths range from 10 to 35 ft.

☆☆ **Southwest Reef**, a wall dive encompassing several other dives, has depths from 15 to 30 ft. Sunken aircraft, small wrecks, and a profuse fish population await. Gigantic southern stingrays bury themselves in the sandy plateaus.

☆☆ **Gouldings Cay,** a tiny island located off the west end of New Providence, shelters a very pretty coral reef which was used as the setting in the films, Cocoon, Never Say Never, 20,000 Leagues Under the Sea and Splash. The area encompasses several acres and offers shallow snorkeling sites. Eagle rays, turtles, old wreck sections, schools of tropicals, morays, and acres of elkhorn coral make this area a prime site.

Blue Lagoon Island (aka Salt Cay)

Fast ferry service to Blue Lagoon Island (242-363-1000), a small watersports and picnic island located approximately one-half mile from Paradise Island in Nassau, is provided by Nassau Cruise and Ferry Service from Paradise Island. Watersports programs, (listed below) on the island are also offered by Nassau Cruise and Ferry ☎ 242-363-3577 or 242-363-1653. Email: info@dolphin encounters.com. Boats depart the Paradise Island Ferry Terminal at 8:30 am, 10:30 am, 1:30 pm and 3:30 pm.

☆☆ **Stingray City** on Blue Lagoon Island is surrounded by a three-acre marine park, home to grouper, moray eels, crawfish, barracuda and a group of affectionate southern stingrays who will eagerly rub up against you looking for a treat. *Brutus*, the largest female at Stingray City is the favorite. She stands out because she has no tail, a mishap she encountered in the wild. She arrived one day with an old rusty fish hook in her mouth which she allowed one of the staff members to remove and has been an endearing presence ever since.

☆☆☆ **Dolphin Encounters** at Blue Lagoon offers a Swim-With-The-Dolphins Program that includes a lengthy learn-about-dolphin session that allows you to get close up, followed by a half-hour swim. The entire trip takes approximately two hours including the boat ride to and from Blue Lagoon Island and the educational lecture. ☎800-327-1584 or 242-327-5066.

New Providence Snorkeling Tours & Rentals

Stuart Coves Dive South Ocean, located at the South Ocean Resort offers snorkeling trips aboard a custom, roomy boat, the *Zambezi* and new "sub" tours, which are sort of self-contained underwater motorcycles with a large two-foot clear dome over your head—no scuba or snorkeling experience needed. They offer gear rentals and sales. Snorkeling trips visit shallow reefs with depths between 15 and 40 ft. Pick up from cruise ships and all major resorts. ☎ 800-879-9832 or 242-362-4171, fax 954-524-5925. Write to: P.O. Box CB-13137, Nassau, Bahamas. E-mail: info@ stuartcove.com. Website: www.stuartcove.com.

Nassau Scuba Centre caters primarily to scuba divers, but will take snorkelers along if space on the boat is available. Nearby Chub Cay is the favorite shore-snorkeling spot. ☎ 800-327-8150 or 242-362-1964. E-mail: info@ divenassau.com. Website: www.divenassau.com

Dive, Dive, Dive ☎ 800-368-3483. Website: www.divedivedive.com. Snorkelers accompany scuba divers on tours.

Where to Stay on New Providence Island

South Ocean Golf, Beach & Dive Resort features 250 guest rooms, two pools, a 1500-ft beach, golf course, tennis, restaurants . The on-premise dive shop entertains snorkelers with reef and wreck tours and sailing. Baby sitting. The resort sits four miles from the airport. ☎ 800-879-9832 or 954-524-5755, fax 954-524-5924.

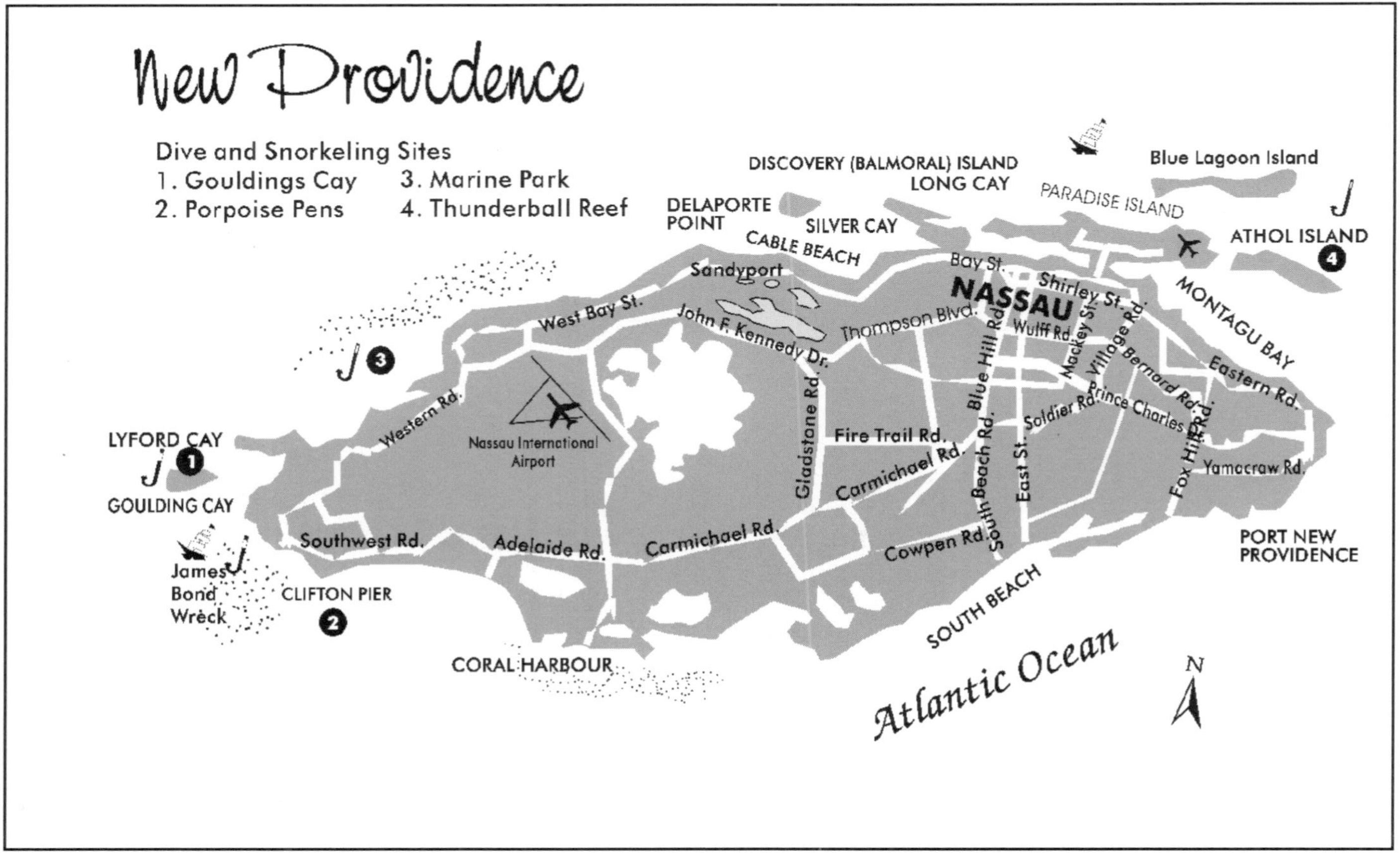

New Providence

Dive and Snorkeling Sites

1. Gouldings Cay   3. Marine Park
2. Porpoise Pens   4. Thunderball Reef

LYFORD CAY
GOULDING CAY
James Bond Wreck
CLIFTON PIER
CORAL HARBOUR
Southwest Rd.
Western Rd.
Nassau International Airport
Adelaide Rd.
West Bay St.
Carmichael Rd.
Sandyport
John F. Kennedy Dr.
Gladstone Rd.
Fire Trail Rd.
Carmichael Rd.
Cowpen Rd.
Thompson Blvd.
Blue Hill Rd.
Bay St.
NASSAU
Mackey St.
Shirley St.
Village Rd.
Wulff Rd.
East St.
Prince Charles
Soldier
South Beach Rd.
South Beach
Bernard Rd.
Fox Hill Rd.
Eastern Rd.
Yamacraw Rd.
MONTAGU BAY
PORT NEW PROVIDENCE

CABLE BEACH
SILVER CAY
DELAPORTE POINT
DISCOVERY (BALMORAL) ISLAND
LONG CAY
PARADISE ISLAND
Blue Lagoon Island
ATHOL ISLAND

Atlantic Ocean

N

The Dig, Atlantis Resort, Paradise Island

Photo © 2004, Atlantis Resort

Nassau Beach Hotel offers all-inclusive or super saver packages. The 411-room resort sits on Cable Beach near the center of town, 20 minutes from dive boat docks. Rooms have A©, phone, cable TV, six restaurants, golf course next door.☎ 888-627-7282 or 242-327-7711, fax 242-327-8829. Web: www.nassaubeachhotel.com. Email: info@nassaubeachhotel.com.

Atlantis, Paradise Island, hosts more than 5,000 guests in three, plush accommodations—the Royal Towers, Coral Towers and Beach Tower. Visitors enjoy a seven-acre snorkeling lagoon stocked with tropical fish and more than 40 waterfalls and fountains. An assortment of exhibit lagoons and underwater formations display 200 species of marine life, consisting of 50,000 live animals , two pools, 35 restaurants, bars and lounges and a full-service dive shop. ☎ 800-321-3000 or 242-363-3000, fax 242-363-3524.

Sandals Royal Bahamian Resort & Spa on Cable Beach features eight gourmet restaurants, seven pools, 406 guest rooms, a private off-shore island, a water sports complex, and The Spa. Snorkeling trips are included in their all-inclusive rates ☎ 888-SANDALS or 242-327-6400, fax 242-327-6961. Website: www.sandals.com.

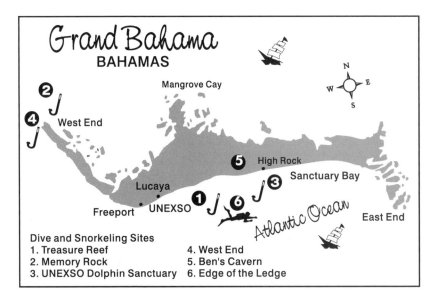

Grand Bahama
BAHAMAS

Mangrove Cay

West End

High Rock

Sanctuary Bay

Lucaya

Freeport   UNEXSO

East End

Atlantic Ocean

Dive and Snorkeling Sites
1. Treasure Reef
2. Memory Rock
3. UNEXSO Dolphin Sanctuary
4. West End
5. Ben's Cavern
6. Edge of the Ledge

GRAND BAHAMA

Grand Bahama Island, the locale of Treasure Reef where over a million dollars worth of treasure was discovered in 1962, is home port to the Underwater Explorers Society (UNEXSO) in Freeport/Lucaya.

UNEXSOs Dolphin Swims

UNEXSO no longer offers snorkeling trips, but their Dolphin Dive Experience provides plenty of time with the dolphins, unique photo opportunities and the opportunity to talk one-on-one with the trainers. The program includes an open-ocean training session (weather permitting) where you'll watch as leaping dolphins follow your boat about mile off shore. The boat stops in an area where you'll be able to meet and interact with dolphins. After this open-ocean training session, you'll return to The Dolphin Experience for a Swim With Dolphins in the private natural environment of their 9 acre lagoon. During your dolphin swim, you will have the opportunity to learn hand signals and the dolphins will perform trained behaviors for you..

Minimum height requirement is 55 (4 ft. 7 in.) and children under 16 must be accompanied by a participating parent or guardian. Not advised for pregnant women. ☎ 800-992-DIVE (3483). E-Mail: info@unexso.com. Website: www.unexso.com

Best Snorkeling Sites of Grand Bahama

The Gulf Stream passes through many of the best snorkeling sites around the island, providing visibility that can exceed 200 ft at times. Shore diving exists off West End and at Paradise Cove. Good for all skill levels.

☆☆ **Treasure Reef**, the site where more than $2.4 million in Spanish Treasure was discovered in the 1960s, provides habitat to large schools of grunts, snapper, goatfish, and sergeant majors. Depths from four to 15 ft.

☆☆ **Memory Rock** offers a look at spectacular brain, pillar and star coral formations. Expect friendly fish and calm seas.

☆☆☆ **Deadmans Reef** at Paradise Cove shelters hordes of fish and corals at shallow depths. Beach and boat access. Resort shop at the cove rents equipment and offers tours.

☆☆☆☆ **West End** has seven new snorkeling trails on the ocean and bay side that feature a shipwreck, walls of fish and lush corals. Beach entry. Check with the on-site dive shop for conditions.

Where to Stay on Grand Bahama

For a list of all Grand Bahama resorts visit www.grand-bahama.com.

Xanadu Beach Resort & Marina, once the home of Howard Hughes, sits on the southwest coast of the island featuring two restaurants, tennis courts, a dive center, 77-slip marina, baby sitting, and huge beach. ☎ 242-352-6782, fax 242-352-5799. Website: xanadubeachhotel.com. Email: info@xanadu beach hotel.com.

Paradise Watersports, located at the Xanadu Beach Resort and Marina (☎ 242/352-2887), offers snorkeling trips aboard a 48-ft. catamaran.

Port Lucaya Resort & Yacht Club, adjacent to the Port Lucaya Market-place, sports ten low-rise buildings that encircle a huge, lush garden and fresh-water pool, restaurant, and 50 slip marina. First floor guest rooms have private patios overlooking gardens or pool area. Second floor rooms have balconies that overlook a huge marina. Book Dolphin swims with UNEXSO at the resort desk. ☎ 800-582-2921 direct, 242-373-6618. Website: portlucayaresort.com. E-mail: vacation@coralwave.com.

The Inn at Old Bahama Bay, located off the beaten trail at West End, features 49 spacious, beach- front suites, seven pristine snorkeling trails across ship- wrecks and coral reefs, two accessible from their beach. The Old Bahama Bay snorkel program guides offer a different underwater site for every day of the week that will challenge veteran and novice snorkeler alike.

Old Bahama Bay Resort, West End, Grand Bahama Island

Settlement Point Reef is heavily populated with colorful coral and hundreds of fish - its unusual to see this type of lush reef in shallow waters. ***Sea Fan Gardens*** is another excellent shallow site, which contains hundreds of colorful sea fans and a variety of tropical fish. ***North Beach*** explores the unique ecosystem of Little Bahama Bank, with its rich undersea grasslands — it is also home to many juvenile fish. ***Indian Cay Trail*** (¼ mile by boat) crisscrosses the shallow areas south of Indian Cay, from the center of the Cay to its eastern end. Excellent fish life and small varieties of coral are present. Sheltered snorkeling area, gorgeous beach, pool, café, sea kayak rentals, dive shop. Guest rooms have every amenity. ☎ 800-572-5711. Website: www.old bahamabay.com.

Paradise Cove Beach Resort, off the beaten trail, offers low-cost apartments and cottages; fine, beachfront snorkeling on ***Deadmans Reef***, glass-bottom kayaks, snack bar, sunset bonfires, secluded beach. All units have a full kitchen and bath, with AC, TV, and VCR. ☎ 242-349-2677, Website: www.deadmansreef.com.

THE OUT ISLANDS

Twenty six resorts offer **Jean-Michel Cousteau's Bahama Out Islands Snorkeling Adventures,** which entail guided reef excursions with pro instructors. Participating resorts are listed under each island description.

ABACO

The Abaco Islands, the northern most group in the Bahamas, stretch south 130 miles from Walkers Cay to Great Abaco. There are two main islands,

Great Abaco and Little Abaco flanked by hundreds of smaller cays. Marsh Harbour is centrally located on Great Abaco. Cars, scooters and bicycles are readily available for rent to explore north or south. Scheduled ferry service runs to the outer cays. Boat rentals are also available. Although Marsh Harbour is the third largest town in the Bahamas, it has only one traffic light! Virtually everything is within

View from Old Bahama Bay

walking distance bars, restaurants, boutiques, grocery and liquor stores.

Best Snorkeling Sites of Abaco

☆ **Charlies Canyons** just 10 minutes from Walkers Cay by boat, is decked with ancient cannons, anchors and fish-filled crevices in 25ft of water. Friendly Nassau grouped, wide-eyed squirrelfish, octopi and schools of French grunts reside in the canyons.

☆☆ to the west lies **Travel Agent Reef**, a perfect for new snorkelers, with a stunning coral garden at depths from five to 10 feet.

☆☆ **North of Tom Browns**, another Walkers Cay site, is a beautiful dive through shallow coral gardens colored with delicate vase sponges and a multitude of reef fish. Depths average 25 ft.

☆☆☆ Prime shallow reefs off **Great Guana Cay** sit 50 ft from the white-sand beach off the closed Guana Beach Resort.

☆☆☆☆ Shallow reefs, populated by every imaginable fish and critter, sit 30 ft out from the shoreline at Hopetown.

☆☆☆☆☆ To the south lies *Pelican Cay National Park*, a 2,000-acre maze of coral tunnels, walls, pinnacles littered with the remains of modern and ancient wrecks. Shallow reef depths range from breaking the surface to about 30 ft. Spectacular marine life includes eagle rays, jacks, angels, huge groupers, and colorful sponges.

☆☆☆ *The USS Adirondack*, a Federal-era battleship, rests in 30 ft of water. Snorkelers exploring the twisted remains of its superstructure might catch a peek at the green moray that lives in one of the old cannons. Hordes of fish inhabit the wreck.

Abaco Snorkeling Tours & Rentals

Dive Abaco, at the Conch Inn Marina, offers reef trips daily at 9:30 am E-mail: dive@diveabaco.com.Website: www.diveabaco.com. Packages with Pelican Beach Villas.☎ 242-367-3600,

Brendals Dive Shop at the Green Turtle Club has two trips daily, rentals, and courses. ☎ 242-359-6226. E-mail: brendal@oii.net. Website: www. brendal.com

Abaco Snorkeling Program Participating Hotels

Abaco Inn, Hope Town, Elbow Cay offers guests eight one-bedroom suites with kitchenettes, private deck, one two-bedroom suite with two baths & kitchenette. The informal club house lounge serves elegant dinners, tropical lunch with a view of the breaking surf. ☎ 800-468-8799 or 242-366-0133, fax 242-366-0113. E- mail: info@abacoinn.com.

Bluff House Resort & Yacht Club, Green Turtle Cay features air-conditioned, suites, deluxe rooms and villas, two restaurants (Historic Main Clubhouse or New Jolly Roger Bar and Bistro), two bars, tennis court,two freshwater pools and a secluded beach. ☎ 800-745-4911or 242-365-4248. Website: www. bluff house.com. bluffhouse@oii.net

The Abaco Beach Resort & Boat Harbour in Marsh Harbour features 76 oceanfront rooms and six two-bedroom cottages The resort harbour has 200 protected slips. Snorkeling trips arranged with Dive Abaco. Web: www. abacoresort com. ☎ 800-468-4799.

Green Turtle Club, Green Turtle Cay, featured on *Lifestyles of the Rich and Famous* offers 32 air-conditioned, pool-side rooms and waterfront villas, each with a patio, ceiling fans and fridge. Boaters enjoy the club's 40-slip, full-service marina . To get there, fly into Treasure Cay Airport (TCB), take a taxi to the ferry dock , then a ferry to Green Turtle Cay's dock. ☎800-688-4752 x417. Web: www.greenturtleclub.com. E-mail: info@ greenturtleclub.com.

Pelican Beach Villas, Marsh Harbour, on a private peninsula with its own beach and 100-foot dock, offers beachfront villas adjacent to Mermaid Reef (nice snorkeling) and the Jib Room Restaurant/Marina. Six villas with tropical furnishing, cable TV, phones, kitchen with dishwasher, house keeping; sleeps up to five. ☎ 800-642-7268; local 242-367-3600. Website: www.pelican beachvillas.com.

Guana Seaside Village, Guana Cay features seven miles of secluded ocean beach. A 50-ft swim from shore brings you over a barrier reef lush with lavender

Rainbow Lighthouse, Elbow Cay, Abaco

sea fans and soft corals. Lots of fish. Guests stay in simple rooms or cottages. ☎ 877-681-3091; direct 242-365-5106. Website: www.guanaseaside.com

Hope Town Harbour Lodge rents 20 newly renovated rooms, each with air conditioning, ceiling fans, and spacious deck. A section of barrier reef lies 20 ft off the inn's lovely two-mile-long beach. With rare exception, its calm and no currents. ☎ 800-316-7844 or 242-366-0095.. E-mail: harbourlodge@ abacoinet.com. Website: www.hopetownlodge.com.   Fly into Marsh Harbour Airport (MHH), take a taxi to the ferry dock, then the ferry to Hope Town's dock.

Getting There

American Eagle, US Airways Express, Continental Connections, Air Sunshine, Island Express and Bel Air Transport serve the area from Florida. There are three airports in the Abacos, Walkers Cay in the north, Treasure Cay in the middle and the largest at Marsh Harbour to the south. Visitors to the Abacos may also take the mail boats, from Potters Cay Dock in Nassau. Contact the dock master in Nassau at ☎ 242-362-4391 for departure times. Schedules subject to weather conditions. Individual resorts may offer private charter flights from Miami or Fort Lauderdale.

ANDROS

Andros, the largest of the Bahama islands, stretches to more than 100 miles long and 40 miles wide. It boasts enormous bird and plant populations, including 48 species of wild orchids. Offshore lies the worlds third largest barrier reef, famous for walls that drop 6,000 feet into the Tongue of the Ocean (TOTO). Between the awesome TOTO and the shore, the reef offers a peaceful haven for snorkelers with depths from nine to 15 ft.

Docking facilities for private boats are limited. At present, San Andros has eight slips with basic facilities, fuel, water, ice, accommodation and a restaurant.

Snorkeling from the beach and off shore is splendid with massive elkhorn and staghorn coral formations inhabited by a diverse marine life population.

Best Snorkeling Sites of Andros

Small Hope Bay Lodge is the center of snorkeling tours and special programs on and around Andros.

☆☆☆ **The Wreck of the Potomac** is 350-ft, steel-hulled cargo ship resting in 25 ft of water. Her hull, split in two, is home to sweeping schools of sergeant majors, squirrel fish, copper sweepers, rays, barracuda and big parrotfish. Boat access.

☆☆☆☆ Excellent snorkeling at **Trumpet Reef**, (near Small Hope Bay Lodge) draws you through a beautiful forest of elk horn, stag horn, brain and soft corals. Hundreds of trumpet fish join striking queen and French angels, schools of grunts and yellowtail in depths from two to 15 ft.

☆☆☆ **Love Hill**, another super snorkeling site near Small Hope Bay Lodge,has a huge thickets of elkhorn and staghorn coral swarming with tropical fish and critters at depths from two to 15 ft.

☆☆☆ **The Dock** at Small Hope Bay Lodge is a great spot for a night snorkel. Fish are abundant and varied amidst 35 years of stuff that's fallen off the dock, including ruins of the previous dock. Sea life includes snappers, blue tangs, parrotfish, barracuda, angelfish, flounder, puffer fish, eagle rays, octopus and an occasional dolphin.

☆☆ **North Beach**, a line of patch shoals that make for pleasurable snorkeling, lies north of The Dock, between two buoy markers. Look for octopus hiding in shells and a variety of starfish.

☆ **Davis Creek** (high tide only), a sandy tidal flat north of the beach and past the point and the rocks, shelters schools of baby barracuda, box fish and hundreds of other juveniles. Expect tidal currents.

☆☆☆☆ **Goat Cay**, a large island visible from the Small Hope Bay Lodge dock, is flanked by sea grasses on one side—good hunting grounds for sea biscuits and sand dollars—and barrier reef shallows on the other side. Abundant coral and sea life.

Andros Accommodations

Small Hope Bay Lodge offers 20 lovely cottages, low-cost air service from Ft. Lauderdale,FL, snorkeling and dive programs. Free snorkeling lesson around the dock. Besides beach snorkeling, the lodge offers daily excursions to the Andros Barrier Reef, ☎ 800- 223-6961, www. smallhope.com.

Andros Lighthouse Yacht Club & Marina on Fresh Creek, offers twenty rooms with king size or double beds, private baths and cable TV. For boaters,

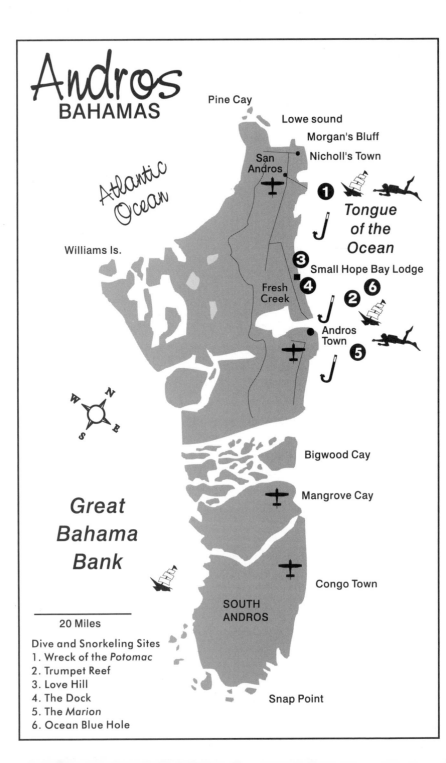

Andros
BAHAMAS

Pine Cay

Lowe sound

Morgan's Bluff

Nicholl's Town

San Andros

Atlantic Ocean

Williams Is.

①

Tongue of the Ocean

③

Small Hope Bay Lodge

④

Fresh Creek

② **⑥**

Andros Town

⑤

Bigwood Cay

Mangrove Cay

Great Bahama Bank

Congo Town

SOUTH ANDROS

20 Miles

Dive and Snorkeling Sites
1. Wreck of the *Potomac*
2. Trumpet Reef
3. Love Hill
4. The Dock
5. The *Marion*
6. Ocean Blue Hole

Snap Point

an 18-slip marina with all amenities. The island's logo, a 107-year-old lighthouse, prom- inently marks the resort.

Adjacent Lighthouse Park has a private beach with decent snorkeling. It is the final resting place of the cannons of the *Cottsac* which sank just north of the Lighthouse. Fly into Andros Town Airport (ASD) then take a taxi to the resort ☎ 242-368-2305, 242-368-2300. Website: www.andros lighthouse.com Email: relax@ andros lighthouse.com.

THE BERRY ISLANDS

This chain of 30 small islands lies off the eastern edge of the Great Bahama Bank, 80 miles southeast of Bimini. **Chub Cay**, a tiny, one-resort island dedicated to fishing, features terrific shore snorkeling. The waters around Great Harbour Cay provide fascinating coral formations and caverns packed with silversides and lobster. A few shipwrecks shelter nurse sharks and southern stingrays. Eagle rays circle the reefs.

Best Snorkeling Sites of the Berry Islands

☆☆☆☆ **The Reef at Chub Cay** sits off the western shore about 15 ft from the shoreline with depths from three to 60 ft. Corals, abundant fish life, pretty sponges and gorgonians make this a terrific snorkeling spot. A more extensive reef sits about 150 yards offshore. Visibility averages about 100 ft, water temperature between 76°F in winter and 86°F in summer.

☆☆☆ Red, pink and lavender sponges splash the shallow walls at **Mama Rhodas Reef** where snorkelers explore coral crevices packed with schools of sergeant majors, eagle rays, grunts, hogfish, huge tiger groupers, jacks and yellowtail. Elkhorn and staghorn corals thrive at 10 to 20 ft. Boat access.

Chub Cay Accommodation

Chub Cay Club, the only resort on the island, specializes in fishing. Guests stay in villas and suites. Snorkeling is off the beach or you can rent a Carolina Skiff. Bring your own gear. ☎ 800-662-8555 Email: info@chubcay.com.

BIMINI

Bimini divides into two islands, North and South Bimini, separated by a shallow, narrow channel. Alice Town, North Bimini, the hub of tourism and commerce, centers around one main road, Kings Highway, where you'll find a half-dozen local restaurants and hometown bars.

Snorkelers enjoy a huge fish population, some patch reefs and the half submerged wreck of the *Sapona*, a large concrete ship. All sites are boat access, averaging 10 to 15 minutes.

Bimini Snorkeling

✫✫✫ **Rainbow Reef**, host to masses of butterfly fish, angels, parrotfish, lobsters, moray eels, grunts is a great spot for fish photos. Average depth: 15 ft. Boat access.

✫✫✫✫ **Wild Spotted Dolphin Pods** off Bimini make for an exciting encounter. Trips, which last three to four hours, are offered by Bimini Undersea. Time to the dolphin grounds runs about an hour. There is no guarantee that the dolphins will always be there, but they have been on four out of five trips and complimentary return tickets are given to passengers of no-see trips. Knowdla Keefe of Bimini Undersea Adventures has devised a program enabling visitors to interact with with these beautiful creatures.

✫✫ **Stones of Atlantis** resemble an undersea highway. Whether its remnants of an ancient civilization or not is yet to be decided, but its definitely a fun dive as you join scores of finned travelers.

Bimini Resort & Snorkeling Tours

Bimini Big Game Club, Alice Town, North Bimini features a club-like atmosphere and beautiful surrounding waters world famous for boating, fishing (deep-sea and bonefishing), diving, kayaking, and wild dolphin encounters. Following a $2 million refurbishment, the resort is snow better than ever. Centrally located, a short stroll from the beach, it has 51 air conditioned rooms, cottages and penthouses, a 74-slip full-service marina, a fine restaurant, a popular bar and complete sporting facilities on the property. ☎ 800-737-1007 or 242-347-3391/3. Website: www.biminibiggame.com .

Bimini Undersea Adventures, headquartered at Bimini Big Game Resort & Marina offers complete snorkeling vacations with a wide choice of resorts in every price range. All are within a five-minute walk of the dive shop. Vacations include use of a mask, fins and snorkel. The shop sells snorkeling gear and rents bikes, kayaks and board sails. Snorkelers join the dive boats on afternoon dives. There is also a swim-with-wild-dolphins program. ☎ 800-348-4644, 242-347-3089, fax 242-347- 3079. E-mail: info@bimini undersea.com.Website: www.biminiundersea. com.

Air transport to North Bimini is provided by CHALKS International airlines

CAT ISLAND

Named for British sea Captain Catt, Cat Island will surprise you with its rolling hills and lush green forests spread over 50 tranquil miles. Located between Eleuthera and Long Island, it is home to the Bahamas tallest summit, Mt.

Alvernia, 206-ft high. Miles of deserted beaches, Indian caves, ruins of early plantations and excellent snorkeling off the beach make this island special.

A single road runs the islands length, making it difficult to get lost while exploring. Appropriately called Main Road, it begins at Arthur's Town in the north and ends at Port Howe in the south.

Cat Island Snorkeling Sites

Good shallow snorkeling exists off the beaches of the Greenwood Beach Resort and Fernandez Bay Village Resort with rocky outcrops between 15 and 40 ft. At Port Howe, numerous coral reef sites start 10 feet from the shore.

Fernandez Bay Snorkeling Sites

☆ A five minute walk from the beach at Fernandez Bay village brings you to **Jumping Rocks Point** where hard and soft corals, purple sea fans, assorted reef fish, crabs and crawfish sprawl along an underwater ledge. Depths run from the surface to 12 ft. Good for beginners.

☆ **Big Lump of Limestone,** a five-minute swim from the Fernandez Bay Resort beach, brings you to hard and soft corals growing from 10 ft to the surface. Grouper and smaller fish inhabit the area. Good for beginners.

☆ ☆ ☆☆ **Dry Head Reef**, which sits 300 yards offshore, shelters vibrant sea fans, lettuce and brain corals, home to grunts, yellowtail, small rays, barracuda and juvenile nurse sharks. The boat ride takes about 35 minutes.

☆☆ ☆ **Naked Point**, a maze of small coral heads, ledges and caves, sits two minutes by boat from Fernandez Bays dock. Sergeant majors, grunts, yellow tail, stone crab, sting rays and spotted eagle rays zip by. Beginner to advanced.

☆ ☆ ☆ **Hazels Hideaway,** a two-mile drive, walk or boat ride from Fernandez Bay offers nice beach-entry snorkeling over coral heads and rocks with plenty of fish. The best spots are in between the little islands scattered about. After your swim, stop in at Hazels Hideaway Bar on the beach and meet Hazel.

Snorkeling Program Participating Hotels

Fernandez Bay Village features accommodations in spacious villas with patios and maid service. Besides the Snorkeling Adventures program, there is wonderful snorkeling off the resort beach in three to six ft of water. Good for children. Snorkeling trips are also offered by the resort. Gear rentals are available for adults, but its best to bring gear for children. ☎ 800-940-1905, 954-474-4821, fax 954-474-4864; local 242-342-3043, fax 242-342-3051. Web: www.fernandezbayvillage.com. E-mail: FBV@batelnet.bs.

Greenwood Beach Resort,a 20-room beachfront inn sits on a lovely eight-mile pink beach.Dine in the large oceanfront dining room or alfresco on the terrace. Ceiling fans. King-sized beds. Guest enjoy beach snorkeling and kayaking. ☎ 877-CAT-7475 or 242-342-3053. Web: www.greenwood beachresort.com. E-mail: info@greenwoodbeachresort.com.

Hawks Nest Resort and Marina is a good choice for private pilots or sailors. The resort offers ten air-conditioned, oceanfront rooms with king size beds, a club house offering games and movies, a 28-slip marina, fresh-water pool, three secluded beaches, sun patio and complimentary use of kayaks to join the Sand Bar Club for shell hunting. Snorkel trips are arranged with **Dive Cat Island**. For reservations call ☎ (800) 688-4752. (242) 342-7050. (242) 342-7051 Website: www.hawks-nest.com. Email: hawksnest@batelnet.bs

Arrive by private plane on Hawks Nest's 4600 private air strip or by regularly scheduled flights from Nassau and Ft Lauderdale.

CROOKED ISLAND

This remote islet, 380 nautical miles from Ft. Lauderdale, offers unexplored reefs and spectacular, uncrowded beaches and fabulous snorkeling. The reef starts at the shoreline, slopes to 40 ft, then plunges to 6000 ft depths in the Crooked Island Passage. The island's sole resort, **Pittstown Point Landing** (☎ 800-752-2322 or 242-344-2507) accommodates all watersports. Web site: pittstownpointlandings.com. Email: info@pittstownlandings.com.

Below: *Inagua National Park, Inagua*   Photo Courtesy Bahamas Tourism

ELEUTHERA

Eleuthera is yet another unspoiled paradise with endless, soft white-sand beaches, peaceful, secluded snorkeling coves and impressive coral reefs. Shaped like a boomerang, the island measures 100 miles long and, less than two miles wide with a population of 10,600 people, the largest of all the Family Islands. It lies 200 miles southeast of Florida and 60 miles west of Nassau. Neighboring out-islands include Spanish Wells, tiny Harbour Island, and a small cay called Current. Spanish Wells, one of the smallest but most progressive islands in the Bahamas, is known for its shallow wrecks.

Best Snorkeling Sites of Eleuthera

There are five beach-entry sites in the Cove Eleuthera Hotel area (Gregory Town) to explore. A four-ft deep artificial lagoon provides a safe spot for beginners to try out gear and meet local fish. More experienced snorkelers will find abundant coral heads surrounded by grunts, angel fish, yellow tail and stingrays in adjacent coves and peninsulas.

A pretty reef 20 yards off the beach at the **Governors Harbour Hatchet Bay** shelters angelfish, yellowtail snappers, southern stingrays, anemones and parrotfish.

Additional beach-entry sites exist at **Rock Sound** where clear water and a throngs of parrotfish, triggerfish, blue tangs and other tropical fish reside.

☆☆ **Mystery Reef**, three miles outside of Current Cut, in the direction of Egg Island, encompasses six coral heads in 25 ft. of water. The heads, centered on a wide sand patch, tower 10 to 20 ft. Exquisite corals and fascinating marine life. Boat access.

☆☆☆☆ **Freighter Wreck.** Approximately five miles from Current Cut lies the rusting hull of a 250-ft Lebanese freighter which caught fire and was purposely run aground. The wreck sits perfectly upright in 20 ft. of water with most of her structure above the surface. Her keel is broke at mid-ship, making salvage out of the question. Although the propeller was removed by scrap metal salvers, furnishings and ships parts are scattered around the hull. Large parrotfish, glasseye snappers, and angels hover the wreck.

☆☆☆☆ **Devils Backbone**, north of Spanish Wells island is a long stretch of shallow coral reefs. Great clumps of razor-sharp elkhorn coral rise to the surface and are often awash at low tide. This treacherous barrier reef is a graveyard for ships, but a paradise for snorkelers. Boat access.

☆☆ Perhaps the most unusual shipwreck in all the Bahamas is **Train Wreck**, the remains of a steam locomotive lying in 15 ft. of water. Still on the barge, which sank during a storm in 1865, it was part of a Union train believed captured by the Confederacy and sold to a Cuban sugar plantation. The wreck site also contains three sets of wheel trucks believed to be part of the same locomotive, and wood beams half buried in the sandy sea floor. The wreckage which is slowly settling in a garden of elkhorn and brain coral formations, offers some great angles for wide-angle photography. Boat access.

☆☆☆ Just a few hundred yards away from the Train Wreck lies the **Cienfuegos Wreck**, the twisted remains of a passenger steamer that sank in 1895. Part of the Ward Line of New York, this 200-ft-long, steel-hulled ship crashed into the reef during a bad storm. All passengers on board survived and her cargo of rice was salvaged. The remaining wreckage lies in 35 ft. of water with some sections at 10 ft. Prominent features are two giant heat exchangers, a big boiler and the main drive shaft. The wreck, looking much like an undersea junk yard with jumbled steel plates, broken ribs and twisted steel beams, makes for a fascinating dive. Boat access.

☆☆ **Potato and Onion Wreck**. *The Vanaheim*, an 86-ft, coastal freighter carrying a cargo of potatoes and onions crashed into Devils Backbone in February, 1969. The force of the heavy seas during the storm pushed her over the barrier reef into 15 ft. of water, an easy dive. Pretty reef surrounds the wreck. Boat access.

Eleuthera Snorkeling Tours & Rentals

Valentines Yacht Club and Dive Center, Harbour Island, offers free snorkel lessons. Snorkel trips come with a tour guide upon request. Sites include three ship wrecks and shallow reefs. They also carry guppy gear for tiny divers.

The reef outside the dive shop breaks the surface in many spots with snorkeling depths starting at five feet. Advanced snorkelers can swim out aways to find more lush growth at depths from 15 to 35 ft. ☎ 242-333-2080. E-mail: dive@ valentinesdive.com. Website: valentinesdive.com.

Snorkeling Program Participating Hotels

Close-in snorkeling sites exist off the beaches surrounding the Cove Eleuthera Hotel and Rainbow Inn.

The Cove-Eleuthera, a 24-room resort, sits on two beautiful snorkeling coves. ☎ 800-552-5960 or 242-335-5142. Web: www.cove eleuthera. com. **Palmetto Shores Villas**, ☎ 800-688-4752 or 242-332-1305.

Rainbow Inn offers miles of deserted beaches, great snorkeling from the shore. Accommodations in studio apartments or villas. A five-minute walk from the resort brings you to additional shore-entry reef snorkeling spots. Free use of equipment. ☎ 800-688-0047 or direct: 242-335-0294. Web: www. rainbowinn. com. E-mail: vacation@ rainbowinn.com

EXUMA

The Exumas, a sandy chain of more than 350 mostly uninhabited islands and cays, extend more than 100 miles between New Providence and Long Island, 35 miles southeast of Nassau. Offshore lie 200 miles of magnificent coral reefs.

Great Exuma, accessible by plane from Nassau and southern Florida, provides visitors with a selection of fine hotels, restaurants, shops and nightlife. In George Town, the capital city, waterside inns such as Peace and Plenty provide a modern base to venture into the uninhabited utopias of the neighboring cays where you can snorkel, beachcomb and birdwatch.

Snorkel trips to **Pigeon Cay** and **Stocking Island**, a shell collector's haven, are readily available. The reefs lie about 100 yards from the beaches. Marinas rent small boats to those who wish to explore the offshore sites on their own.

Best Snorkeling Sites of Exuma

☆☆☆☆ Snorkelers can explore **Exuma National Land and Sea Park**, a magnifi- cent underwater preserve and the **Thunder ball Grotto**, a super fish-feeding area near Staniel Cay, where the famous James Bond movie was filmed. Off the capital city, George Town, lies Stocking Island, where excellent snorkeling and shelling abound.

☆☆☆ **Stingray Reef**, adjacent to Uly Cay and north of Stocking Island is formed of elk horn stands and soft-coral patches, shelter for trumpet fish, barracuda, big turtles, and large schools of grunts and yellowtail. Depths range from 15 to 40 ft.

☆☆☆☆ **Conch Cay**, a northern dive area, offers shallow walls and wide ledges for easy exploration. Marine life offers the big attraction huge turtles, rays and occasional sharks. The reef ranges in depth from six to 20 ft.

Where to Stay on Exuma

Coconut Cove Hotel features eleven air-conditioned, beach front, and garden rooms with terraces and baths, refrigerator, mini bars and ceiling fans. Freshwater pool and pool bar for beverages. ☎ 800) 688-475 . (242) 336-2659. Website: www.coconutcoveexumabahamas.com. Write to: P.O. Box EX-29299, George Town, The Exumas

Staniel Cay Yacht Club has five waterfront cottages for two, a new two-story water front suite suitable for a family of four; and a large cottage for up to seven people. All cottages have been recently renovated and uniquely decorated. Each has A/C. private bath, and a small refrigerator. The Club also features a full-service marina, snorkeling gear, air fills, gift shop, TV, fax, phone and internet. Fishing and snorkeling trips can be arranged. Boston Whalers and kayaks available. ☎800-688-4752. 242-355-2024. 242-355-2044. www.stanielcay.com. Email: info@stanielcay.com.

Club Peace & Plenty is named for the English trading ship upon which Lord Denys Rolle arrived in 1783. The hotel's 35 rooms are air-conditioned with private balconies overlooking the harbour. Watersports and charters are nearby. An on-site restaurant offers local fish, conch burgers, steak and seafood. Ferry service to Stocking Island. ☎ 800-525-2210. 242-336-2250. Web: www.peaceandplenty. com. Email: ppbeach@ batelnet.bs

Peace & Plenty Beach Inn offers 16 deluxe air-conditioned rooms with large balconies facing the beach with grand views of Elizabeth Harbour Rooms have ceiling fans, mini fridge, hair dryer and private bath. The property offers a freshwater pool, an indoor restaurant, covered terrace and a pier extending into the bay Fly into Exuma International Airport (GGT) then taxi to hotel. ☎ 800-525-2210 or 242-336-2250. Website: www. peaceand plenty.com. Email: ppbeach@batelnet.bs

LONG ISLAND

Long revered as a mecca for reef explorers, scenic Long Island is the Bahamas only island with significant high terrain. Its perimeter, blessed with sixty miles of snow-white beaches, slopes down to magnificent shallow reefs, drop-offs, crystal-clear waters, and a profusion of marine life. Two resorts cater specifically to visiting divers.

Best Snorkeling Sites of Long Island

The best reefs lie offshore, but several interesting, shore-entry sites exist off Cape Santa Maria and the beaches surrounding the Stella Maris Resort Community. Check with the dive shop at Stella Maris for sea conditions before entering the water.

☆☆ **Coral Gardens** on the Atlantic side of the island, about three-fourths of a mile from the Stella Maris Resort, makes an

Dolphin © 2004 Joyce Huber

impressive dive when the seas and wind are calm. The reef sits on a shelf about 20 yards wide with depths from three to 20 ft. Massive, healthy stands of elkhorn and staghorn coral shelter a variety of angelfish, trumpet fish, small green and hawksbill turtles, barracuda, huge Nassau grouper and rock grouper. The reef parallels the shore for about two miles. Get there by foot, bike or car. A road sign off Ocean View Drive points the way. Entry is over rock steps into a four-ft depth, then swim out about 20 yards to the reef. Beach entry.

☆☆☆ **Poseidons Point** starts at the shoreline with dramatic brain and elkhorn formations. You can jump in or climb down the rocks. Wildlife includes occasional appearances by a mako, reef, bull or hammerhead shark. Residents include huge three- to five-ft tarpon, parrotfish, shrimp, crawfish, Nassau grouper, yellowtail, grunts and sergeant majors. Beach entry points are four miles from Stella Maris Resort. Seas are usually calm except during storms. Guided, night snorkeling tours are offered by the Stella Maris dive shop. Beach or boat entry.

☆☆ **Columbus Harbour**, where Columbus fleet anchored on Oct 16th, 1492, features close-to-shore reef areas for novice snorkelers and deeper reef scenery further out for advanced snorkelers. To reach the site, head north on the main road till you see the Hillside Church. Turn right (or towards the sea) till you cant go any further. Park and walk about 300 yards across the walking bridge to the north end of the island. Following the shoreline to the left (north) brings you into shallow depths from 3 to 25 ft, and a variety of rocks and hard corals. Swim out from the shore for more interesting coral formations. Big parrotfish, Nassau grouper, rockfish, and crawfish hide in the caves and crevices. Good shelling exists along the outer beaches.

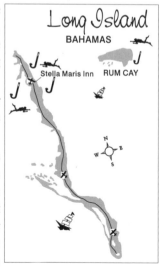

The eight-mile drive to Columbus Harbour takes about 10 minutes from Stella Maris Resort.

☆☆ **Rainbow Reef** has three easy entries from Cape Santa Maria Beach. It lies 20 yards from shore and is completely protected in most weather situations except northwest winds. Encrusting corals and sponges cover the rocky bottom, which is inhabited by a good mix of reef fish. Passing eagle rays are frequently sighted. Some large stingrays bury themselves in the sand. Beach or boat access.

☆☆☆ **Flamingo Tongue Reef** takes its name from the thousands of ruby-colored, Flamingo Tongue shells that adorn its bottom. This spot is also noted for superb sea fans, gorgonia and pillar corals. Walls of schooling reef fish squirrels, grunts, yellow tail roam about. Beware the scorpion fish, stone fish and fire coral. The reef lies six miles from Stella Maris Marina within a half mile of the Cape Santa Maria shoreline. Depths average 25 ft. with shallower areas. Seas are usually calm. Boat access.

☆☆ **The West Bar** is a lovely, 600-ft long, 300-ft wide, bar-shaped shoal within a half-mile of two beautiful beaches. The reef consists of superb brain and staghorn corals, barrel sponges, feather corals, seafans and pillar corals. Depth is 15 ft. Waters are calm. Outstanding visibility. Boat access.

☆☆ **Angelfish Reef** and **Barakuda Heads** are two massive, neighboring coral heads about six miles offshore. Tame groupers, rock fish, barracuda, large schools of jacks, crawfish, and small critters thrive at both sites. Depths vary to 40 ft with many shallow areas perfect for snorkeling.

Snorkeling Program Participating Hotels

Stella Maris Resort offers air-conditioned, two-, three- and four-bedroom villas and bungalows all high atop the islands east shoreline featuring breathtaking views of the ocean. The shoreline is rocky with several hiking paths which will lead to secluded picnic areas. The operation offers guided reef tours and complimentary shuttle bus service to different shore-entry snorkeling spots. Superb beaches. Dive shop. ☎ 800-426-0466. E-mail: smrc@stellamarisresort.com Website stellamaris resort.com.

You can wade out to a beautiful barrier reef from any point along the four-mile long beach at the **Cape Santa Maria Resort** or board the resort's catamaran for offshore snorkeling trips. ☎ 800-663-7090. Website: www.capesantamaria.com.

SAN SALVADOR

Miles of virgin shallow reefs, walls and new wrecks are yet to be explored in the waters around San Salvador, truly one of the diving jewels of the Bahamas. It is so remote the Riding Rock Inns brochure points out that it is NOT IN SOUTH AMERICA. On shore, visitors delight in miles of white-sand beaches including the site where Christopher Columbus first set foot in the New World.

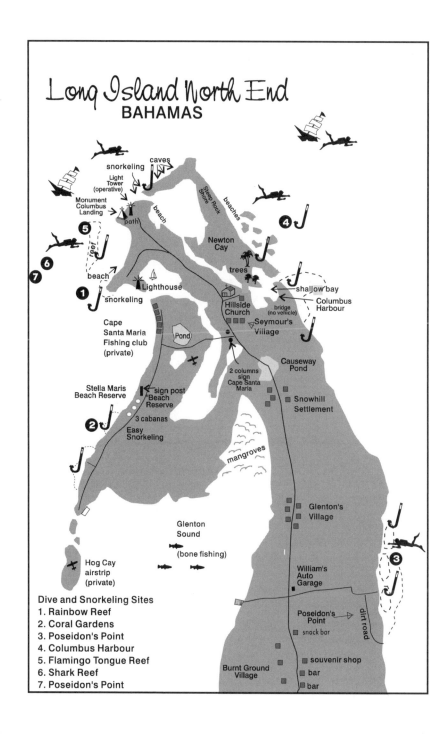

Long Island North End
BAHAMAS

snorkeling

caves

Light
Tower
(operative)

Monument
Columbus
Landing

path

beach

Steep Rock Shore

beaches

Newton
Cay

trees

shallow bay

Columbus
Harbour

bridge
(no vehicle)

beach

Lighthouse

snorkeling

Hillside
Church

Seymour's
Village

Cape
Santa Maria
Fishing club
(private)

Pond

2 columns
sign
Cape Santa
Maria

Causeway
Pond

Stella Maris
Beach Reserve

sign post
Beach
Reserve

3 cabanas

Easy
Snorkeling

Snowhill
Settlement

mangroves

Glenton
Sound

(bone fishing)

Glenton's
Village

Hog Cay
airstrip
(private)

William's
Auto
Garage

Poseidon's
Point

snack bar

dirt road

souvenir shop

bar

bar

Burnt Ground
Village

Dive and Snorkeling Sites
1. Rainbow Reef
2. Coral Gardens
3. Poseidon's Point
4. Columbus Harbour
5. Flamingo Tongue Reef
6. Shark Reef
7. Poseidon's Point

1

2

3

4

5

6

7

Best Snorkeling Sites of San Salvador

San Salvador snorkeling sites range in depth from 10 to 30 ft. Coral and fish can be seen off the Riding Rock Inns beach, but the prettiest beach-entry sites lie about three miles south of the resort. You reach them by bicycle or rental car. There is also nice snorkeling off the end of the runway. Climb down a small slope to get there or swim north from the Riding Rock Inn beach.

☆☆☆ *Snapshot Reef* packs in schools of angelfish, groupers, parrotfish, trumpetfish, damsels, blue chromis, tangs, tarpon, and invertebrates—all waiting for a handout. Boat access.

☆☆ The wreck of the *Frescate*, a 261-ft freighter resting at twenty ft, hit the reefs in 1902 and has since attracted throngs of lobster, silversides, and barracuda. Outstanding visibility. Boat access.

Where to Stay on San Salvador

Club Mediteranee on Columbus Isle offers all-inclusive vacations with ample snorkeling odysseys. ☎ 800-CLUBMED or 242-328-0940.

Riding Rock Inn offers snorkelers all the comforts of home in a relaxed, casual atmosphere. This plush resort features 24 air-conditioned double rooms, conference center, pool, restaurant, and marina. Snorkelers join the dive boats for reef trips. Rental bicycles are available for travel to beach snorkeling sites. Dive shop. ☎ 800-272-1492 or 954-359-8353. Email: info@ridingrock.com. Website: www.ridingrock.com.

Bahamas Live-Aboards (Note: passport needed)

Nekton Diving Cruises cater to scuba divers and snorkelers. The twin-hulled motor yacht carries 32 passengers and 12 staff members. ☎ 800-899-6753 or 954-463-9324 www.nektoncruises.com.

Cruzan Charters captains will tailor guided dives for you. ☎ 800-628-0785 or 305-858-2822, E-mail: charters@ cruzan.com. Website: www.cruzan. com Be sure to specify snorkeling cruise.

Additional Information: *For Nassau and Paradise Island:* ☎ 800-BAHAMAS (224-2627). Website: www.bahamas.com

For Grand Bahama Island: Website: www.grand.bahama.com

☎ 800-448-3386 More about the Bahamas Out Islands resorts may be available through the Family Islands Promotion Board ☎ 800-OUT-ISLANDS (688-4752) Website: www.bahama-out-islands.com

Barbados

Barbados, a tiny island just 21 miles long and 14 miles wide, sits 300 miles from Venezuela—the farthest east and the most isolated of the West Indian Islands. Lush and beautiful, Barbados touts first-rate resorts, vibrant nightlife, duty free shopping and a well-rounded selection of water sports.

The best time to snorkel Barbados is between April and November when fabulous visibility on the barrier reef and calm seas exist. This changes during December through March when a North Swell decreases visibility. During spring, summer and fall, the islands shallow shipwrecks offer a variety of dive experiences. The best wrecks rest on the offshore barrier reef that extends along Barbados western coast. Camouflaged by soft corals, sea fans, and sponges, the wrecks shelter thriving communities of marine animals.

Best Snorkeling Sites

☆☆☆ **Wreck of the 150-ft *Pamir*** was intentionally sunk in 30 ft of water to form an artificial reef. Its superstructure breaks the surface, making it perfect for snorkelers and snorkel-swimmers. Swarms of sergeant majors and butterfly fish inhabit the wreck.

If you don't mind a 200-yard swim, you can reach it from the beach. Although visibility varies, seas are usually calm. Dive operators request no spear fishing or collecting. Beach or boat access.

☆☆☆ **Folkestone Park**, the favorite beach-snorkeling site in Barbados, features an underwater trail around its inshore reef. The park, also a favorite area for boaters and jet skiers, has been roped off near the shore for swimmers to insure safety. Snorkel with or near a group. If you venture out, be sure to tote a floating dive flag.

A 200-yd swim from the beach will take you to a raft anchored over the wreckage of a small barge sitting in 20 ft of water.

During winter when the North Swell rises, visibility can drop drastically for as long as two days. During the rest of the year, Folkestone is the number one snorkeling choice.

☆☆☆ **The Wreck of the *Berwyn***, a 45-ft long, French tugboat that sunk in the early 1900s, sits at the bottom of Carlisle Bay, 200 yards off the island's southwest shore at 25 ft. Encrusted with plate corals, the wreck hosts seahorses, frogfish, wrasses, arrow crabs and other small creatures. It is a favored photo site, with calm sea conditions.

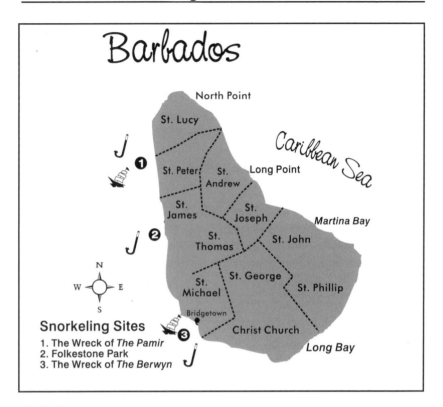

Barbados

North Point

St. Lucy

Caribbean Sea

St. Peter   St.   Long Point
             Andrew

St.   St.
James   Joseph   *Martina Bay*

St.   St. John
Thomas

N
W ─◇─ E
S

St.   St. George
Michael   St. Phillip

Bridgetown
                Christ Church
Snorkeling Sites
1. The Wreck of *The Pamir*   *Long Bay*
2. Folkestone Park
3. The Wreck of *The Berwyn*

☆☆☆ *The Ce-Trek*, an old cement-constructed boat at a depth of 40 ft, has attracted hordes of fish and invertebrates since its sinking in 1986. She sits 300 yards off shore near the *Berwyn*.

Two nice spots for beginning snorkelers are **Mullins Beach** and **Paynes Bay**. Both offer calm waters and ample parking.

Swim with the Turtles

Barbados' healthy, protected population of hawksbill and leatherback turtles is sociable and tends to stay in the same area. In certain monitored areas, where they have become accustomed to humans, you can swim with them as they feed among the coral. Several of the sailboat tours (see below) offer access or E-mail: contactus@justbreezingwatersports.com.

Snorkeling Tours & Rentals

Dive shops are located along the southwest shore.

Bubbles Galore Barbados Dive Shop at the Sandy Beach Island Resort in Christ Church, ☎ (011) 246-430-0354. Website: www.caribsurf.com/ Bubbles/

UnderWater Barbados in Carlisle Bay Centre, ☎ (011) 246-426-0655. Website: www.underwater barbados.com.

Hightide Watersports, at the Coral Reef Club. ☎ (011) 246-432-0931. E-mail: hightide@sunbeach.net. Website: www.divehightide.com.

WestSide Scuba Centre, Holetown, St. James, offers snorkeling tours, free transportation to and from your hotel to the dive boat. ☎ (011) 246-432-2558. E-mail: Westside@funbarbados.com. Website: www.west sidescuba.funbarbados.com.

Rhino Rider Water Safari, at Atlantis Submarines. ☎ (011) 246-436-8929, fax (011) 246-436-8828. E-mail: barbados reservations@ atlantissub marines.com.

Reserve Sail-Snorkeling, sunset, lunch and dinner tours through **Jolly Roger Cruises** and **Tiami Catamaran Sailing Cruises**, Bridgetown offers snorkeling and sunset cruises. ☎ (011) 246-436-6424. E-mail: tallships @sunbeach.net, website: www.tallshipscruises.com.

Where to Stay on Barbados

The following are near snorkeling beaches or reef tour operators.

Almond Beach Club and Spa features 131 air-conditioned guestrooms with ocean or pool views. All inclusive rates include meals, drinks, snorkeling tours, and kayaking. U.S. and Canada: ☎ 800-4-ALMOND (800-425-6663); hotel direct: (011) 246-4900. Website: almondresorts.com.

Grand Barbados Beach Hotel, a luxury, beachfront resort in Carlisle Bay, is just minutes from reef and wreck dives. Write: P.O. Box 639, Aquatic Gap,

Independence Arch, Bridgetown

Courtesy Barbados Tourism

Barbados Reef

Photo © 2004 *Michael Young, Underwater Barbados*

St. Michael, Bridgetown, Barbados, W.I. *In the US* ☎ 800-814-2235, *in Canada* 800-463-1284; or hotel direct: (011) 246-426-4000, E-mail through an e-mail form on www.barbados.org website.

Coral Reef Club, a posh, beachfront resort with its own dive shop (Les Wootens Watersports) sits on 12 acres of gardens adjacent to a superb, white sand beach. Guest activities include cruises on the club's 30-ft catamaran. In the US, ☎ 800-223-1108; hotel direct: (011) 246-422-2372. E-mail: coral@caribsurf.com. Website: coralreef barbados.com

Divi Southwinds Beach Resort, with over 130 fully-equipped, spacious suites, sits on a half-mile of white sand beach near the St. Lawrence Gap, surrounded by 20 acres of lovely gardens. Pool-side bar and snackery. Beachside restaurants. Walking distance of restaurants and nightlife. In the US ☎ 1 800-367-3484; direct (011) 246-7181, fax (011) 246-428-4674. E-mail: comments@diviresorts.com. Website: www.divi southwinds,com.

For Additional Information:

In the US: 800-221-9831; 1-212-986-6516, fax 1-212-573-9850, E-mail: btany@barbados. org.

In Canada: ☎ 1-888-BARBADOS. E-mail: Canada@barbados.org.

For a full, current list of accommodations, contact the Barbados Tourism Authority. In the US ☎ 800-221-9831 or -212-986-6516. E-mail: btany@barbados.org. In Canada: ☎ 888-BARBADOS, fax 416-214-9882, E-mail: Canada@barbados.org.

Belize

Belize offers snorkelers access to the largest barrier reef in the western hemisphere and three beautiful atolls—Lighthouse Reef, the Turneffe Islands and Glovers Reef. Within the reef system are hundreds of uncharted islands.

Just 750 miles from Miami, Belize lies on the Caribbean coast of Central America between Guatemala and Mexico. Its 185-mile-long barrier reef parallels the mainland coastline anywhere from 10 to 30 miles out, with the best snorkeling locations around the out islands.

Most snorkeling vacations center on Ambergris Caye, a bustling re- sort and fishing community and the largest of the out islands or cayes. Its main town, San Pedro, lies a few hundred yards from the Hol Chan Marine Preserve, the northern most point of the Barrier Reef and the jump-off point to Belize's smaller cays and atolls. Ambergris can be reached in 20 minutes by air from Belize City or one hour, fifteen minutes by ferry.

An intriguing adventure spot for snorkeling excursions is Placencia, a small fishing village 100 miles south of Belize City. There are some coral heads off the beaches, but a half-hour boat ride will bring you to Laughing Bird Caye, a small island surrounded by pristine reefs, and the remains of old wrecks. Several Spanish galleons went down in this area over the years and occasionally a gold piece washes up on the beach.

When to Go

Visit Belize during the dry season, from February to May. Annual rainfall ranges from 170 inches in the south to 50 inches in the north. Heaviest rainfall is from September to January.

The climate is sub-tropical with constant, brisk winds from the Caribbean Sea. Summer highs are rarely above 95°F, winter lows seldom below 60°F. Bug repellent is always needed as mosquitoes and sand flies are a constant annoyance.

Note: Crocodiles are occasionally sighted off the atolls and inland swamps. Avoid swimming or snorkeling in areas where sightings are reported.

Best Snorkeling Sites of Belize
THE BARRIER REEF

☆☆☆ **Hol Chan Marine Preserve**, a five-square-mile reef area off the southern tip of Ambergris Caye, is characterized by a natural channel that attracts and shelters huge communities of marine animals. Maximum depth inside the reef is 30 ft, with many shallower areas. Schools of tropicals line the

Braincoral

Photo © Tony Rath
Belize Tourism

walls and you may meet up with big turtles, green and spotted moray eels, six-ft stingrays, eagle rays, spotted dolphins, and nurse sharks.

A constant flow of sea water through the cut promotes the growth of large barrel and basket sponges, sea fans, and beautiful out croppings of staghorn and brain corals. Check tide charts before diving on your own—currents can be very strong in the channel at outgoing tides.

The inner reefs—those facing land—are shallow, with coral slopes that bottom out between 20 and 40 feet. Throngs of juvenile fish, barracuda, invertebrates, grouper, sting rays, conch, nurse shark, and small critters ramble about staghorn and elkhorn coral thickets.

THE ATOLLS

Atolls define ring-shaped islands or island groups surrounding a lagoon. Belize is blessed with three — Lighthouse Reef, Glover's Reef and the Turneffe Islands—all circled by sheltered lagoons dotted with hundreds of shallow coral heads, terrific for snorkeling. Visibility is excellent. Generally,

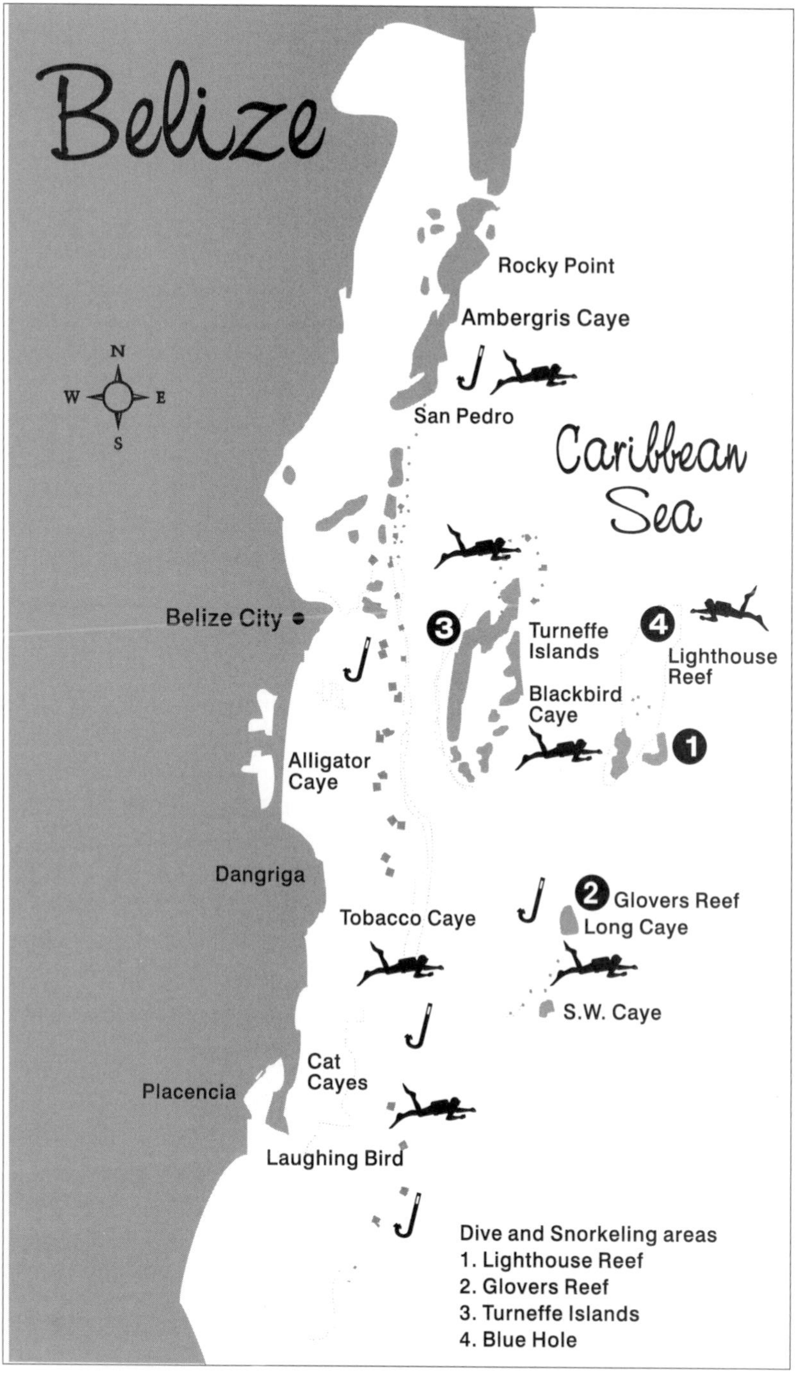

Belize

Rocky Point

Ambergris Caye

San Pedro

Caribbean Sea

Belize City

③ Turneffe Islands ④ Lighthouse Reef

Blackbird Caye ❶

Alligator Caye

Dangriga

Tobacco Caye ❷ Glovers Reef Long Caye

S.W. Caye

Cat Cayes

Placencia

Laughing Bird

Dive and Snorkeling areas
1. Lighthouse Reef
2. Glovers Reef
3. Turneffe Islands
4. Blue Hole

the islands are primitive, remote and largely uninhabited, with the bulk of the population made up of free-roaming chickens—though each location has at least one dive resort.

☆☆☆ **The Turneffe Islands**, 35 miles from Belize City and beyond the barrier reef, encompass 32 low islands bordered with thick growths of mangroves. The lower portion of the chain forms a deep V shape with Cay Bokel at the southernmost point. Cay Bokel is where you'll find the Turneffe Island Lodge, a quaint resort offering dive and snorkeling services. West of the southern point are sheltered reefs at 15 to 30 ft depths with shallower areas. Along the reef are some old anchors overgrown with coral, a small, wooden wreck, the Sayonara, and a healthy fish population. Passing dolphins and stingrays are the big attraction as they upstage the reef's "blue collar workers"—cleaner shrimp, sea cucumbers, patrolling barracuda, defensive damsel fish, schooling yellowtail, grunts, and coral crabs. Snorkeling is excellent—with outstanding water clarity, protected areas, and diverse marine life.

☆☆☆☆ **Lighthouse Reef**, 40 miles from Belize City, is the outermost of the offshore islands within the Belize cruising area. Its circular reef system features several islands and small cayes. Located on its southeast boundaries is a beautiful old lighthouse and Half Moon Caye Natural Monument—the first marine conservation area in Belize and a bird sanctuary for colonies of the red-footed boobie, frigate birds, ospreys and mangrove warblers.

Half Moon Caye Natural Monument features white-sand beaches with a drop-off on the north side and a shallow lagoon on the south end. A dock with a pierhead depth about six ft and an area for amphibious aircraft are on the north side of the island. Dive boats are required to anchor in designated areas to prevent reef damage. All boaters must register with the lighthouse keeper upon arrival. Co-ordinates of an approved anchorage for craft with a length less than 120 ft are 17° 12' 25" N 87° 33' 11" W.

The solar-powered lighthouse, situated on the tapering eastern side of Half Moon Caye, was first built in 1820. It was replaced in 1848 and reinforced by a steel-framed tower in 1931. A climb to the top offers a spectacular view.

Endangered loggerhead turtles and hawksbill turtles come ashore to lay their eggs on the sandy southern beaches.

To the north is the Lighthouse Reef Resort, an air-conditioned colony of English villas catering to divers and fishermen.

☆☆☆☆ South of the Turneffe Islands and Lighthouse Reef is the third and most remote atoll, **Glover's Reef**. It is a reef system formed by coral growing around the edges of a steep, limestone plateau. An almost continuous barrier reef encloses an 80-square- mile lagoon, an outstanding snorkeling spot, with over 700 coral heads. Visibility exceeds 100 ft. Grouper, queen trigger fish, and parrot fish are in abundance. Spotted eagle rays and sea turtles are occasionally spotted on the reefs. It is a spectacular spot with more than 25 coral species to be explored, and thousands of sheltered spots.

Where to Stay in Belize

For a complete listing of all approved accommodations in Belize, contact the Belize Tourism Board. In New York: 317 Madison Avenue, Suite 1704, New York, New York, ☎ 800-624-0686, 1-212-286-9339, fax 1-201-682- 4748. In Belize: P.O. Box 325, Belize City, Belize: ☎ (011) 501-223-1913, fax (011) 501-223-1943. E-mail: info@travelbelize.org. Website: www. travelbelize.org.

Accommodations listed below are near to snorkeling beaches and/or dive operators offering reef trips.

Ambergris Caye

Coconuts Caribbean Hotel (newly remodeled) sits on the beach 20 walking minutes south of San Pedro Town. Features 18 comfortable rooms and two suites all looking out on a private courtyard garden and pool, many with incredible views of the sea. Ceiling fans, air conditioning, cable TV, phone, maid service. Restaurant. Snorkeling trips arranged. Popular resort. ☎ (011) 501-226- 3500/3677/ 3514, fax (011) 501-226-3501. Write: P.O. Box 94, San Pedro, Ambergris Caye, Belize. E-mail: coconuts@btl.net. Website: www.belize net.com/coconuts.html.

Ramon's Village Resort in San Pedro offers 61 lovely, beachfront, air-conditioned, thatched-roof cabanas with a variety of configurations. Poolside bar, lagoon style pool, restaurant, gift shop, two fully-equipped dive shops, and a variety of dive boats. 425-ft pier. Offers snorkel/dive reef trips and basic rentals. Barrier reef 400 yds. from the resort. U.S. reservations ☎ 800-MAGIC 15, 601-649-1990; fax 601-649-1996; direct (011) 501-226-2071, fax (011) 501-226-2214. Write: One Freedom Square, Laurel MS 39440-3325 USA. E-mail: info@ ramons. com. Website: www.ramons.com.

Squirrel Fish
© 2004 Jon Huber

Victoria House (recently renovated) is a full-service, premier, luxury resort situated on its own nine-acre beach. Features 35 casual rooms, suites, casitas, and villas. On-site PADI dive shop, restaurant, beach bar, beachfront pool, tour desk. Several snorkeling tours available. The Barrier Reef lies 3/4 of a mile directly in front of the hotel. In the US, ☎800-247-5159; direct: (011) 501-226-2067. Write: P.O. Box 22, Ambergris Caye, Belize. E-mail: info@victoria-house.com. Website: www.victoria-house.com

Belize Yacht Club Resort and Marina, an oceanfront resort in walking distance of San Pedro Town's shops, and restaurants, features 42 modern, Spanish style, air-conditioned, luxury suites with fully-equipped kitchens, phone, cable TV, private balconies. Outdoor restaurant, pool, marina, bar, gift shop, dive shop, full-service tour desk. Fishing and snorkeling excursions. In the US, ☎ 800-688-0402; E-mail: frontdesk@belizeyachtcub.com. Website: belizeyacht-club.com.

Caribbean Villas Hotel, 3/4 mile from San Pedro Town, features ten air-conditioned, beachfront rooms and suites. In the US (information only): ☎ 785-776-3738; direct: (011) 501-226-2715, Write: P.O. Box 71, San Pedro, Ambergris Caye, Belize. Website: www.caribbeanvillashotel.com.

Exotic Caye Beach Resort, Hotel Playador offers 21 fully-equipped, air-conditioned, one- and two-bedroom condo suites with cable TV, freshwater pool, ocean view restaurant, beach bar, full-service dive shop. In the US ☎ 800-201-9389, fax 770-974-6414; direct: (011) 501-226- 2870, fax (011) 501-226-2871. Write: P.O. Box 11, San Pedro, Ambergris Caye, Belize. E-mail: playador@btl.net. Website: www.belizeisfun.com.

Blue Tang Inn, on the beach in walking distance of San Pedro Town's bars, restaurants and shops, offers newly remodeled, air-conditioned suites with fully equipped kitchens. Arranges a variety of snorkeling trips and other water-sport activities. In the U.S. and Canada: ☎ 1-866-881-1020; direct (011) 501-226-2326. Website: www.bluetanginn.com.

Sunbreeze Hotel, a beachfront hotel near the San Pedro airstrip, features 39 spacious, air-conditioned rooms with private bath, phone, cable TV. On-site dive shop, freshwater pool, beachfront restaurant, gift shop, bicycle rentals. Hotel motto: *No shoes, no shirt, no problem. US* ☎ 800-688-0191. E-mail: sunbreezehtl@sunbreeze.net. Web: www.sunbreezehotel.com.

Tradewinds Paradise Villas features 12 modern, one- and two-bedroom oceanfront and pool side guest suites with fully-equipped kitchens, air conditioning, cable TV and freshwater pool. Full-service tour desk. Short walk to San Pedro restaurants and attractions. A variety of reef snorkeling are offered by local dive shops. Snorkeling off the pier directly in front of the hotel brings you amidst lots of juvenile fish and small coral heads. Barrier reef 1/4 mile from shore. In the US ☎ 800-451-7776; direct: (011) 501-226-2822, E-mail: tradewinds@btl.net. Web: tradewindsparadisevillas.com.

Journey's End Resort sits beachfront on 50-plus acres, away from the mainstream, accessible by water taxi (12 minutes from San Pedro). Offers an assortment of cabana accommodations, all with ceiling fans, air conditioning, mini-frig, coffee maker. Restaurant. Full service activities desk. Huge staff caters to guests' every whim. Good for those seeking pampered seclusion. Snorkeling trips. The Barrier Reef lies one-fourth mile from the beach. Complimentary use of Hobi cats, kayaks, canoes. In the US ☎ 800-460-5665; direct: (011) 501-226-2173. E-mail: info@journeys end resort. com. Website: journeysendresort.com.

South Water Caye

Escape the masses on this private 18-acre island off Dangriga, 35 miles south of Belize City. Transfers from the mainland are by The Blue Marlin Lodge launch or by charter flight. By boat, the trip takes about 90 minutes. Driving from Belize City to Dangriga takes about two hours; by air about 20 minutes.

The big plus for this pristine spot is easy beach snorkeling on the barrier reef that sits 120 feet offshore. Sounds like a short swim, but actually the water is so shallow between the shore and the drop-off, that it's a short walk. Despite Belize's trend towards marine conservation, spear fishing is allowed here.

The Blue Marlin Lodge, South Water Caye's sole resort, spreads over six acres. Catering primarily to divers, snorkelers and fisherman, it features two guest apartments, three domed cabins, and five seaside cottages facing the trade winds. All guestrooms are cozy, cool, and comfortable with fans. The domed cabins are spacious and air-conditioned. The beach cabins are newest; all wood and air-conditioned, with handsome tropical interiors. All rooms have a private bath with hot and cold running water. No phones and no TV in the rooms or cottages, but there is a phone in the office that guests may use, and the bar has one satellite TV. All-inclusive packages. Snorkel trips are aboard a fast Pro 42 dive boat or one of two 26-ft power boats. Or you can wade out to the reef. Bring your own snorkeling gear or rent from the dive shop. In the US ☎ 800-798-1558; direct: (011) 501-522-2243. E-mail: marlin@btl.net. Website: www.bluemarlinlodge.com

The Turneffe Islands

Turneffe Island Lodge, American owned and operated, is a delightful outpost located on a private island approximately 30 miles from Belize City. It accommodates guests in four lodge buildings with multiple rooms—each with private bath and ceiling fan—and in seven luxurious, private, air-conditioned cabanas—each with ocean view. Dining room and lounge. Meals served family style. Outstanding snorkeling reefs lie about 350 yards off the resort beach. Get to the reef by either paddling one of the resort's sea kayaks, sailing a Sunfish, or taking the skiff. Bring your own snorkeling gear; limited rentals available. In the US ☎ 800-874-0118, fax 713-236-7743; direct (011) 501-220-4011. Write: 440 Louisiana, Ste. 900, Houston, Texas 77002. E-mail: info@turneffelodge.com. Website: www.turneffelodge.com.

Blackbird Caye Resort defines eco-tourist paradise. Situated on a private 166-acre jungle island, it is located 35 miles from Belize City on the eastern side of the Turneffe Reef Atoll on Blackbird Cay. Unique and exciting, with miles of deserted beaches and jungle trails, the island sits close to 70 impressive dive sites with depths from 10 ft. Reefs are spectacular—with huge tube and barrel sponges, dramatic overhangs, large loggerhead turtles, dolphins, perfect coral formations. Lots of grouper and reef fish. Manatee sightings. Great snorkeling lies just 400 yards off the shore—a two-minute boat ride. Calm waters inside the reef make it a safe spot for novices. Daily morning and afternoon guided snorkeling excursions. Accommodations feature 15 private, air-conditioned cabanas with ceiling fans, private baths, and private porch—all facing the sea. Restaurant and lounge. Sunfish sailboats, kayaks. Dive and snorkel shop. Resort supplies transfer from airport to dock in Belize city and 1-1/4 hr fast and scenic boat ride to island. In the U.S. ☎ 888-271-DIVE (3483), fax 305-969-7946; Write: P.O. Box 428, Belize City, Belize. E-mail: bb.mresort@btl.net. Website: blackbirdresort.com.

Lighthouse Reef

Lighthouse Reef Resort on Northern Cay, a private island at the northern end of the Lighthouse Reef Reserve, boasts a protected lagoon perfect for snorkelers of all ages. The resort offers 11 villas, suites, mini-suites, and cabanas—all beachfront, with air-conditioning, private baths, porches. E-6 film processing. Camera rentals. Kayaks. Radiotelephone and radio-fax service for emergencies. A private charter meets incoming flights at Belize International Airport to deliver guests to the resort's private airstrip. Flight time is 20 minutes. In the US ☎ 800-423-3114, 1-863-439-6600. E-mail: donna@ scuba-dive-belize.com or through form on website. Website: www.scubabelize.com.

Placencia

Placencia, a great spot for off-the-beaten-track adventures and for those on a low budget, offers pristine snorkeling around forty small cayes between the mainland and the offshore barrier reef. Placencia Village has guest rooms for all budgets. Terrific open-air bars serve pizza and Creole fish dishes.

Rum Point Inn, three miles from the Village, comprises ten seaside cabanas and 12 luxury, air-conditioned garden suites. Restaurant, bar, garden pool, gift shop, large private library, dive shop. Snorkel gear and instructions. Spa services. Small sandy swimming beach. Complimentary use of bicycles, kayaks, sailing dinghy. Pro-42 Auriga II dive boat. Rum Point Tours arranges a variety of marine excursions, fishing activities, and land-based trips. US ☎ 888-235-4031; direct: (011) 501-523-3239. E-mail: rupel@direcway.com. Website: www.rumpoint. com.

Turtle Inn, a mile north of the Village, offers six thatch-roofed cabanas along 500 feet of Caribbean beach front. Cabanas have private baths, ceiling fans. Open-air dining room; sunken sand-floor bar. Guests are offered snorkeling and jungle trips. In the US ☎ 800-746-3743; direct: (011) 501-824-4912. E-mail: info@ blancaneaux.com. Website: www.turtleinn.com.

Nautical Inn Resort, one of the area's newest resorts, sits on 4 acres of the peninsula in Seine Bight Village. Features 12 spacious beachfront rooms with private baths, air-conditioning, ceiling fans, cable TV, phone. Oar House Restaurant, bar, gift shop, freshwater pool, dive shop. Coconut bowling. Entertainment by Garifuna drummers and dancers. Snorkeling, fishing, and jungle tours. Transfers from Placencia airstrip.

To book online, go to the website, then hotels. Click on E-mail to book with the hotel of your choice. 800-688-0377; direct: (011) 501-523-3595. E-mail: nautical@blt.net. Website: www.nauticalinnbelize.com.

Singing Sands Inn houses guests in six individual, thatch-roofed cabanas, modern on the inside with private bathrooms, refrigerators, ceiling fans. ☎ and fax (011) 501-523-2243/8017. Website: www.singingsands.com

Soulshine Resort and Spa, a small dive resort located on a private island, features spacious thatched-roofed cabanas with microwave, refrigerator, full bath, air-conditioning, porch. Restaurant, bar, spa tubs, and spa services. Private beach. Kayaks. Offers a unique whale shark tour, jungle tours, fishing, kayaking, and more. Snorkeling/diving tours take off to Laughing Bird Caye, Ranguana Caye and Little Caye. Direct ☎ (011) 501-523-3347. E-mail: bookings@soulshine.com. Web: www.soulshine.com.

Belize Snorkeling Tours & Rentals

In addition to the dive shops that are associated with, or located on the premises of, the individual resorts listed above, there other dive operators in Belize who offer or can customize snorkeling/diving trips as well. Some are listed below.

Hugh Parkey's Belize Dive Connection, in Belize City at the Radisson Fort George Hotel and Marina pier, offers day snorkel trips to Barrier Reef, Turneffe, and Lighthouse. In the US ☎ 888-223-5403; direct (011) 501-223-4526. Website: www.belize diving.com.

Aqua Dives, on Ambergris Caye on the beach at the Sunbreeze Hotel, offers snorkeling trips, gear rental. In the US ☎ 800-641-2994; direct: (011) 501-226-3415/3222. Website: www.aquadives.com.

Amigos del Mar, on Ambergris Caye, specializes in full-service diving, instruction, snorkeling, and fishing trips. Pick-up service from local, water front resorts. ☎ (011) 501-226-2706. E-mail: amigosdive@btl.net. Website: www.amigosdive.com.

Sea Sports Belize, offers daily guided snorkeling adventures to the Barrier Reef and to Turneffe and Lighthouse Atolls. Trips are available for snorkelers who are visiting Belize for the day on a cruise ship, staying in Belize City, Cayo, or on St George's Caye, or are passing through on a sailing charter. E-mail: through on website, www.seasportsbelize.com.

SeaHorse Dive Shop, in Placencia, offers half- and full-day snorkeling trips (customized to suit your snorkeling abilities), many from the beaches at one of the many cayes in the area. ☎ 800-991-1969. E-mail: seahorse@btl.net. Website: www.belizescuba.com.

Advanced Diving Dive Shop is a full-service dive shop located in the heart of Placencia Village, on the sidewalk next to Cozy Corner. Professional licensed dive masters offer snorkeling tours as well as other marine tours. ☎ (011) 501-523-4037. Website: www.beautifulbelize.com.

Belize Tours, Cruises and Expeditions

The following tour companies offer pre-planned packages for groups and individuals or design-your-own. Package rates for week-long trips are less costly than buying air fare, accommodations, meals, and transfers separately.

American Canadian Caribbean Line Inc. features luxurious, small ship cruises from Belize to the Rio Dulce, Guatemala or Roatan, Honduras and cayes between. They stop for snorkeling at the best spots. ☎ 800-556-7450, 1-401-247-0955, Website: www.accl-small.ships.com.

Landfall Productions Dive and Adventure Travel features well planned, money-saving vacations from the US, including transfers, and accommodations. Group rates. ☎ 800-525-3833, fax 1-916-924-1059. E-mail: lndfall@ aol. com. Website: www.landfallproductions. com.

International Expeditions Inc. has custom-guided trips for the naturalist. Tours are well organized to consider both skilled and novice snorkelers. ☎ 800-633-4734, 1-205-428-1700, fax 1-205-428-1714. Write: One Environs Park, Helena AL 35080. E-mail: nature@ietravel.com. Website: www. internationalexpeditions.com.

Oceanic Society Expeditions offers several Belize five-, seven-, and eight-day snorkeling programs, Belize/Honduras snorkeling tours, and a Whale Shark Reef (marine ecology and snorkeling) trip. Land excursions are available to see Mayan ruins and the Cockscomb Jaguar Preserve. ☎ 800-326-7491, 415-441-1106. E-mail: oceanic society@btl.net. Website: www.oceanic-society.org.

Travel Tips

Additional Information: Belize Tourism Board. In New York: 317 Madison Avenue, Suite 1704, New York, New York, ☎ 800-624-0686, 1-212-286-9339, fax 1-201-682-4748. In Belize: ☎ (011) 501-223-1913,. E-mail: info@travelbelize.org. Website: www.travelbelize.org.

Bermuda

Lying hundreds of miles from anywhere, or more precisely 650 miles off the coast of North Carolina, Bermuda is noted for its delightful powder-soft beaches, secluded coves and lush vegetation. Considered one island, it is actually more than 150 islands surrounded by one of the largest fringing reef systems in the world where three centuries of shipwrecks lie at rest.

The best time to visit Bermuda is from June through October. During this period the Gulf Stream moves close to shore and air and water temperatures reach as high as 85. During the winter the main flow of this warm water moves away from Bermuda, causing local air temperatures to drop as low as 55.

Shipwrecks

The Government officially acknowledges the existence of as many as 400 shipwrecks, though local historian and author Robert Marx notes that there are at least 1500 shipwrecks and possibly 2000 in Bermuda waters based on original photographs of ships that sank in the past 100 years or so and drawings of older ships or their sister ships. Local divers agree that figure may not be an exaggeration. Some of the older and more historically important wrecks are protected sites, off limits.

Best Snorkeling Sites of Bermuda

Beach-Entry Sites

☆☆ **The Snorkel Park** at The Royal Naval Dockyard (fort) is adjacent to the Maritime Museum, a short walk from the cruise ship dock, ferry and bus stops. It open daily from 10:30am to 6pm.

The park, a protected coral reef preserve, has well marked reef trails, floating rest stations and a helpful staff, including experienced life guards. Depths are shallow and the seas calm. Bottom terrain consists of plate corals and gorgonians. Schools of grunts, doctor fish and parrot fish roam about. Several historic cannons dating back to the 1500s are marked off. Look along the base of the fort for ceramic shards, musket mini balls and insulators dating from the forts use as a radio station in WWII.

Rental equipment is available on site, including flotation vests, masks and snorkels. ☎ 234-1006. E-mail: bic@ibl.bm

☆☆ The reef at **Elbow Beach** starts 10 yards from the shoreline then stretches seaward for a mile. If you are not staying at the Elbow Beach Hotel, be sure to enter the water from the public beach to the west of the resort and swim east towards the restaurant. Marine life is quite good with swarms of squirrelfish, parrotfish, grunts and critters. Further out, tarpon and horse-eyed jacks roam the cuts and ledges in the reef. A rocky bottom terrain supports encrusting corals and sponges. Visibility averages 60 ft.s

A 300-yard swim from Elbow Beach seaward takes you over the wreck of the **Pollockshields**, a 323-ft German built steamer, originally called the **Herodot** that was captured by the English in World War I. While carrying ammunition and provisions for WWI, the ship hit heavy fog and ran aground during a hurricane on September 7, 1915. Many of the ships shell casings are embedded in the reef. Some are considered unstable and are best left untouched.

The easiest route to the wreck runs along a break in the reef line that starts directly in front of the Surf Club Restaurant. The swim out takes about 10 to 15 minutes. A strong surge makes this a bad choice on windy or choppy days. For advanced snorkelers only.

☆☆☆ **Church Bay**, a terrific spot when seas are calm, may be entered anywhere along the

Shipwreck, Courtesy Bermuda Tourism

beach. A shallow reef that parallels the shoreline acts as a barrier to most wind- and storm-driven waves. Armies of fish and invertebrates inhabit the reefs nooks and crannies. Soft and hard corals abound. Park along the road above the beach and climb down the steep stairway.

☆☆☆ **John Smiths Bay**, on the beautiful south shore, is handicapped accessible and has a lifeguard from April through October. A 50-yard swim brings you over a shallow reef, alive with midnight parrotfish, grunts, goatfish, squirrelfish, rock beauties, surgeonfish and lobster. The reefs caves and tunnels, easily seen from the surface, shelter small fish, crabs and shrimp. Usually calm with exceptional visibility.

Small caves at one end of the beach provide shelter for people who enjoy the view but not the sun. A mobile vendor offering snacks frequents the area.

☆☆ **Tobacco Bay's** grassy subsea terrain shelters soft corals, eels, sea horses, crabs, octopi, and schools of juvenile fish. A rocky breakwater separating the bay from the ocean keeps this area calm. Depths run from 3 to 10 ft. Most interest is along the shoreline. Beach access.

In season, the beach shack rents snorkeling gear and sells beverages . To reach this site take Duke of Kent Street from St. Georges till you reach the sea.

Bermuda

St. Catherine Pt.

St. Georges Harbour

St. Georges Harbour

Castle Harbour

St. Georges

Atlantic Ocean

HAMILTON

Harrington Sound

Smiths

DEVONSHIRE

Clarence Cove

Deep Bay

PEMBROKE

Hamilton

Paget

Albouy's Pt

WARWICK

Gibbs Hill Lighthouse

The Great Sound

Ireland Island North

Somerset Village

SANDYS

Daniel's Head

SOUTHAMPTON

Wreck of the Darlington

Wreck of the North Carolina

Dive and Snorkeling Sites

1. Blue Holes
2. *The Lartington*
3. *The Constellation/Montana*
4. *L'Herminie*
5. *The Darlington*
6. *The North Carolina*
7. The Snorkel Park
8. Somerset Long Bay
9. Church Bay
10. Southwest Breaker
11. *The Mary Celestia*
12. Horseshoe Bay
13. Warwick Long Bay
14. *The Minnie Breslaur*
15. Elbow Beach
16. *The Pollockshields*
17. *The Hermes*
18. Devonshire Bay
19. John Smith's Bay
20. Tobacco Bay
21. Shelly Bay

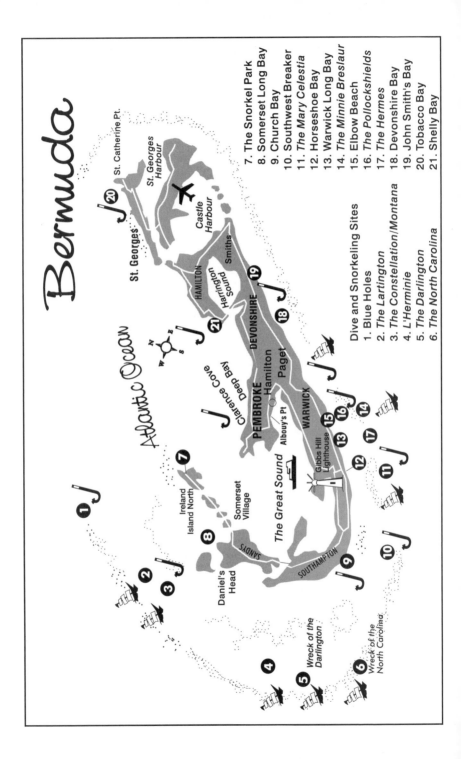

✰✰ Rocky outcrops and ledges make **Warwick Long Bay** tricky to enter and tricky to snorkel without getting scraped by the rocks, but visibility and fish life are excellent and make it worth a try for advanced snorkelers. Neighboring **Jobsons Cove** is an easier, though narrow, entrance. Expect some wave action. Beach access.

✰ **Somerset Long Bay** on Bermudas southwest end, appeals to first time snorkelers with calm, shallow water and a wealth of marine life. Expect rocks, grass and good visibility. Nice spot for a picnic.

The rocks encircling **Devonshire Bay**, on the south shore, harbor a wealth of fish and invertebrates. Bigger fish hang out along mouth of the bay.

✰ On a calm day, **Shelly Bay**, on the north shore, features easy access and impressive marine life. Swim out 50 yards to the reef where you'll find a good variety of fish, including peacock flounder, octopi, and parrotfish. Avoid this spot on windy day unless you want to go board sailing. The long beach, shallow water and recently renovated park complete with jungle gym, slides and swings make it a good choice for children. The parking lot and surrounding area are accessible to people with disabilities.

Offshore Snorkeling Sites

More dramatic reef structures and shipwrecks lie offshore. Several tour companies offer boat trips and instruction on ocean snorkeling.

✰✰✰ **The Blue Holes**, seven miles offshore north of Somerset, are deep sand pockets that drop straight down into an iridescent teal blue, reaching a maximum depth of nearly 60 ft. The surrounding shallow reef, between three and six ft depths, displays vibrant sea fans, soft corals and black coral bushes. An occasional enormous (150-200 lb.) black grouper storms by. Prolific fish life, lobsters and invertebrates.

✰✰✰✰ *The Constellation/Montana.* Located a few miles off the northwestern coast of Bermuda, these two ships sank on exactly the same site, although 80 years apart. *The Montana*, also known as the *Nola, Gloria* and *Paramount*, was an English paddle wheel steamer that was on her maiden voyage as a Confederate Blockade runner during the American Civil War. She was a sleek vessel, 236 ft. in length, with a beam of 25 ft. Her steam engines and twin paddle wheels were capable of turning 260 hp. She ground to a halt in shallow reefs some five and one-half miles from the west end of Bermuda on December 30, 1863. As she was an iron-hulled ship, a great deal of her hull and boilers are remarkably intact and make for an excellent dive. Numerous reef fish and rather large barracuda make the *Montana* their home. Overlapping the *Montana* are the remains of the **Constellation.** This four-masted, 192-ft., wooden-hulled schooner sank on the Bermuda reefs enroute from New York to Venezuela on July 31, 1943. Hers was a general 2,000 ton cargo, but on her deck she carried 700 cases of Scotch whiskey, an assortment of drugs and hundreds of bags of cement which, when washed with seawater, solidified into concrete and so remains.

Used as a cargo vessel during World War II, the wreck is often referred to as the Woolworth or Dime Store Wreck because of the wide variety of artifacts that have been recovered, including red glass, cut glass, china, glasses, tea and coffee cups and saucers, tickets to Coney Island (in Spanish), Yo Yos, 78 rpm records by RCA (with labels in Spanish), cases of pistachio nuts, parts for radios, radios, religious artifacts, devotion altars of pewter, crucifixes, cosmetic supplies by Mennen and Elizabeth Arden, cold cream, Vaseline, pharmaceutical products, including at least eight different types of drug ampules, which provided Peter Benchley with the premise for the movie, *The Deep*. When seas are calm, this is a very enjoyable snorkeling spot. The site lies about five miles offshore and is recommended for ocean-experienced snorkelers. Areas of the reef are as shallow as eight ft. Sea conditions vary with the wind direction and speed.

☆☆☆☆ *The Lartington,* listed on the Bermuda wreck chart as an unidentified 19th-century wreck, was often referred to as the *Nola*, until one of Blue Water Divers guides discovered her name under the port side of the partially intact bow. After writing to Harland & Wolf, a builder of this type of vessel during the 1800s, we learned that this sort of ship, a sailing steamer, was very common in the late 1800s. She gave rise to the expression, tramp steamer, because every time the coal burning engines were fired up, she belched out a cloud of coal dust, liberally coating everything and everyone aboard with black soot. As a result, they resembled railroad hoboes, or tramps, and the name stuck.

When visibility is good, the *Lartington's* saturation steam boilers are visible amidships and, at the stern, the drive shaft and propeller. The steering controls located on the fantail are now well encrusted with over 100 years of coral growth. The bow, partially destroyed, lies a few feet above the 30-ft.-deep sand bottom. The surrounding reef is honeycombed with small caves and some tunnels. Many places come to within 10 ft. of the surface. The entire length of the wreck is visible from the surface, although its too long to explore in its entirety on one snorkeling trip. Sea conditions vary with the wind.

☆☆☆ *LHerminie* sank on a flat calm day in 1838. This huge French ship was lumbering along in the doldrums with her crew of 495 returning to France after seeing action against Maxmillian in Mexico. She ground to a halt on the very shallow flats of Bermudas western ledge. The reef in this area is bland, visibility is rarely in excess of 60 to 80 ft., and the water has a greenish tone, but it is an exciting dive with 40 cannons, easily visible from the surface. The wreck rests at 30 ft.

✩✩✩ **Southwest Breaker,** a massive breaking reef, has caused at least one wreck along Bermudas south shore. The reef rises from a 30-ft. bottom and actually protrudes through the surface, casting up considerable white water even on the calmest days. Through the center of the breaker is a massive tunnel, actually large enough to drive a boat through. The tunnel is often occupied by one or two black grouper and a resident barracuda who is none too shy of photographers. In early summer, clouds of fry or glass eye minnow now feed in the nutrient rich and oxygenated waters here. They draw others and then more still until the breaker is home to more fish than you can count. The surrounding reef is very colorful and appears quite lush with many smaller non-breaking heads known locally as "blind- breakers." These are carved with numerous ledges and caves, excellent for experienced snorkelers and is particularly interesting to photograph. Surface swells.

✩✩✩ *The Mary Celestia*, after making at least five round trips to Wilmington, NC, successfully running the Northern blockade of Confederate ports, ran aground on the Blind Breakers and sank on September 13, 1846, only nine months after her sister ship, the *Montana* was wrecked on the northern reefs. The story, as reported in the *Royal Gazette,* a week later, states that her captain, knowing the waters of Bermuda, warned the navigator to steer clear of the dangerous breakers. The navigator, in turn, remarked with a certain surety, "I know these waters like I know my own house!" He apparently hadn't spent much time at home, for within minutes the *Mary Celestia* struck bottom. She was towed off the reef early the next morning and sank within ten minutes, the seas rushing in through a great hole torn in her underside.

Today, the *Mary* sits quietly in just shy of 60 ft. of water as if she were still steaming along. More than 120 years accumulation of sand covers most of her hull, but her two rectangular steam boilers and engine machinery are visible from the surface. One of her paddle wheels stands upright, with the other lying on its back next to the boilers. The entire wreck is surrounded by a high reef, honeycombed with caverns, canyons and cuts that open onto the sand bottom. Her anchor lies in 30 ft. of water. Schools of very large parrotfish are common. The reef around the wreck starts at 15 ft. Expect surface swells.

Snorkeling Tours & Rentals
Snorkeling cruises cost from $25 for a short tour to $65 for a half day.

Blue Water Divers and Water- sports offers a Guided Snorkel Certificate Program where they teach mask defogging, clearing and adjustment,

Daniels Head beach, located off Bermuda's rocky, northwest coast.
Courtesy of Bermuda Tourism

removing and replacing the mask on the surface. swimming in waves, surface exit and entry techniques, surface breathing, basic knowledge of marine life, clearing the snorkel, submerging, exploring, resurfacing and regaining position, use of a snorkel vest, first aid, clearing the snorkel, dive techniques, use of weight belt, and fish identifying. ☎ 441-234-1034. www. divebermuda.com.E-mail: bwdivers@ibl.bm

Bermuda Barefoot Cruises Ltd. departs Darrells Wharf, Devonshire for snorkeling and sightseeing aboard the 32-ft *Minnow*. Equipment and instruction provided. Complimentary refreshment on return trip. ☎ 441-236-3498.

M.V. Bermuda Longtail Party Boat operates a 65-ft motor catamaran that carries 200 people. Tours depart Flag Pole, Front Street, Hamilton. Snacks and drinks sold on board. ☎ 292-0282, fax 441-295-6459.

Bermuda Water Tours offers both glass-bottom and snorkeling cruises aboard the 50-ft, 75-passenger *Bottom Peeper*. Tours depart near the Ferry Terminal, Hamilton. Gear provided. Full bar and changing facilities on board. Refreshments on return trip. Operates from the end of April 1 to November 30. ☎ 236-1500, fax 441-292-0801.

Bermuda Water Sports, departs St. Georges for half-day snorkel cruises aboard the 100-passenger, glass-bottom boat, Sun Deck Too. Anchors in shallow, waist high water on an island beach. Guides feed and identify fish and corals. Instruction and equipment provided. Full bar and snack bar on board. May to November. ☎ 293-2640 or 441-293-8333 ext. 1938.

Fantasea Diving and Snorkeling, on Darrells Wharf on the Warwick Ferry Route, takes snorkelers and divers to the favorite spots. ☎ 236-6339, 888-DO-A-DIVE. Website: www.bermuda.com/scuba

Haywards Cruises 54-ft, 35-passenger, snorkeling and glass-bottom boat, Explorer departs next to the Ferry Terminal in Hamilton. Bring swim suit and towels. Snorkeling gear provided. Instruction. Changing facilities on board. Cameras available for rent. Complimentary swizzle on return trip. Operates from May to Nov- ember. ☎ 292-8652.

**Jessie James Cruises'
snorkeling tour boats,** the
40-ft Rambler and 48-ft
Consort depart Albouys
Point, Hamilton. They also
will pick you up at Darrells and
Belmont wharves. 236-4804.

Pitman's snorkeling and
glass-bottom boat trip departs
the Somerset Bridge Hotel
dock, and cruises five miles
northwest to the perimeter
reef. Snorkeling instruction

Horseshoe Bay,
Courtesy Bermuda Tourism

on ancient shipwrecks and coral reefs. Gear supplied. Changing facilities on
board. No children under 5 years. ☎ 234-0700.

Salt Kettle Boat Rentals Ltd., Salt Kettle, Paget, offers snorkeling cruises
to the barrier reef and shipwrecks. Refreshments. ☎ 236-4863 or 236-3612.

Sand Dollar Cruises are aboard the 40-ft, 189-passenger, *Bristol Sloop
Sand Dollar*, departing Marriotts Castle Harbour dock, Hamilton. Gear
provided. This boat may be chartered. ☎ 236-1967 or 234-8218.

Nautilus Diving Ltd., at the Southampton Princess Hotel, offers morning
and afternoon reef and wreck tours. All equipment provided. Snorkeling is
from a 40-ft. boat to reefs within 10 minutes of shore. ☎ 238-2332 or
441-238-8000.

Tobacco Bay Beach House on Tobacco Bay, St. Georges. Snorkeling and
underwater cameras for rent. Ideal for beginners. ☎ 293-9711.

Helmet Diving is fun for all ages. No lessons needed. Depth 10 to 14 ft. Does
not get your hair wet. Available at **Hartleys Helmet, Flatts Village
Smiths,** ☎ 292-4434, or **Greg Hartleys Under Sea Adventure, Village
Inn dock,** Somerset. ☎ 234-2861.

Sailing Yachts
The following may also be chartered for private groups. Three-hour cruises
rates start at about $45 per person. Complimentary snorkeling gear.

Allegro Charters 32-ft, eight-passenger *Allegro* departs Barr's Bay Park ☎
441-295-4074, fax 441-295-1314.

Bermuda Caribbean Yacht Charters 52-ft ketch, *Night Wind* carries 25
people. Departs Waterlot Inn. ☎ 238-8578.

Golden Rule Cruise Charters 60-ft, *Golden Rule,* de parts Kings Steps, Dockyard and Darrells Wharf. ☎ 238-1962.

Harbour Island Cruises 50-ft ketch *Sundancer* carries 24 passengers. Departs Albuoys Point.

Longtail Cruises offers snorkeling tours aboard the *Longtail of Hinsons,* a 40-ft, 10-passenger Cheoy Lee ketch. Departs Darrells Wharf or hotel docks in Hamilton harbour. ☎ 236-4482.

Sail Bermuda Yacht Charters carries 15 people on their 40-ft ketch *Alibi*. Departs Albouy Point and the hotel docks in Hamilton Harbour. ☎ 234-9279.

Where to Stay

Accommodations range from ultra-luxurious resorts to inexpensive house-keeping cottages. A complete list is available by calling 800-223-6106 (US), 800-BERMUDA; Canada, 416-923-9600; UK 071-734-8813. Online: www.bermudatourism.com. Following resorts are popular with snorkelers.

The Fairmont Southampton Hotel sits on one of the highest points in Bermuda with ocean views from all guest rooms. Air conditioned. ☎ 866-540-4497 or hotel direct 441-238-8000 or 800-268-7176. Write to P.O. Box HM 1379, Hamilton HM FX, Bermuda.

The Reefs Resort sits on a cliff overlooking lovely Christian Bay, Southampton. Snorkeling off the adjacent sand beach. ☎ 800-742-2008.. Website: www.thereefs.com. Email: generalinfo@thereefs.com.

Sonesta Beach Hotel & Spa is a modern luxury resort hotel with 25 acres of picturesque grounds. Dive shop on premises. ☎ 441-238-8122 or 800-SONESTA (US), fax 441-238-8463.

Grotto Bay Beach Hotel & Tennis Club sits on 21 acres of beachfront gardens in Hamilton Parish. Dive shop on premises. A private beach features two small coves in an enclosed bay. Deep water dock. All rooms have private balconies and panoramic sea views. Air conditioned. ☎ 800-582-3190 (US) or 441-293-8333,

For Additional Information

In the US, write to Bermuda Tourism, Suite 201, 310 Madison Avenue, New York, NY 10017, ☎ 800-223-6106. ☎ 416-923-9600. United Kingdom, Bermuda Tourism, BCB Ltd., 1 Battersea Church Road, London SW11 3LY, England. ☎ 071-734-8813.

Websites: www.bermudatourism.com or www.bermuda.bm.

Bonaire

Bonaire, located 50 miles off the northern coast of Venezuela, is a mountain in the sea surrounded by dense coral reefs that grow to its shoreline. With only 22 inches of rain annually, there is no freshwater run-off, which insures good visibility, often exceeding 70 feet. Excellent snorkeling exists off all the south coast beaches, which are sheltered from high winds and waves.

Dependably dry weather and calm seas prevail most of the year, though changing global weather patterns bring an occasional storm, wind shift, and water temperature drop during mid winter.

Bright yellow painted rocks along the coast road mark the dive sites, most of which can be explored from the beach.

Bonaire Marine Park

In 1979, the Netherlands Antilles National Parks Foundation (STINAPA) received a grant from the World Wildlife Fund for the creation of the Bonaire Marine Park. The park was created to maintain the coral reef ecosystem and to ensure continuing returns from diving, fishing, and other recreational activities.

Photo: *Bonaire Countryside*

Photo © 2004 Jon Huber

The park incorporates the entire coastline of Bonaire and neighboring Klein Bonaire. It is defined as the sea bottom and the overlying waters from the high-water tidemark down to 200 ft (60 m).

All visitors are asked to respect the marine park rules—no sitting on corals; no fishing or collecting of fish while scuba diving; no collecting of shells or corals, dead or alive. Spearfishing is forbidden. Anchoring is not permitted except in the harbor area off town (from the yacht club to the pier). All craft must use permanent moorings, except for emergency anchoring. Boats of less than 12 ft may use a stone anchor.

Popular dive sites are periodically shut down to rejuvenate the corals. Moorings are removed and placed on different sites.

Bonaire's Best Snorkeling Sites

Hotels and dive shops offer daily trips to nearby offshore sites. Most are less than a 10-minute boat ride, but you don't need a boat or even a mask to see Bonaire's reefs. They grow to the surface in many areas and are visible from the shore. Excellent beach dives exist along the shores on the leeward side where channels have been cut allowing access to deeper water. These reefs slope down to a narrow ledge at 30 ft. then drop off to great depth. Expect to pay a $10 annual fee for using the marine park. Most of the resorts and dive shops offer guided snorkeling trips.

☆☆☆☆ To reach **Red Slave,** drive south from Kralendijk, past the Solar Salt Works beyond the second set of slave huts. Strong currents and surf limit this site to experienced open-water divers.

The size and number of fish at Red Slave is spectacular. It is not unusual to spot four-foot tiger, yellowfin, or Nassau groupers. Gorgonians, orange crinoids, and black corals are found on the southern slope. Artifacts from pre-lighthouse wrecks rest on the slope, such as anchors and ballast stones from the 1829 shipwreck *H.M.S. Barham.*

☆☆☆☆ **Salt City** is a boat or shore dive located at the southern end of the island where you'll spot mountains of glistening white salt. To reach it, drive south from Kralendijk past the salt loading pier (very visible). You'll spot a large buoy south of the pier. Enter along the left bank formed by the large sand river—a wide, sand stretch which eventually drops off the shallow terrace into a short, reef slope island.

The terrace is landscaped with star, fire, elkhorn and staghorn corals. Sea life is superb, featuring scad, palometa, big groupers, snappers, garden eels, tilefish and French angelfish. Check currents with one of the local dive shops before entering the water.

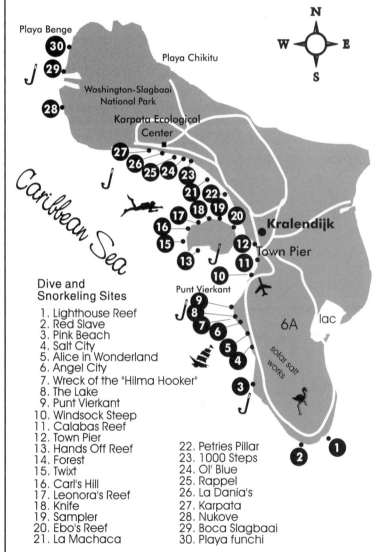

Bonaire

Playa Benge
30
29
28

Playa Chikitu

Washington-Slagbaai
National Park

Karpata Ecological
Center

27
26 **25** **24** **23**
21 **22**
18 **19**
17 **20**
16
15
13

N
W · E
S

Caribbean Sea

Kralendijk
12
11 Town Pier
10

Punt Vierkant
9
8
7 **6**
5
4
3

6A
lac

solar salt
works

2 **1**

Dive and Snorkeling Sites

1. Lighthouse Reef
2. Red Slave
3. Pink Beach
4. Salt City
5. Alice in Wonderland
6. Angel City
7. Wreck of the "Hilma Hooker"
8. The Lake
9. Punt Vierkant
10. Windsock Steep
11. Calabas Reef
12. Town Pier
13. Hands Off Reef
14. Forest
15. Twixt
16. Carl's Hill
17. Leonora's Reef
18. Knife
19. Sampler
20. Ebo's Reef
21. La Machaca

22. Petries Pillar
23. 1000 Steps
24. Ol' Blue
25. Rappel
26. La Dania's
27. Karpata
28. Nukove
29. Boca Slagbaai
30. Playa funchi

Note: Bonaire sites are periodically closed down for rejuvenation.

Slave huts line the beach area south of Kralendijk.

Photo © 2004 Jon Huber

☆☆☆ **Windsock Steep** is known for great snorkeling. This dive is off the small sand beach opposite the airport runway. Check local dive shops for currents before entering the water. Watch out for fire coral as you explore the shallow terrace. The bottom is sandy, but stacked up with sergeant majors, angelfish, snappers, trumpetfish, and barracuda.

☆☆ **Calabas Reef**, just off the beach in front of the Divi Flamingo Resort, is reached by swimming over a sand shelf. Giant brain and star corals grow from the slope. Old anchors are scattered about. To the north is a small sailboat wreck. Reef inhabitants are parrotfish, French angels, damsels, Spanish hogfish, and yellow snappers. Spotted, goldentail, and chain morays peek out from the crevices.

☆☆☆ **La Machaca** lies off the main road in front of the Habitat Resort and dive shop. Named after a small, wrecked fishing boat, La Machaca is noted for its huge and varied fish population. Mr. Roger, a huge green moray, an old tiger grouper, friendly rock beauties, and two black margate inhabit the area.

☆☆☆ **Petries Pillar** derives its name from the colony of pillar coral that grows on the reef face. To reach this site, travel north toward Gotomeer, turn left about 4/10 of a mile after the last house onto an unpaved road. Follow that road down to the sea. Fine for boat or shore entry.

☆☆☆☆ **1000 Steps** (*Piedra Haltu*) may be either a boat or a shore dive, though a boat dive may be easier and will definitely save you carrying your gear down the (actual count, 67) steps. To reach 1000 Steps, drive north from town along the scenic road towards Gotomeer until you reach the entrance of the Radio Nederland transmitting station. On your left are steep concrete steps leading down the mountainside to a sandy beach and the dive site. Swim through the marked channel to a sandy shallow terrace. Gorgonians and flower corals are abundant. Lavender shrimp, barracuda, black durgons, yellowtail snappers, horse-eye jacks, and schoolmasters populate the reef.

☆☆☆☆ **Ol Blue**, a favorite with snorkelers for its walls of reef fish, cleaning stations and calm waters, may get choppy when the wind kicks up. Get there by driving north along the scenic road to Gotomeer past the transmitting station to the white coral-rubble beach. The dive site is at the point where the road descends to the ocean and the cliff bends away from the road.

☆☆☆☆☆ **Nukove** lies off a little road between Boca Dreifi and Playa Frans. It is a particularly nice shore dive with a channel cut through the jungle of elkhorn coral, which grows to the surface. Numerous juveniles, shrimp, and anemones may be seen in the cut. Scrawled filefish, black durgons, grouper, wrasses, and barracuda are in residence.

☆☆☆☆ **Boca Slagbaai** provides opportunity to see the best examples of buttress formations in Bonaire water. In addition, green morays, white spotted filefish, tarpon, and barracuda are in abundance. Slagbaai boasts six concrete cannon replicas, halved and buried for the 1974 film, Shark Treasure. To reach this dive site, drive through the village of Rincon and into Washington/Slagbaai National Park where you will follow the green arrows to Slagbaai. Excellent snorkeling is to the south where two real cannons may be viewed at the southernmost point of the bay.

☆☆☆☆ **Playa Funchi,** located in Washington Slagbaai National Park, is another popular snorkeling beach area. From Rincon, follow the green or

Sea Turtle, Courtesy Bonaire Tourism & Rick Sammon

yellow signs. Enter next to the man-made pier and swim north for the best snorkeling. Rays, parrotfish, rock hinds, jacks, groupers and angels swim through fields of staghorn coral. On shore, picnickers are greeted by hoards of fearless lizards in search of scraps.

Klein Bonaire

The dive sites surrounding Klein Bonaire, a nearby, uninhabited island, offers terrific snorkeling. Some may be closed down for rejuvenation.

☆☆☆ **Leonora's Reef**, on the north side, is a snorkelers' paradise with a heavy cover of yellow pencil coral, fire coral, star coral, and elkhorn stands on a narrow shallow terrace. West of the mooring are pillar coral formations. Expect to be greeted by masses of fish. Attack yellowtail snappers and tiny, royal blue fish are joined by tiger, yellow mount and rare yellowfin groupers at "cleaning stations" (areas where fish line up to have barber or cleaner shrimp pick parasites from their mouths).

☆☆☆☆ **The Forest**, another fabulous snorkeling spot, starts at 15 ft, then drops off to great depths. Two-foot-long queen triggerfish, morays, black durgons, puffers, and an abundance of small critters roam the forest.

☆☆☆☆ **Twixt**, just north of Forest, around the southwest bend of Klein Bonaire, provides excellent opportunities for wide-angle photography—with huge basket sponges, sea whips, black coral, huge pastel fans, tube sponges, and star corals. Depths range from 15 feet. The coral wall slopes down to a sandy bottom. Seas are almost always calm and flat here.

Large groupers frequent the pillar coral cleaning station at the upper edge of ☆☆☆☆☆ **Carl's Hill**. Named after photographer Carl Roessler, this delightful spot tops at 15 ft and drops sharply. An occasional strong current cleanses the huge purple finger sponges on the slope. West of the mooring, keep an eye out for cleaning stations.

☆☆☆☆ **Ebo's Reef** (aka Jerry's Jam) provides superb video and still photography opportun- ities. Dramatic overhangs of black coral grow in less than 30 ft of water. Masses of grunts, Spanish hogfish, groupers, sergeant majors, parrotfish, and yellowtail swarm the shelf. The drop-off starts at 15 ft and slopes off to a sandy bottom.

☆☆☆☆ **At Knife Reef**, a shallow, half-circle of elkhorn coral creates a mini lagoon protecting star coral heads, gorgonians, and a multitude of fish. Bermuda chubs, peacock flounders, lizardfish, and yellowhead jawfish rove the terrace.

☆☆☆☆ **Sampler** shelters spotted eels and hordes of tamed, friendly fish that will charm you as you investigate the lovely pillar and staghorn corals.

Bonaire Snorkeling Tours

Bonaire's unique Guided Snorkeling Program offers a series of 12 different guided snorkeling tours to selected sites around Bonaire and Klein Bonaire that, together, represent Bonaire's reef life. Most sites are accessible from shore, while others involve short boat trips. The Snorkeling Program is offered by the following companies—and all dive shops on the island welcome snorkelers on their scuba boat tours.

Sea & Discover, Bonaire's Marine Education Center, offers snorkel programs for children as well as the Guided Snorkel program. Groups are kept purposely small (4 adult snorkelers or 8 children) to maximize fun and learning, minimize confusion in the water, and allow the sessions to be tailored to individual interests. ☎ and fax (011) 599-717-5322. E-mail: info@seandiscover.com. Website: www.seandiscover.com.

Bon Bini Divers, at the Lions Dive & Beach Resort, offers guided tours, courses, and rentals. ☎ 717-5425, Website: www.bonbinidivers.com.

Buddy Dive, at the Buddy Dive Resort, features boats, guided and regular snorkeling tours, rentals, courses. ☎ 1-866-GO-BUDDY; local: 717-5080. Website: www.buddydive. com E-mail: info@BuddyDive .com.

Dive Inn Bonaire offers snorkeling courses and guided snorkeling tours. Wheel-chair accessible dive boat has same height as pier. ☎ (011) 599-717-8761. E-mail: info@diveinn-bonaire.com. Website: www.divein bonaire.com.

Great Adventures, at Harbour Village Beach Club, offers boat trips, rentals, guided snorkeling tours, kids' programs and more. ☎ (011) 599-717-7500. Website: www.harbourvillage.com.

Discover Bonaire, based at the Sand Dollar Condominium Resort complex, offers a variety of guided snorkeling trips and snorkel trips from kayaks, as well as other activitites. ☎ (011)599-717-2229. E-mail: info@discover bonaire.com. Website: www.discoverbonaire.com

Where to Stay on Bonaire

NOTE: For a complete list, contact the Tourism Corporation Bonaire, 10 Rockefeller Plaza, Suite 900, New York, NY 10020. ☎ 800-BONAIRE (1-800-266-2473), 1-212-956-5912, E-mail: usa@tourismbonaire.com. Website: www.infobonaire.com.

Bonaire's entire tourist trade revolves around its beautiful reefs. All but three of the island's hotels were built in the last 20 years—all especially to accommodate divers.

Buddy Dive Resort features 1-, 2-, 3-bedroom, fully-equipped apartments with kitchen, AC, TV, phones. Dive center, pools, restaurant, bar. ☎ 866-GO-BUDDY; E-mail: info@BuddyDive.com. Web: www.buddy dive. com.

Bruce Bowker's Carib Inn is one of Bonaire's most intimate dive resorts, with only 10 units. Oceanfront accommodations are air conditioned and have cable TV. Maid service, pool. Full-service dive shop, snorkel equipment rentals. ☎ (011) 599-717-8819, fax (011) 599-717-5295. Write: P.O. Box 68, Bonaire, NA. E-mail: info@caribinn.com. Website: www.caribinn.com.

Divi Flamingo Beach Resort & Casino, on the beach overlooking Calabas Reef, features standard, deluxe, and studio rooms in hotel or villa settings. A few rooms have balconies directly over the water where you can view the reef and fish swimming by. Two pools, two open-air, beachfront restaurants, casino, fitness center, dive shop. Kids' programs, guided snorkeling tours. Wheel-chair accessible custom dive boats and accom- modations. ☎ In the U.S.: 800-367-3484; E-mail: comments@diviresorts.com. Website: www.diviflamingo.com.

The Dive-Inn Dive Shop and Studios, in Kralendijk, features a small public beach and reef just across the street, and its own pier. All 7 studios feature air-conditioning, cable TV. Dive-Inn offers guided snorkel trips. Both studios and dive boat are wheel-chair accessible. ☎ (011) 599-717-8761. E-mail: info@diveinnbonaire. Website: www.diveinnbonaire.com.

Lions Dive & Beach Resort Bonaire features 31 apartments with patio or balcony, fully-equipped kitchen, cable TV, phones, AC, room safes. Four restaurants, sundeck. ☎ 1-866-LIONSDIVE (1-866-546-6734) hotel direct: (011) 599-7-5580. Website: www.lionsdive bonaire.com.

Plaza Resort Bonaire, a 224-unit, deluxe, beachfront hotel (with spacious villas and suites), offers snorkeling, a variety of watersports, Kids' programs, dive shop. Three restaurants, casino. In the U.S./Canada: ☎ 1-800-766-6016; hotel direct: (011) 599-717-2500, fax (011) 599-717-7133. E-mail: usa@plazaresortbonaire.com or info@plazaresort bonaire. com. Website: www.plazaresortbonaire.com

Captain Don's Habitat offers deluxe, oceanfront cottages, villas, studios. Good snorkeling off the beach. In the US/Canada: ☎ 1-800-327-6709; hotel direct: (011) 599-717-8290; fax (011) 599-717-8240. E-mail: info@ habitat bonaire.com. Website: www.Habitat Bonaire.com.

Harbour Village sits opposite Klein Bonaire on a powdery sand beach encompasses Harbour Village Beach Club, the Portofino Hotel and Yacht Club, two restaurants, a marina, pools, fitness and tennis facilities, and a dive shop. Guided snorkeling tours, Kids' Club, snorkeling off the beach. ☎ 1-800-424-0004. Website: www.harbourvillage.com.

Sand Dollar Resort features 75 oceanfront, fully-equipped condos (studio, 1-, 2-, 3-bedroom). Snorkeling from the shore. Sundeck at water's edge; no beach. Tennis courts, pool, restaurant overlooking the sea, pool bar, watersports. The new Bonaire Dive & Adventure (dive center) features diving, snorkeling, kayaking, nature tours, kids' programs. Bari Reef lies directly in front of the condo property. In the U.S.: ☎ -800-288-4773. Website: www.sand dollarbonaire.com.

For Additional Information

In the US and Canada: Write to the Bonaire Tourism Corporation, 10 Rockefeller Plaza, Suite 900, New York, NY 10020. ☎ 1-800-BONAIRE (800-266-2473), 212-956-5912, E-mail: usa@tourismbonaire.com.

Website: www.infobonaire.com.

British Virgin Islands

The British Virgin Islands encompass more than 60 islands with most tourist activity around the four largest—Tortola, Anegada, Virgin Gorda and Jost Van Dyke. Except for Anegada, a flat coral slab surrounded by shallow reefs, the islands are mountainous and of volcanic origin.

Clustered around the Sir Francis Drake Channel and protected from high wind and waves, the BVI rate particularly high with sailors. In fact, half the tourist beds are aboard the hundreds of yachts in Tortolas marinas.

Snorkeling is superb amidst towering coral pinnacles, canyons, massive boulders, lava chutes and almost 200 different shipwrecks. Most areas have little or no surge and only gentle currents. Visibility may reach anywhere from 50 to over 100 ft.

The best time to visit the BVI is between Mid November and June, with warmest water temperatures between mid-March and early December. Reduced rates at hotels and for charter boats exist during hurricane season, July through October. Air temperature ranges between 80° and 90° F year-round with an occasional drop in February.

British Virgin Islands Best Snorkeling Sites

Reef and wreck dives are easily arranged through the dive shops. Many offer rendezvous service which means they will pick you up from your charter boat or arrange a meeting place convenient to all. Snorkeling gear may be rented or borrowed. Bring your camera. A wetsuit top, shortie, or wetskin is recommended for winter snorkeling.

The BVI reefs are protected by law, and no living thing may be taken. Take only pictures, leave only bubbles.

Beach Entry Sites

☆☆☆☆ **The Baths**, at the southern tip of Virgin Gorda, encompasses the islands most famous beaches. The area, a natural landscape of partially submerged grottoes and caves formed by a jumble of enormous granite boulders, is a favorite beach-access snorkeling area and one of the biggest tourist attractions in the BVI. The caves shelter a variety of tropical fish. Find this area by taking the trail which starts at the end of the Baths Road. A small bar just off the beach rents snorkel equipment. Beware of dinghies! The Baths is a favorite of cruise ship visitors.

The Baths, Photo Courtesy British Virgin Islands Tourism

☆☆ **Spring Bay**, neighboring the Baths, has a gorgeous sandy beach and good snorkeling amidst the rocks.

☆☆**Crawl National Park**, a great spot for beginning snorkelers, also on Virgin Gorda, is reached via a palm-lined trail from Tower Road, just north of the Baths. A natural pond created by a boulder formation is ideal for children.

☆☆☆ **Smugglers Cove**, off the beaten path on the northwest end of Tortola, may be tough to find but, well worth the effort. The last mile leading to this spot is rough driving. There are two lovely reefs, about 100 ft out, with crowds of grunts, squirrel fish, parrot fish and some good-sized trunk fish to keep you company. Depths are shallow and seas usually calm. Good for children. The beach is shaded by palms and sea grape trees. No rest rooms or changing facilities, but there is an honor bar with sodas, beer and some snacks and a phone with a couple of taxi numbers.

Guests of the neighboring **Long Bay Beach Resort** are shuttled to Smugglers Cove twice a day.

☆☆ **Brewers Bay**, on Tortolas north coast road, has two good snorkeling sites, one to the left along the cliffs with depths from eight to 10 ft , the other in the center of the beach opposite the rock wall edging the road. The reef starts close to shore and stretches out in shallow depths for a long way. Schools of trumpet fish, octopus, stingrays and sergeant majors inhabit the area.

☆☆☆☆☆ **Loblolly Beach**, on Anegadas northern shore, is one of the best shore-entry snorkeling spots in the Caribbean when winds are calm. Coral heads teaming with fish and invertebrates are close to shore. Visibility can exceed 100 ft. There is usually some surf, but it breaks on the front of the reef which is quite a distance from shore. The Big Bamboo Bar and Restaurant on the beach is worth the trip. Owner Aubrey Levons welcomes everyone with island stories and hospitality. Loblolly Beach may be reached by taxi, bike or jeep from the Anegada Reef Resort docks.

Avoid this area during strong winds. The sea gets stirred up and visibility drops from super to silty, the beach becomes a sand blast area. Spring and summer are usually the best times to dive and snorkel Anegada.

Anchoring on Anegada Reef is prohibited. Dive and snorkeling day trips can be arranged through the dive operators. Dive BVI offers a particularly nice snorkeling trip aboard their fast 45-ft Sea Lion to Anegada which also includes beach combing and a local lobster lunch at the Anegada Reef Hotel.

Additional excellent snorkeling sites are found on the northeast corner of **Benures Bay, Norman Island**; the **Bight** and **Little Bight** also off Norman Island. At Peter Island, try the south shore at **Little Harbor** and the western shore at **Great Harbor. Diamond Reef** on the southeast side of Great Camanoe can be reached by dinghy fom Marina Cay. The shallow reef sits straight out from the utility pole on the shore.

Long Bay, near Smugglers Cove, Tortola, has pretty corals and the biggest fish, but water entry is difficult as the coral grows to the surface.

Boat Access Sites

☆☆☆☆ **The Caves at Norman Island**, accessible by boat, shelter bright sponges, corals and schools of small fish. The reef slopes down to 40 ft. Norman Island is rumored to have inspired Robert Louis Stevenson's *Treasure Island* and the Caves are reputed to be old hiding places for pirate treasure. Moorings are maintained by the National Park Trust.

☆☆☆☆☆ *Wreck of the R.M.S. Rhone*, featured in the movie *The Deep*, is by far the most popular dive in the BVI. Struck by a ferocious hurricane in October, 1867, the **Royal Mail Steamer, Rhone** was hurled onto the rocks at Salt Island as its captain, Robert F. Wooley, struggled desperately to reach open sea.

The force with which the 310-ft vessel crashed upon the rocks broke the hull in two leaving a great snorkeling area at the stern, which lies in 30 ft of water amid rocks and boulders. The top of the rudder sits just 15 ft below the surface. Its superstructure, encrusted with corals, sponges, and sea fans, provides a dramatic setting for underwater photography.

British Virgin Islands

Caribbean Sea

N
W · E
S

Jost Van Dyke

Tortola

Sir Francis Drake Channel

St. John (U.S.V.I.)

Peter Island

Norman Island

Salt Island

Cooper

Ginger

Virgin Gorda

Anegada

Dive and Snorkeling Sites

1. The "RMS Rhone"
2. "Chikuzen"
3. Chimney
4. Gary's Grottos
   (Great Dog Island)
5. "Rokus"
6. Alice in Wonderland
7. P.O. S.
8. Joe's Cave
9. Van Ryans Rock
10. Invisibles
11. Paramatta
12. The Baths
13. Crawl National Park
14. The Caves
15. Manchioneel Bay

11 |—| (3 mi.)

5 |—→| (11 mi.)

Fish greet snorkelers upon entering the water. Living among the wreckage are a 300-pound jew fish, a very curious 4 ft barracuda named Fang, schools of snappers, grunts, jacks, arrow crabs, squirrel fish, and yellow tail.

Usually calm sea conditions make this a good spot for surface snorkeling or free diving. Excellent visibility runs between 50 to over 100 ft. Also, the *Rhone* is a national park and off limits to coral collecting and spear fishing. The wreck sits off Black Rock Point on the southwest tip of Salt Island. Boat-access.

☆☆☆☆ **The Chimney**, located at Great Dog Island off the west end of Virgin Gorda, features a spectacular coral archway and canyon, covered with a wide variety of soft corals, sponges and rare white coral. Hundreds of fish follow snorkelers across the archway to a coral-wrapped, tube-like formation resembling a huge chimney. The many shallow areas and protected-cove location make this a terrific snorkeling spot. Boat access only. Some surge and currents when wind is out of the north.

☆☆☆ **Garys Grottos** lies near the shoreline, four miles north of Spanish Town on Virgin Gorda. It is a shallow reef characterized by three huge arches which resemble a tunnel. This rocky area is teeming with shrimp, squid and sponges. Depths average 30 ft.

☆☆ **Great Dog Island's** south side drops off to a shallow reef with 10-to-60 ft depths. Nice elkhorn stands hide spotted and golden moray eels, spiny lobster and barber shrimp. Good for snorkeling when seas are calm.

☆☆☆☆☆ **Alice in Wonderland**, a coral wall at South Bay off Ginger Island, slopes from 15 ft. Named for its huge mushroom corals, villainous overhangs, and gallant brain corals, this ornate reef shelters longnose butterfly fish, rays, conch and garden eels. Visibility is good and seas are usually calm. Boat dive, good for photography, and free diving.

Private yachts should choose the eastern mooring which is closer to the larger coral ridges.

☆☆☆ **Blonde Rock**, a pinnacle between Dead Chest and Salt Island, starts at 15 ft below the surface. Coral encrusted tunnels, caves and over-hangs support a wealth of crabs, lobsters and reef fish. Good for snorkeling when seas are calm. Boat access.

☆☆ **Van Ryans Rock**, a seamount in Drakes Channel, sits between Beef Island and Virgin Gorda. The top is at 16 ft with boulders and coral leading down to a sandy plain. Nurse sharks, eels, huge turtles, lobster, jacks, spade fish, and barracuda circle. Snorkelers should take care to avoid the huge clumps of fire coral. A light current is occasionally encountered.

☆☆☆ **Invisibles** , a sea mount off Tortolas northeast tip, is a haven for nurse shark, eels, turtles and all types of reef fish from the smallest to the largest. Diver, Gayla Kilbride describes this area as a Symphony of Fish. Depths go from three ft to 65 ft.

☆☆☆☆ *Wreck of the Paramatta*, which ran aground on her maiden voyage in 1853, rests at 30 ft off the southeast end of Anegada. The ship sits on a dense coral reef perfect for snorkelers. If you stand on the ships engine, youll be shoulder deep. Enormous reef fish swim around the wreck, including a 200-pound jew fish, 30-pound groupers, butterfly fish, turtles, and rays. Still remaining are the stern and bow sections, long chain, port holes, and cleats of the wreck, all sitting amid beautiful elkhorn and staghorn coral formations, large sea fans, brain corals and red and orange sponges. This is a great spot for underwater portraits.

☆☆ **Manchioneel Bay**, Cooper Island, has a beautiful shallow reef with packs of fish around the moorings.

Snorkeling Tours & Rentals

Dive BVI Ltd., a PADI five-star shop, operates out of Leverick Bay, Virgin Gorda Yacht Harbour, Peter Island and Marina Cay. Owner Joe Giacinto has been diving and snorkeling the BVI for 29 years and knows all the best spots. Snorkeling trips are offered to Anegada and other spots aboard the SeaCat or Sealion, fast, large, wave-piercing catamarans. Write: P.O. Box 1040, Virgin Gorda, BVI ☎ 800-848-7078/284-495-5513. E-mail: info@divebvi.com.

Underwater Safaris, at the Moorings Mariner Inn on Tortola and Cooper Island, offers fast 42- and 30-ft dive boats. The Tortola shop is the BVIs largest retail dive shop. Write: P.O. Box 139, Road Town, Tortola. ☎ 800-537-7032 or 284-494-3235, fax 284-494-5322. Web: underwater safaris.com.

Dive Shops in the Sun at the Prospect Reef Resort Marina offers reef and wreck trips for snorkelers of all ages and abilities. Skilled guides and instructors. Small groups allow personal attention. Comfortable, fast boat. Snorkel vests for your safety. Full-day and half-day packages. ☎ 284-494-1147 Fax: 284-494-8599. Email: caribimages10@hotmail.com.

Kilbrides Sunchaser Scuba, at the famous Bitter End Yacht Club on Virgin Gorda, features tours to 50 different dive locations. Snorkelers join the scuba divers on reef and wreck tours. Prices lower on the afternoon trips. ☎ 800-932-4286 or 284-495-9638; fax 284-495-7549. Most sites are near islands with superb snorkeling. Website: www.sunchasersscuba.com. Email: info@sunchasersscuba.com. Live-Aboards Vacations

Sail-dive vacations are an easy way to enjoy a variety of snorkeling sites and destinations. Live-aboard yachts are chartered with captain, captain and crew, or bare to qualified sailors. Navigation is uncomplicated, you can tour most of the area without ever leaving sight of land.

With sailing almost a religion in the BVI, it is easy to customize a live-aboard snorkeling vacation. If you are an experienced sailor you can charter a bareboat and see the sights on your own. If you've never sailed before, you can captain a crewed yacht to find the best snorkeling spots. Or book a week-long cruise on a commercial live-aboard where you'll meet other avid snorkelers. Prices on private charters vary with the number of people in your party. With four to six people, a crewed yacht will average about the same cost as a stay at a resort. Be sure to specify that you are a snorkeler.

Cuan Law. One of the worlds largest trimarans (105 ft long, 44 wide), *Cuan Law* was specifically designed with divers and snorkelers in mind. As with most live-aboards, you are offered all the diving you can stand. *Cuan Law* accommodates 18 passengers in 10 large, airy double cabins, each with private head and shower. The captain visits all the best snorkeling spots. Cruises are booked up from three months to a year in advance. Plan early. ☎ 800-648- 3393 or 284-494-2490. E-mail: cuanlaw@surfbvi.com. Website: www.cuanlaw.com.

Yacht Promenade, a sleek, 65-ft tri-hull sailing yacht for couples or groups of six to 12 features spacious air-conditioned cabins, full breakfasts, lunches, cocktails, hors d'oeuvres and three-course gourmet dinners. There are five guest staterooms, one in each outer hull and three at the rear of the center hull, three queen-sized berths and two that are larger than king and can be converted into four single berths. Vacations include use of 11-ft kayaks, a banana boat, and a board sail. Snorkelers go in off the back of the boat. Pick up at Village Cay Marina, Road Town, Tortola. ☎ (US) 800-526-5503 or 284-494-3853. Website: www.yachtpromenade.com.

The Moorings Ltd. offers Cabin N Cruise tours for those wishing to enjoy a fully crewed sailing vacation without having to charter an entire yacht. ☎ 800-535-7289. See listing below.

Bareboating

Private sailing yachts with diving guides and instructors are available from most of the charter operators listed below. You can arrange for your own personal live-aboard snorkeling vacation. Be sure to specify your needs before going.

Bareboating can be surprisingly affordable for groups of four or more. Boats must be reserved six to nine months in advance for winter vacations and at least three months in advance for summer vacations.

Experience cruising on a similar yacht is required and you will be asked to fill out a questionnaire or produce a sailing resume. Instructor-skippers are available for refresher sailing. A cruising permit, available from the Customs Department, is required. For a complete list of charter companies contact the BVI Tourist Board at ☎800-835-8530 or write 370 Lexington Ave. Suite 1605, New York, NY 10017. Www.bviwelcome.com

The Moorings Ltd., Tortola, has been operating for 35 years. Their charter boats range from 32 ft to 60 ft luxury yachts, both mono-hulled and catamarans. The Moorings cruise guide, shows aerial photographs of the best anchorages in the British Virgin Islands.

A three-day sailing vacation can be combined with a four day resort vacation at the Moorings Mariner Inn. Write to The Moorings, Ltd., 19345 US Hwy 19 North, Clearwater, Florida. 34624. ☎ 800-535-7289, 800-669-6529 or 727-535-1446. Website: www. moorings.com. Email: yacht@ moorings. com.

A Fast Track to Cruising course, offered by **Offshore Sailing School**, includes the complete Learn to Sail course and Moorings/Offshore Live Aboard Cruising course on consecutive weeks. Available starting Sundays year-round (two person minimum for Live Aboard cruising), the package includes 10 days/nine nights accommodations ashore, six days/five nights aboard a Moorings yacht, Learn to Sail and Live Aboard Cruising courses, textbooks, certificates, wallet cards, logbook, full day practice sail, split yacht provisioning during onboard portion of Live Aboard Cruising course (five breakfasts, five lunches, three dinners) graduation dinners ashore, airport or ferry transfers in Tortola. ☎ 800-454-8002 or 239-454-1700. Website: www.offshore-sailing.com. Email: sail@offshore-sailing.com. Write to: Offshore Sailing School, 16731 McGregor Blvd., Ft. Myers, FL 33908.

Where to Stay in the British Virgin Islands
Web site: www.bviwelcome.com.

Tortola

Every type of accommodation is available in the BVI from tents to cottages, guesthouses, condos, luxury resorts to live aboard sailboats and motor yachts. Reservations can be made through your travel agent or the BVI Tourist Board at ☎ 800-835-8530 or online. Resorts listed below cater to divers and snorkelers, however simpler accommodations exist and may be found on the website: www.bviwelcome.com.

BVI Villas rents upscale private homes and villas. ☎ 800-862-863

Long Bay Beach Resort on Tortolas north shore has 82 deluxe hillside and beachfront accommodations. ☎ 800-729-9599. Write: P.O. Box 433, Road Town Tortola, BVI. Website: www.longbay.com.

The Moorings-Mariner Inn, Tortola, is home port to The Moorings charter boat operation. No beach. The poolside bar and restaurant are just a few steps from Underwater Safaris, the largest retail shop in the BVI.

The resort offers a new **Shore N Sail** vacation with three nights aboard a luxurious sailing yacht (snorkeling included) with your own skipper and provisions and four nights at the resort. ☎ 800-535-7289, 284-494-2332, fax 813-530-9747, or write The Moorings Mariner Inn, 1305 US 19 S., Suite 402, Clearwater, FL 34624. E-mail: yacht@moorings.com Website: www.moorings.com

Nanny Cay Resort & Marina, two miles southwest of Road Town, has 41 air-conditioned guest rooms with TV and phones. Amenities include a fresh water pool, restaurant, bar, tennis, board surfing school and Blue Water Divers. Marina. ☎ 284-494-4895. Web: www.nannycay.com. Email: hotel@nannycay.com.

Prospect Reef Resort is a sprawling 130-room, oceanfront resort on the west end of Road Town, Tortola, facing Sir Francis Drake Channel. Guest accommodations range from studios to full apartments, and luxury villas. Amenities include six tennis courts, miniature golf, two restaurants and three pools. Rooms are cooled by ceiling fans and sea breezes. ☎ 800-356-8937 or 284-494-3311.

Prospect Reef Marina offers snorkeling for all skill levels. Website: www.prospectreef.com.

Sugarmill, at Apple Bay on the northwest shore of Tortola, is the best small hotel on the island with good snorkeling off the beach, which is sheltered by two reefs. Hillside cottages built around the remains of a 360-year-old sugar mill are air conditioned and have internet connections. Proprietors, Jeff and Jinx Morgan, are famous for their gourmet meals. Snorkeling tours arranged. Email: sugmill@surfbvi.com. Website: www.sugarmillhotel.com. ☎ 800-462-8834 or 284-495-4355, fax 284-495-4696.

Treasure Isle Hotel, Roadtown, has 40 air-conditioned rooms, pool, restaurant, bar. ☎ 284- 494-2501. Snorkeling trips with Underwater Safaris. ☎ 800-223-1108 or 877-903-2525. Email: info@treasureislehotel.net.

MARINA CAY

Pusser's Marina Cay, a six-acre island off the northeast tip of Tortola, features Dive BVIs newest dive and water sports center offering daily snorkeling trips, ocean kayaks, two new Hobe catamarans, Pusser's Fine Dining and a large Company Store.

Marina Cay Resort offers four one-bedroom units and two two-bedroom villas that accommodate up to 16 guests. ☎ 284-494-2174. Web info on www.bviwelcome.com. Email: marinacay@pussers.com

VIRGIN GORDA

The Bitter End Yacht Club on Virgin Gorda's North Sound offers guest rooms in luxury villas along the shore and hillside or bare boat a Freedom 30 live-aboard yacht. The club bar is the favorite story-swapping place for sailing and diving folk. Daily snorkeling trips, arranged through Kilbrides Sunchaser Scuba, leave from the Bitter End Docks every morning. ☎ 800-872-2392, or 284-494-2746 or write P.O. Box 46, Virgin Gorda, BVI.

Biras Creek Estate, located on a 140-acre peninsula, can be reached by scheduled ferry from Tortola. The resort has 34 luxury villas with garden and ocean views overlooking North Sound. Recently refurbished, the resort provides complimentary use of Boston Whalers and 25-ft sailboats.☎ 800-608-9661 or 284-494-3555, fax 284-494-3557. In the US ☎ 800-223-1108; from the UK 0-800-894. 057 Write: P.O. Box 54, Virgin Gorda, BVI. Website: www.biras.com. Email: biras@biras.com

Little Dix Bay features 90 luxury suites and guest rooms on a half-mile of pristine beach surrounded by tropical gardens. Watersports center on premises offers snorkeling tours. ☎ 800-928-3000, 888-767-3966 or book through your travel agent. Website: www.littledixbay.com.

Peter Island Resort & Yacht Harbour offers luxurious beachfront rooms overlooking Sprat Bay and the Sir Francis Drake Channel. Excellent snorkeling off the beach. Dive facility on site. ☎ 800-346-4451, 770-476-9988 or 284-495-2000, fax 284-495-2500. Website: peterisland. com. Email: reservations@peterisland.com.

ANEGADA

Tiny Anegada, 12 miles northwest of Virgin Gorda, covers just 15 square miles. This off-the-beaten-track coral atoll, surrounded by uninterrupted beaches and gorgeous reefs, is home to 250 residents and a huge community of exotic Caribbean birds including a flamingo colony, herons, terns and ospreys. Shipwrecks and coral heads abound, a delight for snorkelers, but sailors beware approaching the island by boat can be treacherous without local knowledge and eyeball navigation. Snorkeling, diving and fly fishing, done from shore, is outstanding

Much of the islands interior is a preserve for 2,000 wild goats, donkeys and cattle. Not for the average tourist, but a great spot if you want to get away from it all. Expect encounters with a ferocious mosquito population—carry as much repellent as you can. Fly in from Beef Island, Tortola or go by boat from any of the marinas.

Anegada Reef Hotel, on Setting Point, offers great beaches, snorkeling and fly fishing, 16 lovely, air-conditioned rooms, tackle shop, tank fills. Informal restaurant. Jeep and bicycle rentals. Resort shuttle to snorkeling areas. 284-495-8002, fax 284-495-9362. Website: www.anegadareef.com. Email: info@anegadareef.com.

Anegada Beach Campground offers 8 x 10 and 10 x 12' tents, a restaurant, beach bar and snorkeling tours. Bare sites cost $7 per person, per night, equipped tents are $20 per person. ☎ 284-495-9466 or write to Box 2710, Anegada, BVI.

Additional Information

For a list of all guesthouses, apartments, hotels, campgrounds, charter operators, and restaurants contact the British Virgin Islands Tourist Board.

In Tortola: 2nd Floor, Akara Building, DeCastro Street, Road Town, ☎ (284) 494-3134, fax: (284) 494-3866. Email: bvitourb@surfbvi.com.

In New York: 370 Lexington Avenue, Suite 1605, New York, NY 10017, E-mail: bvitouristboard@worldnet.att.net; ☎ (800) 835-8530, or 212-696-0400.

In Atlanta: BVI Tourist Board, 3390 Peachtree Road, NE, Suite 1000, Lenox Towers Atlanta, GA 30326, ☎ 404- 240-8018, fax: (404) 364-6582.

In London: W1P 3PG, ☎ (44) 207 947 820, fax: (44) 207 947 8279, E-mail: bvi@bho.fcb.com.

Website: www.bviwelcome.com

Cayman Islands

The Cayman Islands—Grand Cayman, Cayman Brac and Little Cayman —host more than 200,000 watersports enthusiasts each year. Located 480 miles south of Miami (a two-hour flight), the islands boast some of the most exciting snorkeling spots in the world with outstanding visibility, diverse marine life, and robust coral communities—many a short swim from shore.

Physically beautiful, both above and beneath the sea, each island is blessed with an extraordinary fringing reef, superb marine life, and long stretches of sparkling, palm-lined beaches.

Underwater Cayman is a submerged mountain range—complete with cliffs, drop-offs, gullies, caverns, sink holes, and forests of coral. The islands are the visible above-the-sea portions of the mountains. At depth, the Cayman Trench drops off to more than 23,000 ft.

Grand Cayman, the largest and the most developed of the three islands, has several snorkeling boat operators and a wide choice of beachfront resorts. Cayman Brac and Little Cayman lie 89 miles northeast of the big island and are separated by a seven-mile-wide channel. Both wildly beautiful, each has its own special personality.

With daily direct flights from North America and easy access from many other parts of the globe, most vacationers head first for Grand Cayman. Its

Photo: *Seafeather Bay, Cayman Brac*
Photo © 2004 Jon Huber

famed Seven Mile Beach is headquarters for snorkeling Activity—with several terrific beach-entry sites.

When To Go

Late summer and fall bring chance of a hurricane, but snorkeling is possible year round. Conditions are generally mild, although steady winds can kick up some chop. When this happens, dive boats simply move to the leeward side of the island and calmer waters. Air temperature averages 77°F. Water temperature averages 80°F.

Marine Park Regulations

With a dramatic growth in tourism and an increase in cruise ship arrivals, the islands have enacted comprehensive legislation to protect the fragile marine environment. Marine areas are divided into three types: Marine Park Zone, Replenishment Zone, and Environmental Zone.

The Marine Park Zones outlaw the taking of any marine life, living or dead, and only line fishing from shore and beyond the dropoff is permitted. Anchoring is allowed only at fixed moorings. (There are more than 200 permanent moorings around the islands.)

It is an offense for any vessel to cause reef damage with anchors or chains anywhere in Cayman waters.

In a Replenishment Zone, the taking of conch or lobster is prohibited, and spear guns, pole spears, fish traps and nets are prohibited. Line fishing and anchoring (at fixed moorings) are permitted. (Spearguns and Hawaiian slings may not be brought into the country.)

Environmental Zones are the most strictly regulated. There is an absolute ban on the taking of any kind of marine life, alive or dead; anchoring is prohibited and no in-water activities of any kind are tolerated. These areas are a breeding ground and nursery for the fish and other creatures which will later populate the reef and other waters.

The Marine Conservation Board employs full-time officers who may search any vessel or vehicle thought to contain marine life taken illegally. Penalties may include a maximum fine of CI$5,000 or imprisonment, or both.

Best Snorkeling Sites of Grand Cayman
BEACH SITES

Patch reefs and coral heads teeming with reef fish lie just a few yards off several of the island's swimming beaches. The best shore spots exist off **West Bay Cemetery, Seven Mile Beach, the Eden Rock Dive Center** in Georgetown, **Smith Cove, The Treasure Island Resort beach, Rum Point Club, Parrots Landing, Seaview Hotel, Coconut Harbour,**

Sunset House, Pirates Inn, Frank Sound, Half Moon Bay, East End Diving Lodge and **Morritt's Tortuga Club**. Depths range from three to 20 ft. Clearer water and more dramatic coral formations are found farther offshore and may be reached by boat. Snorkeling cruises, some with dinner or lunch, are offered by the hotels and dive shops. Snorkelers are urged to inquire about currents and local conditions in unfamiliar areas before attempting to explore on their own.

Swimmers off the Rum Point Club beach should stay clear of the channels, which have rip tides. Grand Cayman's Southwest Point shows a good variety of juvenile reef fish and invertebrates on a rocky bottom close to shore. Currents beyond 100 yards are dangerous.

A trail marked by a round blue and white sign with a swimmer outline denotes access through private property to the beach. All Cayman beaches are free for public use.

☆☆ **Smith's Cove**, south of George Town, shelters a shallow reef whiskered with pastel sea fans and plumes. Trumpet fish, squirrel fish, schools of grunts, sergeant majors, butterfly fish, parrot fish, and angels offer constant entertainment. The reef sits 150 ft from the beach at Southwest Point. Depths are from 15ft.

☆☆ **Eden Rocks**, favored by cruise ship groups, lies less than 200 yds offshore from the Eden Rock Diving Center. Depths range from five to 40 ft. The reef features beautiful coral grottoes, walls, caves and tunnels and tame fish. If you've yet to befriend a fish, this area offers the proper social climate. Good visibility and light currents are the norm here.

Boat Sites

☆☆☆☆ **Sand Bar at Stingray City** in North Sound is home to several tame stingrays. Depths are shallow to 12 ft. Boat tours departing from George Town or Seven Mile Beach are either a half- or full-day tour.

Stingray City is the most photographed dive site in the Caymans, if not the entire Caribbean. Pictured in all the tourist board ads, the subject of endless travel articles and an Emmy-award film by Stan Waterman, this gathering of Southern stingrays in the shallow area of North Sound is a marine phenomenon which has thrilled divers and snorkelers since its discovery by two dive instructors, Pat Kinney and Jay Ireland, early in 1986.

Today, the 20-member cast of rays are big celebrities, luring curious visitors—as many as 150-200 per day—from across the globe. Feeding time occurs whenever a snorkeling boat shows up.

Grand Cayman Snorkeling Tours

Ambassador Divers offers snorkeling trips, gear rental, video rental, trips to Stingray City. ☎ (011) 345-949-8839, fax (011) 345-949-8838. E-mail: ambadive @candw.ky. Website: www.ambassadordivers.com.

Bob Soto's Reef Divers, at the Treasure Island Hotel and the Scuba Centre (near to Soto's Reef), has snorkeling trips, photo and video services, gear rentals, and comfortable, custom dive boats. In the US ☎ 800-BOB-SOTO (800-262-7686); direct: (011) 345-949-2022; fax 345-949-8731. E-mail: bobsotos@candw.ky. Website: www.bobsotos diving.com.ky.

Capt. Marvin's Watersports. Located in West Bay. Private/group snorkeling trips, Stingray City tours, courses, and gear rental. ☎ 866-978-0022, (011) 345-945-6975. E-mail: info@captainmarvins.com. Website: www.captainmarvins.com.

Captain Crosby's Watersports, at Coconut Place Tropic Center, specializes in snorkeling and dive trips to Stingray City. Half- and full-day. Snorkeling equipment and lunch included. 47-ft trimaran sailboat. Gear, photo, and video rentals. ☎ (011) 345-945-4049. E-mail: crosby@cayman.org. Website: www.cayman.org/crosby.

Don Foster's Dive Cayman, a full-service facility based at the Comfort Suites and in George Town, offers snorkeling excursions, Stingray City trips. Gear and photo equipment rentals. A reef with depths from 18-60 feet is located right in front of the shop at Casuarina Point in George Town. Snorkelers are also welcome to use the facilities at any time at no charge. In the U.S. and Canada: ☎ 1-800-83-DIVER (1-800-833-4837); direct: (011) 345-949-6579; Comfort Suites Dive Shop (011) 345-946-3483. E-mail: donfosters@cayman.org. Website: www.donfosters.com.

Eden Rock Diving Center, in George Town, touts unlimited shore diving on George Town's Waterfront. Eden Rock Reef and Devil's Grotto are a short swim from the dive shop. Snorkel trips. Photo, video, and snorkel gear rentals. ☎ (011) 345-949-7243, fax (011) 345-949-0842. Write: P.O. Box 1907, George Town, Grand Cayman,BWI. Website: www.edenrockdive.com.

Off the Wall Divers offer personalized dive/snorkeling tours. Trips to Stingray City. ☎ and fax (011) 345-945-7525. Write: P.O. Box 30176, Seven Mile Beach, Grand Cayman, BWI. E-mail: info@otwdivers.com. Website: www.otwdivers.com.

Red Baron Divers visits top snorkeling areas. Banana boat, catamaran, ocean kayak, sailboat, parasail rentals. ☎ (011)345-916-1293, fax (011)

345-947-0116. Write: P.O. Box 11369 APO, George Town, Grand Cayman, BWI. E-mail: info@redbarondivers.com. Website: www.redbaron divers.com.

Red Sail Sports, at the Hyatt, Westin, Marriot, Holiday Inn, Morritts Tortuga, Royal Palms, and Rum Point Resorts, offers snorkel and dive trips, dinner sails and cocktail cruises. Photo, video, and snorkel gear rentals. Sailboat, catamaran, kayak, waverunner rentals. SASY. ☎ 1-877-REDSAIL (1-877-733-7245); direct: (011) 345-945-5965, fax (011) 345-945-5808. Write: P.O. Box 31473, Seven Mile Beach, Grand Cayman, Cayman Islands, BWI. E-mail: infocayman@redsailcayman.com. Web: redsailcayman.com.

Resort Sports Limited, at Beach Club Colony Dive Resort and Spanish Bay Reef Resort, offers Stingray City trips and snorkeling tours. ☎ 1-800-48-2DIVE; direct: Beach Club Colony ☎ (011) 345-949-8100, fax (011) 345-949-5167; Spanish Bay Reef ☎ (011) 345-949-3765, fax (011) 345-945-1842.

Sunset Divers, at Sunset House, is best known for its underwater photo center run by Cathy Church. The Photo Centre offers 35mm and video camera rental, processing and photo instruction for all levels. Snorkeling trips, Stingray City Snorkel. In the US ☎ 1-888-854-4767; direct: (011) 345-949-7111, fax (011) 345-949-7101. Write to P.O. Box 479 George Town, Grand Cayman, Cayman Islands, BWI. E-mail: sunsethouse @sunsethouse.com. Website: www.sunsethouse.com.

Treasure Island Divers, at the Treasure Island Resort, offers snorkeling trips and sail cruises to all four sides of Grand Cayman. Their 45-foot boats offer freshwater showers, marine heads and a sundeck which shades the bottom deck. In the U.S. and Canada: ☎ 1-800-872-7552; direct: (011) 345-949-4456, fax (011) 345-946-4348. Write: P.O. Box 30975 Seven Miles Beach, Grand Cayman, Cayman Islands, BWI. E-mail: info@tidivers.com. Website: www.tidivers.com.

Charter Boat Headquarters, in the Coconut Place Shopping Center on West Bay Road, offers snorkel sails, glass-bottom boat rides, submarine rides, dinner cruises, fishing, and more. ☎ (011) 345-945-4340. E-mail: charter@ candw.ky. Website: www.cay man.com.ky/com/ fishing.

Where to Stay on Grand Cayman
Seven Mile Beach Accommodations

The Beachcomber is an older 24-unit, condo complex within walking distance of shops, grocery and restaurants. Each of the air-conditioned, two-bedroom units has a patio with ocean views. Free access to local world-class gym/spa. Snorkel from the beach over patch corals and fish. ☎ (011) 345-945-4470, fax: (011) 345-945-5019. Write: P.O. Box 1799, George town, Grand Cayman, Cayman Islands, BWI. E-mail: beachcom@candw.ky. Website: www.beachcomber1.com.

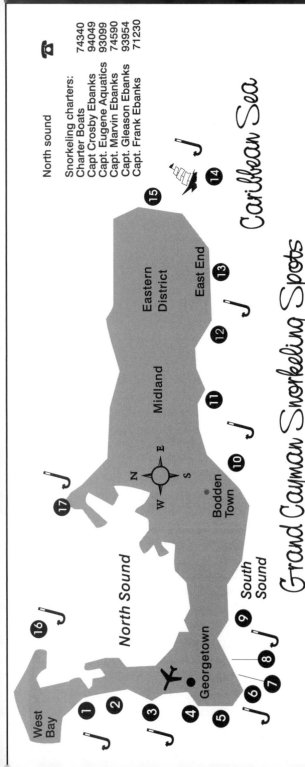

Grand Cayman Snorkeling Spots

Caribbean Sea

North sound

Snorkeling charters:
Charter Boats   74340
Capt Crosby Ebanks   94049
Capt. Eugene Aquatics   93099
Capt. Marvin Ebanks   74590
Capt. Gleason Ebanks   93954
Capt. Frank Ebanks   71230

1. West Bay Cemetery
2. Seven Mile Beach
3. Ramada Hotel Beach
4. Bob Soto's Scuba Center
5. Eden Rock Smith's Cove
6. Southwest Point
   (Stay near shore, dangerous
   currents beyond 100 yards)
7. Lighthouse Cay (boat access only)

8. Cemetery & public-access
   beach
9. Prospect Community Centre
   (stay inside bay to east)
10. Pirates Inn
11. Frank sound
    (long swim to reef)
12. Halfmoon Bay
    (Nice shallows, protected area)
13. East End Diving Lodge
    (Shallow reef)

14. Wreck of the *Ridgefield*
    (boat access only. Superb snorkeling
    inside reef on calm days)
15. Morritt's Tortuga Club
16. Stingray City & Sand Bar
17. Rum Point Club
    (Excellent snorkeling, but avoid
    getting close to the channels
    where dangerous rip tides exist)

Note: Snorkeling trips may be booked through
most dive shops or arranged through the hotel desks

Caribbean Club features 18 individual, oceanfront and garden, one-two-bedroom villas. Restaurant, bar, air-conditioning, tennis court, beach, Laundromat. ☎ (011) 345-945-4099, fax (011) 345-945-4443. Write: P.O. Box 30499, Seven Mile Beach, Grand Cayman, Cayman Islands, BWI. E-mail: info@caribclub.com. Website: www.caribclub.com.

Treasure Island Resort, a 25-acre beachfront, hotel features 277 spacious, air-conditioned rooms. Restaurants, bar, three pools, dive shop. Scooter and bicycle rentals. In the US ☎ 1-800-992-2015; hotel direct: (011) 345-949-7777, fax (011) 345-949-8672. Write: P.O. Box 1817 George Town, Grand Cayman, Cayman Islands, BWI. E-mail: info@icon-hotels.com. Website: www.tresureislandresort.net.

Hyatt Regency Grand Cayman, adjacent to the Britannia Golf Course. A complete beachfront luxury resort in British Colonial design, with 289 deluxe rooms, including new beach-view suites and 85 villas. Restaurants, bars, pools, salon, hot tub, massage, tennis, croquet, dive shop, spa, snorkeling, boating, board sailing, parasailing, waterskiing, shops, children's programs, car rentals. Red Sail Watersports on premises. Handicapped accessible. ☎ 1-800-233-1234; hotel direct: (011) 345-949-1234, fax (011) 345-949-8528. Write: P.O. Box 1588, George Town, Grand Cayman, Cayman Islands, BWI. E-mail: dunck@camapo.hyatt.com. Website: www.grandcayman.hyatt.com.

Westin Casuarina Resort and Villas offers 343 guest rooms, pools, swim-up bar, salon, tennis, dive shop, beach, and shops on a lovely stretch of Seven Mile Beach. ☎ 1-800-WESTIN-1 (1-800-937-8461); hotel direct: (011) 345-945-3800, fax (011) 345-949-5825. Write: P.O. Box 30620, Seven Mile Beach, Grand Cayman, Cayman Islands, BWI. E-mail: fommgr@candw.ky. Website: www.starwood.com/Westin.

Indies Suites Grand Cayman Resort Hotel, a luxurious beachfront, 40-suite hotel, features snorkeling trips to Stingray City, the North and West Walls, gear rental. Red Sail Water Sports on premises. In the U.S. and Canada: ☎ 1-866-846-3437; hotel direct: (011) 345-945-5025. Website: www.indiessuites.com.

Sunset House, a 59-room resort owned and operated by divers for divers, sits south of Seven Mile Beach. Good snorkeling exists off the property's shoreline. In the US ☎ 1-800-854-4767; hotel direct: (011) 345-949-7111. Website: www.sunsethouse.com.

Treasure Island Condominiums offers 96 beachfront condos, with all the amenities of a hotel resort. 1-, 2-, 3-bedroom. Great snorkeling right in front.

☎ 1-800-999-1338; hotel direct: (011) 345-949-8533, fax (011) 345-949-8531. Write: Airport P.O. Box 11513, Grand Cayman, Cayman Islands, BWI. E-mail: cayman@ticondos.com. Web: www.ticondos.com.

CocoPlum Condominiums, about a half mile from George Town on a secluded section of Seven Mile Beach, offers one-, two- and three-bedroom oceanview and oceanfront fully furnished apartments with central air conditioning, T.V., phone. Two fresh water pools, tennis courts, beach, snorkeling, and daily maid service. ☎ (011) 345-949-5959, fax (011) 345-949-0150. Website: www.cocoplumcayman.com.

Grand Cayman Marriott Beach Resort towers five stories over Seven Mile Beach. Offers 305 spacious rooms, four deluxe suites, and stunning views. There's a snorkeling reef about 50 feet out, restaurants, bar, snack bar, pool, spa, dive shop. ☎ 800-228-9290. Website: www.marriotthotels.com/gcmgc.

West Bay Accommodations

Discovery Point Club, a 40-unit beach condo at the north end of Seven Mile Beach at West Bay, offers a terrific beach with nice snorkeling. Hot tub, pool, tennis courts, Laundromat. Children six and under stay free. ☎ (011) 345-945-4724, E-mail: vacation@discoverypointclub.com. Website: www.discoverypointclub.com.

CAYMAN BRAC

Often called the loveliest of the islands, Cayman Brac (brac is Gaelic for bluff) is rumored to be the resting place of pirates' treasure. Its most striking feature is a 140-foot-high limestone formation covered by unusual foliage, including flowering cactus, orchids, and tropical fruits such as mango and papaya. Rare species of birds (including the endangered green, blue, and red Caymanian parrot) inhabit the island—which is a major flyway for migratory birds. Resident brown booby birds soar the cliffs.

Best Snorkeling Sites of Cayman Brac

Several excellent shore-entry points exist off the north and south shores. Wind conditions determine which area is calm. Usually, if the north shore spots are choppy, the south shore is calm. Check with area dive shops for daily conditions.

☆☆☆ **WindSock Reef** and the ***Wreck of the Tibbetts***, in White Bay off the northwest coast, is the Brac's most popular beach-entry snorkeling spot. A spur and groove reef encircles gardens of elkhorn, pillar corals, sea fans, orange sponges, and gorgonians. Expect good visibility and usually calm seas. Typical inhabitants are stoplight parrot fish, blue tangs, midnight parrot fish, sergeant majors, turtles, grey angels, grunts, trumpet fish, and triggerfish. Shore area depths range from four to 20 ft.

Farther out lies the wreck of the *Tibbetts*, a 330-ft Russian destroyer built for the Cuban Navy that was renamed the Captain Keith Tibbets and deliberately sunk on September 17, 1996. The vessel, the Caymans' most exciting new dive attraction, can be reached from shore if you don't mind a 200-yard swim. Fore and aft cannons, a missile launcher and machine gun turrets remain on the ship. Snorkelers may easily view the top of the radar tower at 12 feet and the bridge at 32 feet below the surface. Check with area dive shops before venturing out. Visibility usually 100 ft or better.

To reach White Bay, travel the North Shore Rd (A6) west from the airport main gate to Promise Lane. Turn right down the road.

☆☆ **Stake Bay**. Find this spot by turning off the North Shore Rd at the Cayman Brac Museum. Reef terrain, depths, and fish life are similar to White Bay. Sea conditions are usually calm, but will kick up when the wind is out of the North. A steel stairway leads to the reef. Lots of parking.

☆☆ **Scotts Jetty**, behind Scotts Development building has lots of corals and fishes along the rocks. This is across from the Tibetts Square parking lot.

☆☆ **Creek** lies off the north shore. A turn towards the shore from Cliffs Store on the North Shore Rd (A6) will lead to the Island Dock. Enter from the beach area left of the dock, facing seaward. Dense patches of elkhorn predominate. Depths are shallow to 30 ft. Angels, small turtles, and sergeant majors swarm the reef. Wind speed and direction determine the conditions, though seas are usually calm with a light current.

Additional entry points are found at the boat launching areas where cuts through the dense coral have been blasted. Parking is available alongside the north road.

South Shore

☆☆ **Sea Feather Bay**, located off the South Shore Rd. at the Bluff Road crossing, provides haven for pretty wrasses, turtles, blue parrot fish, grouper, indigo hamlets, squirrelfish, porkfish, blue tangs, and rockfish. Reef terrain comprises long stretches of dense elkhorn interspersed with tube sponges, fire coral, rose coral, and gorgonians. After a big storm, this area becomes a wash-up zone for some strange cargo, such as rubber doll parts and unusual bottles which may come from Jamaica or Cuba. Expect some surge and shallow breakers. Visibility good, though silt may churn up the shallows following a storm.

Experienced snorkelers may want to dive the barrier reef at the south western tip of the island. Water entry is best by boat, but if you enjoy a long swim you can get out to the reef from either the public beach or one of the hotel beaches.

Cayman Brac Snorkeling Tours

Dive Tiara, at the Divi Tiara Dive Resort offers snorkel trips, photo and gear rentals. Photo Tiara offers the Nikon School of Underwater Photography, a full-service photo and video center with equipment rental and instruction. ☎ 800-661-DIVE or 345-948-1553, E-mail: divetiara@candw.ky. Website: www.divi tiara.com.

Reef Divers Cayman Brac, at Brac Reef Beach Resort. features personalized dive/snorkel service. Photo, video, snorkel gear rentals. Ocean kayak rentals. SASY. ☎ 800-327-3835; direct: (011) 345-948-1642, fax (011) 345-948-1270. E-mail: reefdiving@candw.ky. Web: www.bracreef. com.

Where to Stay on Cayman Brac

Brac Caribbean Beach Village, offers 16 modern rooms, air conditioning, restaurant, Laundromat, sailing, kayaks, bicycles, and a relaxed atmosphere. ☎ 1-866-843-2722; hotel direct: (011) 345-948-2265, fax (011) 345-948-1111. Website: www.866 the brac.com.

Brac Reef Beach Resort offers 40 comfortable, air conditioned rooms with satellite TV. Restaurant, bar, air-conditioning, pool, hot tub, tennis court, dive shop, snorkeling, bicycles. ☎ 800-594-0843, hotel direct: (011) 345-948-1323. Website: www.bracreef.com.

Divi Tiara Beach Resort caters to divers and snorkelers. This first-class resort features 71 spacious, air-conditioned rooms, auto rentals, sailboards, bicycles and paddleboats. Restaurant, bar, pool, tennis court, volleyball, dive shop, snorkeling, fishing, shops. Resort shuttle will take you across the island to top snorkeling spots. Wheelchair accessible. PhotoTiara, located on premises, offers the Nikon School of Underwater Photography—a full service underwater photo and video center with equipment rental and instruction In the US ☎ 800-367-3484; hotel direct: (011) 345-948-1553, fax (011) 345-948-1657 . Write: P.O. Box 238, Cayman Brac, Cayman Islands, BWI. E-mail: tiarares@candw.ky. Website: www.diviresorts.com.

LITTLE CAYMAN

Populated by fewer than 70 people, Little Cayman retains a rural and unhurried ambiance. Its grass runway, unpaved roads and limited phone service attest to its long-standing reputation as a great get-away vacation spot.

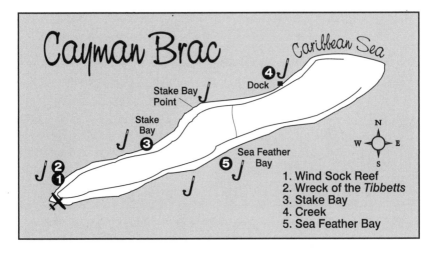

Activities include diving, snorkeling, fly fishing, and counting iguanas. Bring aspirin, bug repellent, decongestants, and suntan lotion from home.

Best Snorkeling Sites of Little Cayman

Little Cayman offers several superb snorkeling spots with visibility often exceeding 100 ft. Ground transportation to beach-access sites is easily arranged through the dive operators. For the ultimate in free diving, head out to Bloody Bay and Spot Bay off the north shore—where the seas are calm, and the marine life spectacular. The boat ride takes about 25 minutes. Average depth on top of the North Wall is 25 feet. Note: The Western half of the wall is called the Bloody Bay Wall and the eastern half Jackson Wall.

☆☆☆☆☆ **Bloody Bay Wall i**s one of the top five dives in all the Caymans. The Wall peaks as a shallow reef at 15 ft and drops off to an unfathomed bottom. Bright orange and lavender tube sponges, pastel gorgonians, and soft corals flourish in the shallows. An extremely friendly six-foot barracuda named Snort may join your dive—flashing his pearly whites while cheerfully posing for videos and still photos. Eagle rays blast by the wall along with slow-moving turtles and huge parrot fish. Spotted morays peek from the walls. Sea conditions are usually calm, although a stiff wind will churn the surface. Super snorkeling in the shallows. Boat access.

☆☆☆☆ **Little Cayman Wall**, off the island's west end, starts shallow—with a blaze of yellow, orange, and blue sponges at 15 ft, then drops off to unknown depths. Soft corals and big barrel sponges decorate the wall. Great for snorkeling. Boat access.

Seven Mile Beach, Grand Cayman
Courtesy Cayman Islands Tourism

☆☆☆ **Point of Sand**, off the southeast end of Little Cayman, is excellent for experienced and beginning snorkelers. A gentle current flowing from west to east maintains excellent visibility. The bottom is sandy with many coral heads scattered about. Marine life is fine and the site is accessible from the shore. Ground transportation can be arranged from the resorts.

☆ Good snorkeling for beginners at **Mary's Bay** starts 50 yards from the beach—inside the barrier reef. There is no current, and visibility runs about 30 to 50 ft. A host of fish and invertebrates is found in the shallows. Depth averages three to eight ft. The bottom is turtle grass—requiring booties or other submersible footwear. An old shack on an otherwise deserted shore marks the spot.

☆☆ **Jackson Point,** aka School Bus, is for experienced snorkelers only. Swim out about 75 yards from the beach where you'll see a small wall towering from a sandy bottom at 40 ft to 15 ft. Hundreds of fish, rays, and turtles congregate in the shallows. Corals and sponges carpet the area. Swimming another 50 to 60 ft brings you to a much larger wall, which drops off to extraordinary depths.

☆☆ **Jackson Bay** resembles Jackson Point except for the bottom of the mini wall, which drops off to a depth of 50 to 60 ft. Beach access.

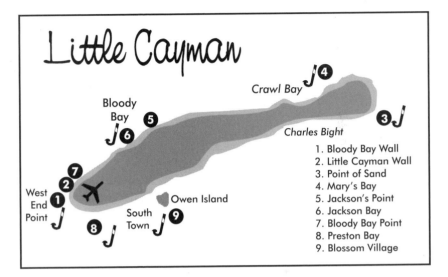

Little Cayman

Crawl Bay

Bloody Bay

Charles Bight

West End Point

Owen Island

South Town

1. Bloody Bay Wall
2. Little Cayman Wall
3. Point of Sand
4. Mary's Bay
5. Jackson's Point
6. Jackson Bay
7. Bloody Bay Point
8. Preston Bay
9. Blossom Village

☆☆☆ **Bloody Bay Point**, recommended for seasoned snorkelers, requires a 100-yard swim out to the reef. The bottom eases down to about 30 ft before the drop-off to The Great Wall begins. Well worth a visit for the spectacular coral and marine life.

☆ **Preston Bay**, just east of the lighthouse, provides another good shore entry choice for beginning snorkelers. Maximum shoreline depth is six ft and visibility 30 to 50 ft. Swarming fish and a white sandy bottom offer endless photo opportunities.

☆☆ **Blossom Village**, a lovely, shallow reef, displays crowds of reef fish and critters amidst staghorn and brain corals at depths from four to eight ft. Boat access. A light current maintains 50-100 ft visibility.

Little Cayman Snorkel Tour Operators and Rentals

Dive shops are located on the premises of several area accommodations and offer snorkel trips and gear rentals. See listings below.

Where to Stay on Little Cayman

Little Cayman Beach Resort features 40 spacious, air-conditioned rooms with balcony or patio. Fresh water pool, restaurant, bar, and a full-service dive/photo operation. In the U.S. and Canada: ☎ 800-327-3835; hotel direct: (011) 345-948-1033, fax (011) 345-948-1040. Write: P.O. Box 51, Little Cayman, Cayman Islands, BWI. E-mail: bestdiving@reefseas.com. Website: www.littlecayman.com.

Paradise Villas, an oceanfront resort, offers 12 duplex units with kitchens, air-conditioning, and terraces. Adjacent restaurant. Pool, dive shop. ☎ 1-877-3CAYMAN (1-877-322-9626); hotel direct: (011)345-948-0001, fax (011) 345-948-0002. Write: P.O. Box 48, Little Cayman, BWI. E-mail: iggy@candw.ky. Website: www.paradisevillas.com.

Southern Cross Club, a fishing and diving resort comprised of five double cottages on a pretty beach, warmly welcomes snorkelers. Features sea views, air-conditioning, and ceiling fans. Service and meals are tops. Restaurant, bar, dive shop, snorkeling, fishing, kayaks, bicycles, airport shuttle. Snorkelers mix with scuba groups on morning trips. Friendly, family atmosphere. ☎ 800-899-2582; hotel direct: (011) 345-948-1099, fax (011) 345-948-1098. Write: P.O. Box 44, Grand Cayman, BWI. E-mail: info@southerncrossclub.com. Web: www.southerncrossclub.com.

Sam McCoy's Diving and Fishing Lodge, on the north shore, offers rustic accommodations for up to 14 divers (seven rooms). Rooms in the main lodge are air-conditioned with private bath. Pool. Relaxed family-style dining. Twenty-ft fiberglass runabouts are used for reef trips. Shore diving from Jackson's Point. ☎ 800-626-0496. E-mail: info@mccoyslodge.com.ky. Web: www.mccoyslodge.com.ky. Write: P.O. Box 12, Little Cayman, BWI.

Pirates Point Resort features 10 rustic guest cottages and a guest house on seven acres of secluded white beach. Owner Gladys Howard offers friendly service, superb, gourmet cooking. Good snorkeling directly in front of the resort, only 10 feet from shore. ☎ (011) 345-948-1010, fax (011) 345-948-1011. Write: P.O. Box 43, Little Cayman, Cayman Islands, BWI. Website: www.piratespointresort.com.

Additional Information:

The following websites and phone numbers will bring you to the most up to date On line: www.caymanislands.ky. *In New York:* 877-4-CAYMAN, 1-212-889-9009.

In Canada: Website: www.caymanislands.ky/canada. ☎ 800-263-5805 or, 416-485-1550, In the United Kingdom ☎ +44 (0) 20 7491 7771, www. Caymanislands.co.uk. In the Cayman Islands: Box 67 George Town, Grand Cayman, Cayman Islands, BWI. ☎ (011) 345-949-0623; fax (011) 345-949-4053.

©XCARET

Cozumel, Akumal & Cancun

Vacationers based on Cancun can easily arrange for bus trips to Akumal and boat trips to neighboring Isla Mujeres and Cozumel.

ISLA MUJERES

A lovely, snorkeling-depth reef aprons the south end of *Isla Mujeres*, a small island between Cancun and Cozumel, which can be easily reached via ferry from either spot. When you arrive, enter from the shore at *Playa Garrafon*, four miles from town. This spot—*El Garrafon* (the carafe)is one of the most populated (by fish and swimmers) in the Caribbean. Just wade out from the beach with some cracker crumbs and you'll immediately be surrounded by crowds of friendly fish. Ideal for first time snorkelers. The beach has a dive shop, showers, refreshment stands and shops.

COZUMEL

Cozumel, Mexico's largest island, lies 12 miles off the Yucatan Peninsula, separated by a 3,000 ft-deep channel. Dense jungle covers most of this islands interior, but its surrounding coast sparkles with miles of luxuriant, white sand beaches.

Noted for its incredible water clarity and marine life, Cozumel's fringing reef system is fed by warm, fast-moving Yucatan currents (a part of the Gulf Stream) as they sweep through the deep channel on the west side of the island. These currents bring a constant wash of plankton and other nutrients that support thousands of exotic fish. Most reef dive sites have too strong a current for snorkeling, but protected areas exist near the shore that are suitable. Visibility remains a constant 70 to 100 ft year round, except during and after major storms.

Tourist activity centers around San Miguel, the islands cultural and commercial center which boasts an impressive seaside shops, *cantinas* and restaurants. An ultra-modern cruise-ship terminal accommodates daily-arriving ocean liners and ferries from the mainland. Most resorts scatter along the west coast where calm waters prevail.

When to Go

The best time to visit Cozumel is from December till June. Water and air temperatures average 80F year round with hotter conditions from June to October. Summer and fall often bring heavy rains or hurricanes.

Best Snorkeling Sites of Cozumel

Good snorkeling may be found all along Cozumel's east coast beaches. The shallow reefs have nice stands of elk horn and brain coral with lots of fish and a constant show of juvenile tropicals and invertebrates.

Snorkelers should avoid the strong currents associated with drift diving on the outer reefs and stick to the inner reefs on calm days. Cozumel is recommended for experienced ocean snorkelers. Novices should ferry over to *Isla Mujeres*.

☆☆☆ **Paraiso Reef North** is a popular shallow dive just north of the cruise ship pier in San Miguel. The reef is accessible by swimming straight out 200 yds from the beach at the Hotel Sol Caribe or by dive boat. The remains of a twin engine airplane, sunk intentionally as part of a movie set, rests at 30 ft creating a home for a vast array of fish life. Huge green morays, eagle rays, turtles, yellowtail, French angels, schools of pork fish, butterfly fish, and queen trigger fish may be found. Check with the local dive shop before entering the water.

☆☆☆ **Chancanab National Park**, south of the cruise ship pier at Laguna Beach is protected from wind and waves. Ideal for snorkeling, depths range from very shallow to about 30 ft. Schools of grunts, angel fish, damsel fish, trumpet fish, turtles, and snapper dart between the clumps of coral. Sea fans and soft corals adorn the reef. Visibility runs about 75 ft, sometimes better. Snorkeling gear may be rented from shops on the beach. Changing rooms, freshwater showers and lockers are available. Admission fee. A botanical garden and restaurant are on the premises.

Cozumel Snorkeling Tours & Rentals

NOTE: To telephone or fax any of the Mexican listings from the US, dial 011 52 + 987 + the seven digit number. In Mexico just dial the last five digits.

Most of the dive shops offer three to seven day, reduced-rate dive packages where you pay to go out with scuba divers. Before forking over your money, ask if refunds are given for missed boat trips and whether you can get that in writing. Some snorkelers prefer to pay each day rather than risk missing the boat or discovering the currents are too strong for snorkeling and losing the price of a trip.

Dive Palancar at the Diamond Resort has trips aboard a 44 custom dive boat to Palancar and Santa Rosa Reefs. Beach diving tours. Dive and snorkeling courses. English speaking guides. Boats on time. Check for currents before signing up for a tour. ☎ 800- 247-3483, (011) 52-987-23443 ext. 895.

Dive Paradise offers fast, shaded boats and mixed tours for snorkelers and scuba divers. www.dive paradise.com. ☎ 52-987-21007,

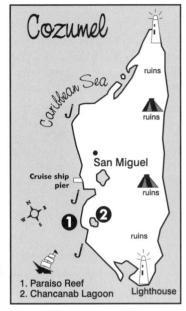

1. Paraiso Reef
2. Chancanab Lagoon   Lighthouse

Where to Stay in Cozumel

Hotel Presidente Inter-Continental, sits seven minutes from down town and 15 minutes from the airport. Each room is equipped with a private terrace that overlooks the sea. It has a large, freshwater pool, tennis courts and restaurants. Snorkeling off the beach. www.cozumel.inter-continental.com. ☎ 800-327-0200.

Casa Del Mar Located just 5 minutes south of San Miguel, the newly renovated Casa del Mar features 98 rooms with air conditioning, fans, satellite TV, telephone, pool, hot tub, tennis court, car rental and dive shop. Beach club. ☎ 800-435-3240. Email: casamar@ cozumel.com.mx

Fiesta Americana Cozumel Dive Resort on the south side of the island, features 226 rooms—122 with two double beds; four junior suites with a king size bed, dining room, large balcony with ocean view, cable TV, telephone with direct access, A/C, purified water, hair dryer, bathroom. An on-site dive

Caves, Xcaret, Yucatan

Photo Courtesy Mexican Tourism

shop offers snorkeling, kayaking, and board surfing. ☎ 800-FIESTA-1. Email: dive@fiestaamericana.com. mx. Web: www.divehouse.com

Melia Cozumel, (formerly known as the Paradisus) sits on Cozumels longest stretch of natural beach. Located 2.5 miles from town on the Northeast side of the island, this all-inclusive hotel offers air-conditioned, deluxe ocean-view and garden view rooms. For diving and snorkeling trips, guests must travel to the Paradisus Beach & Dive Club on the southern side of the island. Hotel guests receive complimentary use of non-motorized sports equipment kayaks, Sailfish, board sails and lunch at no additional charge. ☎ 888-341-5993, (011) 52-987-20411, fax (011) 52-987-21599. Website: www.solmelia.com.mx E-mail: paradisu@cancun.rce.

Plaza Las Glorias. All 168 rooms are ocean view, air conditioned with satellite TV, mini-frig, hair dryer, private terrace, telephone, in-room safety deposit box, pool, Jacuzzi, diving school, motorbikes, travel agency, car rental, shops and a boutique. There is one restaurant located on the property *La Palapa*, surrounded by the pool, and a swim-up bar. ☎ 800-342-AMIGO (for reservations only) 011+52 987 8722000/2400.

AKUMAL

Akumal (place of the turtle) lies 60 miles south of Cancun on Mexico's Yucatan Peninsula in an area known as the Tulum Corridor. Laid back and off the beaten track, this tiny resort community originated as a section of a large coconut plantation. It wasn't until 1958 that Mexican treasure divers salvaging a sunken Spanish galleon discovered great sport diving opportunities along the offshore barrier reef. Pristine corals and sponges, frequent turtle sightings, silky white, sand beaches and terrific beach snorkeling have popularized Akumal with a discriminating group of visitors. Three dive operators serve the area.

Drawbacks exist for those who like pampered tours the boats are open with ladders, no platforms, no sun canopies. On the other hand, most sites lie close to shore, a five-to-ten minute boat ride. Spear fishing is prohibited.

Akumal dive operators also offer snorkelers freshwater tours to jungle pools or cenotes, which are sunken limestone caverns with dazzling stalagmites and stalactites. These inland adventures combine a jungle trek through natures most exotic gardens.

When to Go

The best time to dive Akumal is October through April. Weather is very hot in May and June and rain is heavy during July, August and September.

Best Snorkeling Sites of Akumal

Akumals best snorkeling sites are inside a barrier reef that parallels the shoreline along **Akumal Bay**, neighboring **Half Moon Bay** and nearby **Yalku Lagoon.** Uncrowded beaches, secluded bays and a healthy marine population make Akumal delightful for family snorkeling vacations.

The reef structure comprises three distinct systems running parallel to one another at progressively deeper depths. The inner reef, where most snorkeling takes place is a network of patch reefs with depths from three to 35 feet with huge stands of elk horn and formations of boulder, brain and plate corals. Frequent sightings of loggerhead, green and hawksbill turtles that nest along Yucatan beaches, highlight many dives.

Snorkelers exploring from the beach can swim up to the breakers on the reef. Conditions inside are normally calm with depths from three to 20 ft.

 Akumal Bay's best snorkeling is off the beach in front of the Club Akumal Caribe. Depths range from three feet to 20 feet with coral heads leading out to the breakers at the barrier reef. A variety of corals, sea fans, sponges, reef fish, occasional moray eels, barracudas, jacks, grouper, sting rays, parrot fish and turtles inhabit the bay. Bottom terrain is sandy with coral heads scattered about. Bay conditions inside the barrier reef are almost always tranquil.

☆☆☆ **Half Moon Bay**, about three minutes down the interior road from Akumal Bay, resembles Akumal Bay in terrain and marine life. This is a residential area, but anyone can use the beach.

☆☆☆☆ **Yalcu Lagoon**, at the end of the interior road, a short drive from Half Moon Bay, features several partially submerged caves, throngs of fish and crystal clear, tranquil water. Freshwater mixing with seawater provides nutrients and aquatic plants that attract rich marine life. Big parrot fish, angels, Spanish hogfish, rays, juvenile turtles and spotted eels nibble on the plants

The Cross of the Bay,,
Manchones Reef, Cancun
Photo Courtesy Cancun Tourism

The Cross of the Bay was placed in the water between Manchones and Isla in 1994, as a memorial to those who have lost their lives at sea. The bronze cross lies 1/2 mile off the southeast tip of Cancun .

around the rocks. A natural entrance from the sea ensures a constant mix of nutrients. The outlying barrier reef protects this natural aquarium from wind driven waves and rough seas.

Enter the lagoon from the head of the bay or climb down the big rocks anywhere along the shore. Guided boat and beach-entry snorkeling tours of Yalcu are offered by the dive shop at Club Akumal Caribe.

Inland Cenote

☆☆☆☆ *Nohoch Nah Chich*, listed in the Guinness Book of World Records as the worlds longest underwater cave system, is also featured in the PBS TV series, The New Explorers as one of Yucatans most exciting caverns. Visitors snorkel in the shallow fresh water amidst hordes of fish, brilliant white stalactites and stalagmites. Unlimited visibility and an openness to the caverns offer breath taking views.

Joining a jungle walk and snorkeling expedition to *Nohoch Nah Chich* involves a mile-and-a- half trek through impressive flora. Horses or donkeys carry your gear. Be sure to apply sun protective lotions and bug repellent and wear a hat that will shade your face. Jungle walks are rugged and not suitable for anyone with severe disabilities or medical problems.

Snorkeling up and down the coast. . .

Several sheltered bays and secluded beaches with good shore-entry snorkeling exist along the coast. About six miles south of Akumal, the dirt road turnoff at KM 249 leads to ☆☆☆☆ *Chemuyil*, a quiet, horseshoe-shaped cove of tranquil water edged by a lovely, powder-white beach. A shallow snorkeling reef crosses the mouth of the bay. A small beach bar (the Marco Polo) serves fresh seafood, cold beer and soft drinks. Full camping facilities and a few tented *palapas* for overnight rental are available.

About 20 miles south of Akumal lies ☆☆ *Xel-Ha* (pronounced shell ha), the worlds largest natural aquarium, covering 10 acres of lagoons, coves and inlets teeming with exotic fish. Platforms above the rocky limestone shore provide sea life viewing for non-swimmers. Unlike Akumal, this well known attraction is packed daily with tourists. In fact, busloads mobbed with avid snorkelers arrive by the moment in season.

A small admission fee is charged. On site showers, shops, a nice maritime museum, seafood restaurant and Subway sandwich shop cater to visitors. Snorkeling gear is available for rent. Despite the crowds, most snorkelers, especially those touring with children, immensely enjoy this spot. Venture across highway 307 to visit some small ruins

☆☆ **Xcaret** (Scaret), Mayan for little inlet, about 40 miles north of Akumal, is a private ranch turned aquatic theme park. Once a busy Mayan port, this novel playground now features varied dolphin swims and snorkeling through an under ground river that flows through a series of open-ended caves. A mix of fresh and saltwater nourishes sea plants, which in turn feed armies of fish that entertain between 400 and 500 snorkelers each day. The effect is like drifting through a very big, very pretty, shaded pool stocked with fish. Holes in the roof of the caves filter light into a spectrum of colors.

Topside features include a wild-bird aviary, butterfly pavilion, saltwater aquarium, botanical garden and a couple of Mayan temple ruins, the Museum of Mayan Archaeological Sites with scale models of 26 Mayan ceremonial sites found on the Yucatan peninsula. There are three restaurants, two snack bars, one cafeteria, showers, lockers, photo center, horse shows, gift shops and a sundeck with spectacular ocean views. Crowded, but very user friendly.

The Mayans prized Xcaret for their belief that its waters could purify bodies and souls, thus it became important as a sacred bath spot before crossing the sea to Cozumel to worship *Ixchel*, Goddess of Fertility.

Cancun Ruins,

Courtesy Mexican
Tourism

We can't guarantee the fertility or soul-purifying prospects, but most snorkelers find Xcaret a fun day or half-day diversion. Michael Cherup, a snorkeling researcher returning from Xcaret, claims relief from back pain!

Akumal Snorkeling Tours & Rentals

Akumal Dive Center at Club Akumal offers boat tours. ☎ 800-351-1622, In Akumal: (011) 52-987-59025,E-mail: clubakumal@aol.com.

Where to Stay in Akumal

Hotel Club Akumal Caribe features a variety of air-conditioned accommodations and an on-site dive shop. Choose from spacious Maya bungalows with garden views or first class hotel rooms facing the pool and ocean. Or try the resort's Cannon House Suite, on the main beach, with two bedrooms, two baths, living room and kitchen or a two-bedroom condo on Half Moon Bay with one king size bed, two twins, kitchens and living room.

Contact the reservation office for additional information: In the US,☎ 800-351-1622, in Canada ☎ 800-343-1440, in Texas, ☎ 915-584-3552, in Mexico, ☎ 95-(800) 351-1622. E-mail: club akumal@aol.com.

For Additional Information

For up-to-date information on hotels, climate, customs, air travel, religious services, island transportation, documents and departure tax contact the Mexican tourist board at ☎ 800-446-3942; Website: www.visitmexico.com. Email: contact@visit mexico.com

Curaçao

Curaçao, the largest of five islands that make up the Netherlands Antilles (which also include Bonaire, Saba, Saint Maarten and St. Eustatius), is a dry and hilly island completely surrounded with rich coral reefs. Its coastline sparkles with beautiful sand beaches, secluded lagoons and coves.

Watersports and tourist activity center around the main resort and beach area off Willemstadt, the capital city, which boasts superb shopping, fine restaurants and a safe environment.

Like its sister islands, Aruba and Bonaire, Curaçao lies far south of the hurricane belt and offers clear skies and good diving year-round. Most dives require a boat. The reefs and wrecks are a stones throw from shore, but the shore adjacent to the best reefs is often formed of jagged, razor-like, ironshore cliffs. Seas along the south coast locale of the Curaçao Underwater Park are usually calm in the morning, but may kick up a three- or four-ft surge in mid-afternoon.

The Curaçao Underwater Park, established in 1983 by the Netherlands Antilles National Park Foundation (STINAPA), stretches 12 miles from the Princess Beach Hotel to East Point and features more than 20 dive sites marked by numbered mooring buoys. Within the park, snorkelers find crystal-clear water and spectacular seascapes. The reefs are in pristine condition with many yet to be explored.

Best Snorkeling Sites of Curaçao

☆☆☆ **Kalki Beach,** a sheltered cove just south of Westpunt on the northern tip of the island, is Curaçao's favorite beach-entry site. A short swim out brings you over hard corals and rocks alive with parrot fish, blue tangs, grunts, small barra- cuda, anemones and en- crusting sponges.

☆☆☆☆ **Jan Thiel Reef**, just outside of Jan Thiel Bay off Willemstadt, has lush, shallow gardens at 15 ft with massive gorgonians, two- foot lavender sea anemones, seafans, long, purple tube sponges, pastel star, leaf, fire, pencil and brain corals. Fishlife is superb with walls of grunts, trumpetfish, parrot fish, angels and small rays. Added buoyancy from a snorkeling vest or shorty wetsuit will help you to stay clear of the fire coral. Swim out from Playa Jan Thiel, just east of the SuperClub's Breezes Hotel. The beach has changing facilities and is a favorite for picnics. Admission fee.

☆☆☆ **Sandys** Plateau (aka Boka Di Sorsaka), is part of a marked snorkeling trail that can be reached by swimming out from Jan Thiel Bay. It is an excellent spot for novice divers and snorkelers. The terrain, a combination

Tugboat wreck, Photo courtesy Curacao Tourism

of walls and steep slopes, supports radiant lavender and pink star corals, yellow pencil corals and orange tube sponges. Lush stands of elk horn coral grow to within 10 ft of the surface. Dense coral flows around an undercut ledge between 10 and 30 ft. Soldierfish, trumpetfish and schools of sergeant majors hover over the ledge.

Nearby, just offshore to the Curaçao Seaquarium, lies the wreck of the ☆☆☆ *S.S. Oranje Nassau*, a Dutch steamer that ran aground on the Koraal Specht over 80 years ago. Also known as *Bopor Kibra*, Papiamento for broken ship, this is a favorite spot for free diving. The seas are always choppy over the wreck. Entry is best from the dive shop docks adjacent to the sea quarium. Check with the divemaster for the days conditions.

This area is known for outstanding corals. Depths start shallow with large pillar and star corals, sea fans, huge brain coral, and gorgeous stands of elk horn. It then terraces off to greater depth. Fish life includes swarms of blue chromis and creole wrasses, French angels, barracuda and jacks. Sea conditions are choppy and recommended for advanced snorkelers with some ocean experience.

The mooring for ☆☆☆ **PBH**, initials for the former Princess Beach Hotel, sits straight out from the SuperClub's Breezes Hotel's beach. This reef starts shallow enough for snorkeling then drops off. Arrow crabs, octopi, and hordes of juvenile fish swim the shallow terrace.

Knip Bay offers good fish watching along the rocks at either end.
Photo © 2004 Jon Huber

☆☆☆ **Bullen Bay,** just north of the park, is an outstanding dive with a protected shallow area for snorkeling. Yellow pencil corals and pretty white sea plumes highlight the reef. Average shallows' depth runs 10 ft. Boat access.

Beaches

Beautiful, white-sand beaches surround Curaçao, from popular hotel beaches to intimate secluded coves. Along the southern coast, you'll find free public beaches at West Point Bay, Knip Bay, Klein Knip, Santa Cruz, Jeremi Bay and Daaibooi Bay. Knip Bay is the largest and loveliest swimming beach on the island. Good fish watching along the cliffs. The main private beaches, which charge a small fee per car, are Blauw Bay, Jan Thiel, Cas Abao, Barbara Beach and Port Marie.

Curaçao Snorkeling Tours

Reef snorkeling trips may be booked through the following operators.

Animal Encounters at the Curaçao Seaquarium offers rentals and guided tours for snorkeling and/or diving with sharks, sea turtles, stingrays, and colorful tropical fish. ☎ 599-9-465-6940 Animal Encounters, 599-9-461-6666 (Seaquarium), fax (011) 599-9-461-3671. Website: Curacao-sea-aquarium.com.

Seascape Curaçao Dive and Watersports, on the beach at the Hilton Curaçao Hotel, has fast, comfortable boats and friendly service. ☎ (011)599-9-462-5000, Website: www.seascapeCuracao.com

Habitat Curaçao Dive Resort, Rif St. Marie. ☎ (011) 599-9-864-8800, E-mail: info@habitatcuracao.com. Website: www.habitatdiveresorts.com

Ocean Encounters Curaçao, at the Lions Dive Resort, the Seaquarium, and Breezes, offers reef trips and educational tours to the Seaquarium lagoon. ☎ 011) 599-9-461-8131, fax (011) 599-9-465-5756. E-Mail: info@ocean encounters.com. Website: www.oceanencounters.com.

Caribbean Sea Sports, at the Marriot Beach Resort, offers reef trips and attentive staff. ☎ 011) 599-9-462-2620, fax (011) 599-9-462-6933. E-mail: css@cura.net. Website: www.caribseasports.com.

Dive Center Scuba Do, at Jan Thiel Beach and Sports Resort offers boat trips, gear rental 767-9300. www.divecenterscubado.com E-mail: scubado @cura. net.

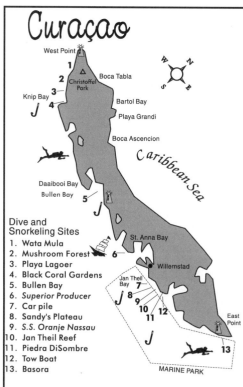

Curaçao

West Point

1
2 Boca Tabla
   Christoffel
   Park
Knip Bay 3
J   4

Bartol Bay

Playa Grandi

Boca Ascencion

Caribbean Sea

Daaibooi Bay
Bullen Bay 5

Dive and
Snorkeling Sites
1. Wata Mula
2. Mushroom Forest 6
3. Playa Lagoer
4. Black Coral Gardens
5. Bullen Bay
6. *Superior Producer*
7. Car pile
8. Sandy's Plateau
9. *S.S. Oranje Nassau*
10. Jan Theil Reef
11. Piedra DiSombre
12. Tow Boat
13. Basora

St. Anna Bay

Willemstad

Jan Theil
Bay 7
J 8 9
  10 12
  11   East
          Point

J   13

MARINE PARK

Where to Stay on Curaçao

The Hilton Curaçao features 196 rooms with balconies, two beaches, two restaurants and bars, free form pools, full- service spa and fitness center, and dive center. In the United States and. and Canada reserve a stay at: ☎ 800-445-8667); Web: www. hiltoncaribbean. com/curaçao.

Habitat Curaçao, on the south west coast in Rif St. Marie, features 56 guest rooms, an international restaurant, fitness center, pool, cable TV, tennis courts and a variety of watersports and activities. In the US and Canada book a stay at: ☎

800-327-6709 or online at, www.habitatdive resorts.com.

Holiday Beach Hotel and Casino, on the west coast, sits on Coconut Beach facing the Curaçao Underwater Park. The newly remodeled 200-room hotel has a complete dive shop, beach, casino, two restaurants, pool, tennis courts and handicapped facilities. Private balconies and terraces. In the US and Canada: ☎ 800-444-5244; hotel direct: (011) 599-9-462-5400, fax (011) 599-9-462-4397. E-mail: usoffice@ hol-beach. com. Website: www.hol-beach.com.

Lions Dive and Beach Resort is a luxurious, 72-room, three-apartment oceanfront dive complex adjacent to the Curaçao Seaquarium. Rooms overlook the Curaçao Marine Park and the Orange Nassau. The resort features an open-air, seaside restaurant and bar, pool, health club and fitness center, and a full-service dive center. In the US: ☎ 1-866-LIONSDIVE (1-866-546-6734), fax 954-217-9980. Hotel direct: (011) 599-9-434-8888. E-mail: us-canada@ lionsdive.com or info@ lionsdive.com. Website: www.lionsdive.com

SuperClub's Breezes Curaçao, with 339 rooms, overlooks a private, 1,500-ft-long, white sand beach with good snorkeling a short swim out. The all-inclusive resort welcomes families, couples, and singles. Four restaurants, three bars, two pools, tennis courts, kids and teen activities. Dive shop. Ocean Encounters on premises offers gear rentals and boat tours. In the US: ☎ 1-877-GO-SUPER (1-877-467-8737); hotel direct: (011) 599-9-736-7888, fax (011) 599-9-461-4131. E-mail: bzc@800go super. com. Website: www.breezesCuraçao.com .

Curaçao Marriot Beach Resort & Emerald Casino sits oceanfront on Piscadera Bay with 247 rooms (each with a private balcony or terrace), casino, four restaurants, two bars, fitness center, pool with swim-up bar, satellite TV, tennis courts and water sports and dive shop. ☎ 800-223-6388; hotel direct: (011) 599-9-736-8800. E-mail: reservations@curacao marriott.vi. Web: www. curacaomarriott.com or www.marriotthotels. com.

Additional Information

In the US and Canada contact the Curaçao Tourist Board at 7951 S.W. 6th Street, Suite 216, Plantation, Florida 33324, ☎ 800-CURACAO (800-328-7222), 1-954-370-5887. Website: www. curacao-tourism.com. In Curaçao: Curaçao Tourist Board, 19 Pietermaai, P.O. Box 3266, Willemstad, Curaçao, NA. ☎ (011)-599-9-434-8200, fax (011) 599-9-461-2305. E-mail: info@ctdb.net. Website: curacao-tourism.com.

Dominica

Dominica, the largest island in the Windward chain, sits off-the-beaten-track between Martinique and Guadeloupe. It is ideal for the snorkeler who also enjoys rugged rainforest hikes and a wilderness environment. Narrow strips of black-sand beaches that encircle the island rise to a mountainous interior where simmering volcanic pools, exotic rain forests and thundering rivers harmonize.

The island's most outstanding feature is water—with more than 365 rivers, thermal springs, pools, and waterfalls fed by 350 inches of rainfall per year in the interior and 50 inches on the drier west coast. Thankfully, all of the resorts and snorkeling sites lie off the *dry* western shores.

Subsea terrain, too, is unique with hot springs bubbling up through the sea floor amidst shallow wrecks and walls of critters.

Roseau, the capital and main city, is a busy area which may be seen in its entirety by way of a half-hour walk. Most interesting are some old French Colonial buildings, botanical gardens at the south end and the Old Market on the waterfront where island crafts are offered.

Visitors arriving by cruise ship at the **Cabrits National Park**, on the north west tip of Dominica, step off the 300-ft pier and are immediately surrounded by twin waterfalls and a lush garden.

When to Go

The best time to snorkel in Dominica is during the driest season, February through April though expect the possibility of "*liquid sunshine*" (rain) all year. Whenever you go, plan on doing combat with a ferocious mosquito population, especially at dawn and dusk.

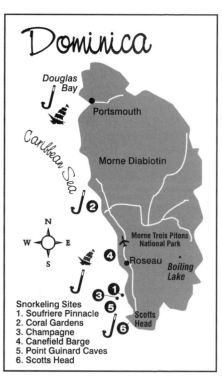

Dominica

Douglas Bay

Portsmouth

Caribbean Sea

Morne Diabiotin

N
W — E
S

Morne Trois Pitons National Park

Roseau

Boiling Lake

Scotts Head

Snorkeling Sites
1. Soufriere Pinnacle
2. Coral Gardens
3. Champagne
4. Canefield Barge
5. Point Guinard Caves
6. Scotts Head

Best Snorkeling Sites of Dominica

None recommended for children.

✩✩✩✩ **Soufriere Pinnacle** rises from the depths of Soufriere Bay to within five feet of the surface. A favorite of macro-photographers, the pinnacle is a delight- ful cornucopia of crabs, shrimp, lobster, octopi, sea anemones, starfish, tree worms, and gorgonians. Calm seas and light currents invite all levels of diver and snorkeler. The site is four miles off the southwest shore—a 15-minute boat ride.

✩✩✩✩ **Coral Gardens**, a short trip from Castaways Beach, is a shallow reef with depths from 15 ft. Good for free diving and surface snorkeling, the reef is vibrant with corkscrew and pink anemones, arrow crabs, violet Peterson shrimp, florescent crinoids and flamingo tongue snails. Spotted and green moray eels, sting rays and scorpion fish hide in the shadows.

✩✩✩ **Scotts Head Dropoff** lies five miles off Scotts Head, a fishing village at the southern tip of the island. Snorkelers will find large sponges and lavish soft corals along the reefs shallow ledge, which starts at five ft. Conditions are light to moderate. Good visibility. Boat access

✩✩ **Champagne** is a shallow site highlighted by sub-aquatic, freshwater, hot springs which emit a continuous profusion of hot bubbles. A fun dive, it's like jumping into a giant glass of hot club soda. Near shore with dependably calm conditions, the site covers an area of about 300 square ft.

Depths range from near the surface, with 10 ft the average. The bottom is uninspiring brown weeds ruffled by schools of tiny sprat, reef fish and lobster. A few divers report the bubbles to be too hot for comfort. Boat access.

✩✩✩ **Canefield Barge**, an overturned barge, rests on patches of shallow reef. Depths from five ft, hordes of friendly reef fish and calm seas make this a good choice for snorkelers. Basket stars, anemones, hydroids and iridescent sponges cover the wreck. Boat access.

✩✩✩ **Point Guinard Caves**, an area of shallow reefs, grottoes and caves, are great fun for all level of snorkelers. Sea horses, blood stars, octopi, crabs, lobster and hordes of sponges inhabit the crevices.

Beach-entry Snorkeling Sites

The best shore-entry snorkeling spots are **Scotts Head** on Sourfriere Bay in the southwest and **Douglas Bay** in the northwest, which has a reef less than 200 feet from the shore. **Point Guinard** off the southwest coast is another popular spot. On the north and northeast coasts try **Woodford Hill Bay**,

Dominica Beach
Photo ©Karen Sabo, Landfall Productions

Hodges Bay, Grand Baptiste Bay and **Hampstead Beach.** Check with dive shops for wind and water conditions before entering the water.

Dominica Snorkeling Tours

Dive Dominica at Castle Comfort Lodge is a full service dive center. Snorkelers join scuba divers. Whale and dolphin-watching cruises. Beach diving in front of the lodge. ☎ 1-888-414-7626, (011) 767-448-2188, fax (011) 767-448-6088. Write: P.O. Box 63, Roseau, Commonwealth of Dominica. E-mail: dive@cwdom.dm. Website: www.divedominica.com

Anchorage Dive Centre offers reef and wreck diving, snorkeling, and whale watching aboard two fast boats (39-ft and 30-ft) and a new 60-ft catamaran. Hotel packages. In the US, reserve through Caribbean Adventures ☎ 800-934-DIVE; dive center direct: (011) 767-448-2638; E-mail: anchorage@cwdom.dm. Website: www. anchorage hotel.dm

Dive Castaways features personalized tours to their own special sights. ☎ (011) 767-449-6245, Web: www.castaways-dominica.com. E-mail: inquirys@castaways-dominica. com.

Nature Island Dive caters to small groups with a variety of water and landsports kayaking and mountain biking. Dive boats visit Soufriere, Scotts Head Reserve and local reefs. Snorkelers join scuba divers on a space available basis. Both sites visited on the boat trips are also accessible from shore, and sea kayaks may be rented for paddling to snorkeling sites. Snorkeling equipment rentals.☎ (011) 757-449-8181, Write: P.O. Box 2345, Soufriere, Commonwealth of Dominica. E-mail: natureidive@ cwdom.dm. Website: www.natureisland dive.com.

Where to Stay on Dominica

Anchorage Hotel & Dive Center, one-mile south of Roseau, features 32 air conditioned, clean, modern rooms, cable TV, phones, squash court, pool, bar, restaurant, and full-service PADI dive center. Whale- and dolphin watching cruises. ☎ (011) 767-448-2638. E-mail: anchorage @cwdom.dm. Website: www. anchorage hotel.dm.

Castle Comfort Dive Lodge is a cozy 15-room inn. Five rooms have ocean-view balconies. All are air-conditioned and have ceiling fans. Great meals! Friendly service. Good snorkeling off the shore. Snorkeling and whale-watching excursions. On site dive shop. ☎ 800-525-3833; hotel 1-888-414-7626. E-mail: dive@cwdom.cm. Website: www.castlecomfort divelodge.com.

The Castaways Beach Hotel and Resort, a charming 27-room waterfront resort surrounded by botanical gardens, features modern, spacious guest rooms with ceiling fans and air conditioning. A beachfront terrace overlooks the sea. Adjacent dive shop. ☎ (011) 767-449-6245, E-mail: enquirys@castaways-dominica.com. Web: www.castaways-dominica.com.

Package Tours

Landfall Dive and Adventure Travel offers complete air, hotel and boat trips. ☎ 800-525-3833. Website: www.landfall productions.com.

Additional Information: Get up-to-date accommodation and travel information for snorkeling in Dominica by contacting the National Development Corp. ☎ (011) 767-448-2045, fax (011) 767-448-5840. Write: P.O. Box 293, Roseau, Common wealth of Dominica, W.I. E-mail: tourism@dominica.dm. In the US Dominica Tourist Office ☎ 888-645-5637, 718-261-9615, fax 718-261-0702. Write: 110-64 Queens Blvd., P.O. Box 427, Forest Hills, NY, 11375-6347. E-mail: dominicany@msn.com. Website: www.dominica.dm.

Florida Keys

A wealth of topside attractions, fabulous resorts and restaurants combined with spectacular offshore coral reefs attract more than a million divers and snorkelers to the Florida Keys each year. Key Largo, the jumping off point to the Keys lies 42 miles south-southwest of Miami. All points from Key Largo to Key West connect to the mainland and to each other by the Overseas Highway, a continuation of US Route 1.

Dive shops offering snorkeling tours pave the 100-mile route from Key Largo to Key West. Whether you choose to stay in Key West for its wealth of topside attractions, Key Largo for the John Pennekamp Marine Sanctuary or the middle keys, you wont be disappointed. Patches of finger-like, spur and groove reefs parallel the islands from Key Biscayne to Key West and are inhabited by more than 500 varieties of fish and corals. Shallow depths, ideal for underwater video and still photography, range from just below the surface to an average maximum of 40 feet. There are shallow shipwrecks, such as the wreck of the *San Pedro,* an underwater archaeological preserve off Islamorada, miles of coral canyons and pinnacles, the famous Statue of Christ in Key Largo, and every imaginable fish along the entire coast.

The reef lies between four and eight miles offshore. There are no beach-entry reef sites, but small boat rentals and guided snorkeling trips are offered throughout the Keys.

Before venturing off shore, be sure to pick up a copy of the rules and regulations for boaters and divers. Everything living is protected in Florida's marine parks. Wearing gloves, touching corals and feeding fish are prohibited. Spear fishing is outlawed. Certain foods eaten by humans can be unhealthy and often fatal to fish. Touching corals may kill them or cause infection or disease which can spread to surrounding corals. The entire area has recently gained status as The Florida Keys National Marine Sanctuary, an underwater park administered by the National Park Service.

When to Go

The official high season in the Keys runs from mid December to mid-March, but many snorkelers prefer springtime March, April and May for the usually dry skies and warm seas. The rainy season starts the end of June and continues till late mid October. Winter, especially January and February bring an occasional drop in air temperature.

When to book a tour

Good snorkeling conditions on the Florida Keys shallow reefs depends on good weather conditions. High winds that churn up surface swells also stir up the sandy bottom. You might plan a reef trip the morning after a storm and find visibility as low as 25 ft, yet return in the afternoon to calm seas and visibility in excess of 100 ft.

When storms rule out trips to the outer reefs, visit the Content Keys, a sheltered area which is almost always calm, located on the Gulf side of Marathon. The corals and sponges don't rival the outer reefs, but the fish life is good and there are some nice hard corals and encrusting sponges.

In Key Largo you might explore the swimming lagoon at John Pennekamp State Park. There are some old cannons and a sunken car. This artificial reef attracts numerous fish and crustaceans. An occasional manatee has been spotted too.

Places to Avoid

Snorkeling is unsafe in the brackish and fresh waters of the Everglades, home to alligators. There is a crocodile sanctuary on the northernmost tip of Key Largo which must be avoided. Alligators and, even more so, crocodiles are unpredictable and despite a sluggish appearance must be considered extremely dangerous to humans. If you're unfamiliar with the area, stick to the ocean, avoid the bays, especially in the northern keys.

Dolphin Swims

An opportunity to swim with the dolphins awaits you in any one of three Florida Keys facilities. You must be at least 13 years old, know how to swim and attend an orientation session with a dolphin trainer. Advance reservations are a must. Each of the facilities provides in-depth briefings prior to in-water encounters that cover dolphin behavior, proper interaction with and facts about dolphins. During the encounters, the ever-curious dolphins use their sensitive bottle-shaped noses to give humans the once-over, often presenting their chins to be scratched or, occasionally, even kissed. Prices subject to change.

The Dolphin Research Center, mile marker (MM) 59 bayside on Grassy Key, specializes in behavioral research and maintains liaisons with university research programs and independent scientists around the world. Founded in 1984 as a not-for-profit teaching and research facility, the center and its staff have received numerous conservation awards for the rescue and rehabilitation of sick and injured marine mammals.

With human attention and kindness, the animals return to good health and provide fun-filled programs that educate visitors about dolphins, sea lions and the environment. Dolphin Encounter, the centers swim program, can be reserved for $155. For $80, visitors can try **Dolphin Splash**, a wade-in program that offers the opportunity to get waist deep in the water with the dolphins. **Hands On Training, Meet the Dolphin** and **Paint With A Dolphin** offer a wide range of interactions.

Dolphin Research Center is open daily, 9 a.m. to 4 p.m., with continuous dolphin and sea lion sessions. Children ages 3 and younger are admitted free of charge; ☎ 305-289-1121 or www.dolphins.org.

At Dolphins Plus on Key Largo, Ocean Bay Drive, MM 100 ocean side, visitors can enjoy natural or unstructured swims with other participants and dolphins for $125 per person, and structured swims or one-on-one inter-active sessions with dolphins for $160 per person. A double session of both the natural and structured swim can also be purchased for $240 per person. In addition, Dolphins Plus offers a *Make Your Own Package Program,* where visitors can choose from the many dolphin encounter programs available to customize their vacation experience.

Dolphins Plus also offers extended group education programs ranging from $550 for three-day programs to $850 for five-day programs that focus on a general study of dolphins and their habitats. Agendas feature seminars on dolphin intelligence, anatomy and communication. Advanced reser-vations are required, and guests are encouraged to call for details.

Coordinated by the not-for-profit Island Dolphin Care, five-day dolphin therapy programs are offered on premises to disabled humans. Scientists believe the unconditional acceptance by dolphins enhances the self-esteem of individuals and complements traditional therapies; ☎ 305-451-5884.

Dolphins Plus is open daily from 8 a.m. to 5 p.m. Non-swimming tours allow visitors to view swim sessions for a fee of $10 per adult and $5 per child . Children under seven free. ☎ (305) 451-1993 or www.dolphinsplus.com.

Islamorada-based **Theater of the Sea**, MM 84.5 oceanside, offers dolphin, sea lion and stingray swim programs, along with glass-bottom boat rides, wildlife exhibits and continuous marine shows featuring dolphins and sea lions. Cost for dolphin swims is $140 per person, for sea lion swims $95 per person and $45 per person for stingray swims.

Theater of the Sea also offers three-hour Trainer for a Day programs for $140, in which participants assist facility trainers with the feeding, care and training of dolphins and sea lions, as well as a wade with baby dolphins. Additional on-site activities include glass-bottom boat tours and snorkel trips. The facility is open 365 days a year from 9:30 a.m. to 4 p.m. Park entrance fees are $18.50 for adults, $11.50 for children between the ages of 3 and 12, and free for children under the age of 3; ☎ 305-664-2431.

Based at Hawks Cay Resort, MM 61 oceanside on Duck Key, **Dolphin Connection** offers a number of dolphin encounter programs. The facility's Dolphin Discovery program allows supervised contact with dolphins from a submerged platform. Costs for the program are $90 for resort guests and $100 for non-guests.

The resorts **Dolphin Detectives** program, priced at $30 for resort guests and $35 for non-guests, allows children ages 5 and older to feed, pet and play with dolphins from the dock. Similar to the Dolphin Detectives program, Dockside Dolphins offers a behind-the-scenes look at dolphin training for $40 per guest and $45 per non-guest; children ages 12 and under must be accompanied by a paying adult. Dolphin Connection is open daily; ☎ 888-814-9154 or 305-743-7000, ext. 3570.

Open daily from 8 a.m. to 5 p.m., the **Dolphin Cove Center**, MM 102 bayside in Key Largo, is the Florida Keys newest dolphin center. In-water dolphin encounters cost $160 per person; ☎ 305-451-4060.

A dolphin-assisted therapy program for children with special needs is provided by **Dolphin Human Therapy** at Dolphin Cove; (305) 378-8670.

Best Snorkeling Sites of the Florida Keys

The Upper Keys

Key Largo to Islamorada

Conditions on the reefs vary with the wind, from flat calm with no current to high seas with strong currents. Two to four-ft seas are the norm with a light current. The inner reefs are always calmer, but visibility isn't as good. Check with individual snorkeling tour companies or dive shops for daily weather and sea conditions.

☆☆☆☆ **The Statue**. Key Largos most popular dive, underwater wedding site and perhaps the one which symbolizes the area, is a nine-foot bronze replica of Christ of the Abyss, created by sculptor Guido Galletti for placement in the Mediterranean Sea. The statue was given to the Underwater Society of American in 1961 by industrialist Egidi Cressi.

The top of the statue is in nine feet of water and can be seen easily from the surface. The base rests on a sandy bottom, 20 feet down, and is surrounded by huge brain corals and elk horn formations. Stingrays and barracuda inhabit the site. A buoy marks the statues location, but small swells make it difficult to pinpoint if you are using your own boat. Extreme shallows in the area provide outstanding snorkeling areas, but make running aground a threat.

☆☆☆☆ More easily found is **Molasses Reef**, marked by a huge, lighted steel tower in the southeast corner of the park. Noted as the areas most popular reef dive, it holds the distinction of having had two shiploads of molasses run aground on its shallows.

The reef provides several dives, depending on where your boat is moored. Moorings M21 through M23 are for scuba diving. M1 through M20 are shallow and better for snorkeling.

Be sure to check the current at Molasses before entering the water since an occasional strong flow makes the area unsafe. Depths vary from very shallow to approximately 40 ft.

☆☆☆☆☆ Slightly northeast of Molasses stands **French Reef**, an area many consider the prettiest in the park with ledges carpeted in pink and lavender sea fans, tube sponges, soft corals and anemones. Shallow depths range from areas where the reef pierces the surface to 20 ft.

☆☆☆☆ Despite pristine reefs and a robust fish population, a long boat ride prevents most dive operators from frequenting **Carysfort Reef**, located in the northeast corner of the park.

If you are fortunate enough to catch a trip out there, expect a good display of fish and the possibility of one huge, resident barracuda, tamed by a local dive master, swimming up to within an inch of your mask. This unique, engaging plea for a handout makes the toothy guy tough to ignore, but sanctuary officials greatly discourage fish feeding so try to resist sharing your lunch. Instead, explore the reefs healthy display of staghorn, elk horn and star corals at depths varying from very shallow.

☆☆☆ South of Pennekamp Park lies **Pickles Reef**, a shallow area rich with marine life, sea fans and boulder corals. Residents of the wreck include parrot fish, schools of grunt, sergeant majors, moray eels and angels.

Wreck of the Benwood

Photo ©2004 Jon Huber

☆☆☆☆ **Alligator Reef**, Another popular Islamorada dive site, is home to walls of grunts, parrotfish, groupers and an occasional nurse shark, who hide betwixt and between nice stands of elk horn and brain corals.

Key Largo Boat Tours

Snorkeling trips to John Pennekamp Park and the National Marine Sanctuary are offered by the following tour operators:

Captain Slate's Atlantis Dive Center. Snorkel, rent a kayak or take a tour on a glass-bottom boat. Located at 51 Garden Cove Drive, Key Largo, FL 33037 ☎ 305-451-3020 or 800-331-DIVE. Email: dive@captainslate.com

Caribbean Watersports offers reef or bay snorkeling tours ecological and sunset cruises, Located at Mile Marker 97, Bayside, Key Largo, FL 33037 on the beach behind the Westin Beach Resort Key Largo. They also rent wave runners, Hobie Cat sailboats, kayaks, paddle boats, masks and fins. ☎ 305-852-4707, Email: cwsports@aol.com

Dive In features uncrowded snorkel trips. Six passengers maximum. Custom charters. Located at MM 97.5, oceanside, Key Largo, FL 33037 ☎ (305) 852-1919 or (877) 453-6179. Email: dawn@diveinflkeys.com.

Dual Porpoise Charters Inc. Provides custom snorkeling tours for both German and English speaking visitors. Two scheduled trips a day. Quality rental equipment. Located at MM 100, Holiday Inn Docks, Slip #2, Key Largo, FL 33037. ☎ 305-394-0417. Email: info@dualporpoise.net.

Book **Sundiver Tours** at the red and white snorkel station, MM 103 on Overseas Highway. Sundiver offers dry snorkels, which prevent you from inhaling salt water. ☎ 305-451-2220 or 800-654-7369.

Horizon Divers books uncrowded, customized daily dive/snorkel trips on a spacious 45 catamaran. Freshwater. Free ice-cold fruit juices and water. Free gear storage, dockside picnic area. MM 100, Oceanside at Ramada Inn and Shell station, Key Largo, FL 33037 ☎ 305-453-3535 or 800-984-3483. Email: horizon@econch.com. Turn ocean side at Ramada and Shell, go two blocks, we're on the right.

Its A Dive, a full service water sport facility at the Marriott Key Largo Beach Resort, offers morning and afternoon snorkeling trips. Located at 103800 Overseas Highway, Key Largo. ☎ 305.453.9881 or 800-809-9881. Email: info@itsadive.com.

John Pennekamp Coral Reef State Park features terrific, comfortable, glass-bottom boats and sail-snorkel tours. MM 102.5 Overseas Highway, Oceanside, Key Largo, FL 33037. ☎ (305) 451-1621 or 800-326-3521, fax: (305) 451-1427.

Keys Diver Snorkel Tours offering daily snorkel only tours to John Pennekamp Park and The Key Largo National Marine Sanctuary. Dry Snorkels and Prescription Masks. 99696 US 1 MM100 Bayside (next to Wendys) Key Largo, FL 33037-2432, ☎ (305) 451-1177 or 888-289-2402, fax: (305)451-6389. Email: tbfirm@aol.com

Quicksilver Catamaran Charters mixes snorkeling and sailing tours. Daily trips on a 50 ft. catamaran. Sunset sails nightly. Holiday Inn Docks, MM 100, Key Largo, FL 33037. ☎ 305-451-0105 or 800-347-9972. Email: info@quicksilversnorkel.com.

Reef Roamer Snorkel features Catamaran Sailing and Snorkeling tours. Staff is well informed on local reefs and aquatic habitats. MM 100. ☎ (305) 453-0110. Email: info@reefroamersnorkel.com

Capt. Ron's Reel n' Reef Charters offers fishing and snorkel trips aboard The Alessa a restored Bertram 31. Six passengers maximum.☎ 305-853-0636 or 305-394-CAPT (2278). Email: reelreef@aol.com

Islamorada

Offshore Islamorada, on the Atlantic side, lies the remains of the 287-ton Dutch ship, *San Pedro*, one of Florida's oldest artificial reefs. Remains of the ship rest in a sand pocket 18 feet below the surface offering shelter to a host of sea creatures amidst the ballast stones and coral overgrowth. Visibility can't compare with the offshore reefs, but it is an interesting dive nonetheless. Residents include gobies, damsels, moray eels and groupers.

The ship carried 16,000 pesos in Mexican silver and numerous crates of Chinese porcelain when she wrecked in 1733. For tours contact the Long Key

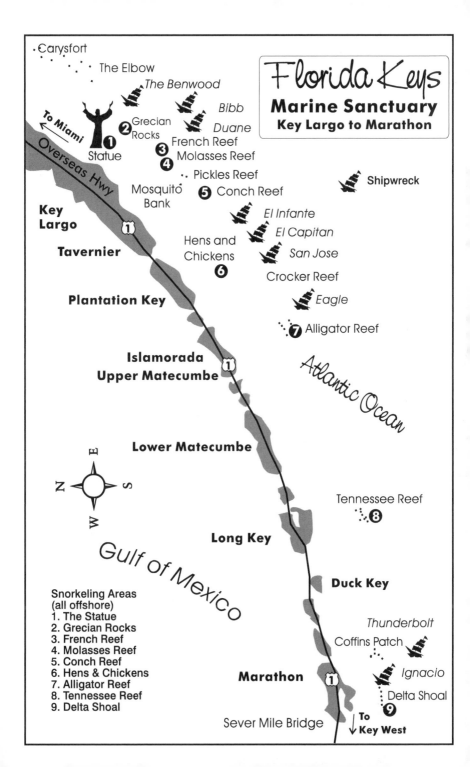

State Park office at 664-4815. Boaters use LORAN coordinates 14082.1, 43320.6. The wreck lies approximately one and one-quarter nautical miles south from Indian Key. Be sure to tie up to the mooring buoys to prevent anchor damage.

Islamorada dive shops visit Molasses, Alligator and Tennessee reefs—all named for a ship wrecked at the site and in depths ranging from extremely shallow to about 40 feet.

Islamorada Boat Tours

Holiday Isle Dive Shop at the Holiday Isle Resort launches daily snorkel trips at 9:00 am and 1:00 pm. Located at MM84 Overseas Hwy., Islamorada, FL 33036. ☎ 305-664-DIVE or 800-327-7070. Email: diveshop@dive holiday isle.com.

The Middle Keys
Marathon - Big Pine Key

Dive sites in the Middle Keys from Long Key Bridge Key to the Seven Mile Bridge are similar to, but often less crowded than those in Key Largo.

Sombrero Reef and Looe Key National Marine Sanctuary both offer superb reef snorkeling. Depths range from two to 35 feet. Corals and fish life are similar to Molasses and French Reef.

☆☆☆☆ **Sombrero Reef,** Marathon's most popular ocean dive and snorkeling spot offers good visibility and a wide depth range from the shallows to 40 feet. Cracks and crevices shot through the coral canyons that comprise the reef overflow with lobster, arrow crabs, octopus, anemones, and resident fish. A huge light tower marks the area. Boaters must tie up to the mooring buoys on the reef.

☆☆☆ Slightly north of Sombrero lies **Coffins Patch**, which has good snorkeling areas with mounds of pillar, elk horn, and brain corals at depths averaging 20- to 30-ft.

Middle Keys Boat Tours

Latigo Private Charters include all meals, snacks, drinks and luxury accom modations aboard a 56 motor yacht. Kayaks, snorkel, dive, water ski and fishing equipment are provided. Take the dinghy or 20 center console boat to explore uninhabited spots. ☎ 305-289-1066, Email: cruise@latigo.net.

Looe Key Reef Resort & Dive Center offers snorkeling reef trips. ☎ 305-872-2215 or 800-942- 5397, Email: looekeydiv@ aol.com

Bahia Honda State Park, Recently named the second most beautiful beach in North America, Bahia Honda (meaning deep bay in Spanish) is the

Top: Snorkeling Kauai, © Seafun Kauai

Below: Pedersen Shrimp, © Charles Seaborn, Bonaire Tourism

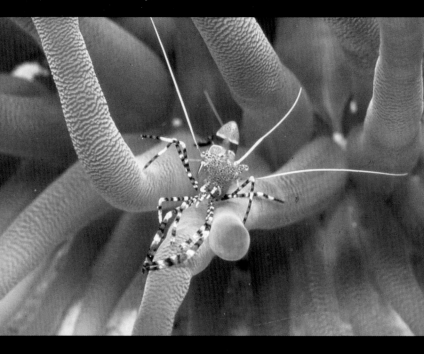

Facing page: Akumal Reef, Akumal Mexico © Myrna Bush
Club Akumal Caribe

Above: Stingray City, Grand Cayman © Wayne Hasson, Cayman Tourism

Left: Seahorses © Marc Bernardi, Aquatic Encounters

Below: Hanauma Bay, Oahu, Hawaii © Robert Coello, Hawaii Visitors Bureau

Facing page: Christ of the Abyss, © 2004 Jon Huber

Top Left, Hiske
Versteeg, Red Sail
Sports, Aruba © 2004
Jon Huber; Top right -
Parrot Fish © 2004
Marc Bernardi,
Aquatic Encounters
Left: South Shore
Snorkeling, Bermuda,
Bermuda Tourism
Below: French Reef,
Key Largo, Florida ©
2004 Jon Huber

Facing page: Bahamas © Jean Michel Cousteau's Out
Islands Snorkeling Adventures

Top , Willemstadt, Curacao ©
2004 Jon Huber; right -
Queen Angel Fish © 2004 Jon
Huber
Below: Giant Clams, Great
Barrier Reef, Australia, © 2004
Maria Shaw

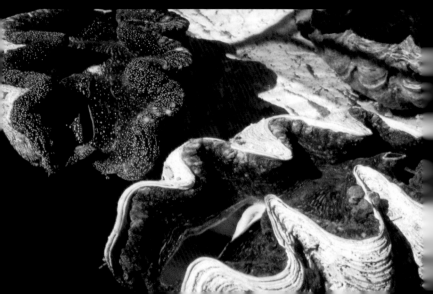

Top , Manatees at Florida Springs © 2004 Francois Fournier;

Below: Pink Sponges off Ponce, Puerto Rico, © 2004 Richard Ockelman

Top , Marble Grouper, Key Largo, Florida © 2004 Jon Huber;

Left - Great Heron, Belize © 2004 John Mazurowski

Below: Tent Reef, Saba © 2004 Joan Bourque, Sea Saba

Above: Sea Lion, Galapagos, © 2004 Marc Bernardi, Aquatic
Encounters
Below: Squirrel Fish , Key Largo, Florida © 2004 Jon Huber

Top , Sea Anemone, Saba, © 2004
Joan Bourque, Sea Saba
Left - Tarpon Basin, Florida © 2004
Joyce Huber
Below: Red-Lipped Batfish,
Galapagos © 2004 Marc Bernardi,
Aquatic Encounters

busiest park in the Keys. An on-site concession runs daily trips aboard a 56-ft boat to Looe Key National Marine Sanctuary. The park features two white sandy beaches, a marina, dive shop, cabins and campsites. Located at Mile Marker 38, Overseas Highway, Big Pine Key, FL 33043. ☎ 305-872-3210.

Strike Zone Charters' five and one-half hour trip to both the ocean reefs and Gulf of Mexico include snorkeling gear, glass-bottom viewing and host a fish fry on the beach. ☎ 800-654-9560 or 305-872-9863. Website: www. strikezonecharter.com.

The Lower Keys
From Big Pine Key to the Dry Tortugas

Dive boats in the Lower Keys—Big Pine Key, Sugar Loaf Key, Summerland Key, Ramrod Key, Cudjoe Key and Torch Key— take off to reefs surrounding American Shoal and Looe Key National Marine Sanctuary.

☆☆☆☆ **The Looe Key Reef Tract**, named for the HMS Looe, a British frigate that ran aground on the shallow reefs in 1744, offers vibrant elk horn and staghorn coral thickets, an abundance of sponges, soft corals and fish.

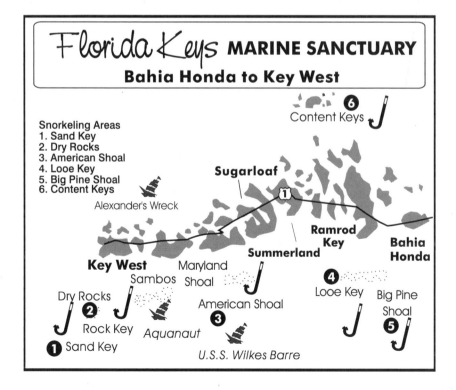

Florida Keys **MARINE SANCTUARY**
Bahia Honda to Key West

Snorkeling Areas
1. Sand Key
2. Dry Rocks
3. American Shoal
4. Looe Key
5. Big Pine Shoal
6. Content Keys

Alexander's Wreck

Content Keys ❻

Sugarloaf ❶

Ramrod Key

Bahia Honda

Key West   Maryland Shoal   Summerland

Sambos

Dry Rocks   Looe Key ❹   Big Pine Shoal

Rock Key   American Shoal ❸   ❺

❷

❶ Sand Key   *Aquanaut*

U.S.S. Wilkes Barre

Constant residents include Cuban hogfish, queen parrotfish, huge barracuda, and long snout butterfly fish. A favorite dive site of the Lower Keys, Looe Key bottoms out at 35 feet. Extreme shallow patches of seagrass and coral rubble provide a calm habitat for juvenile fish and invertebrates.

Snorkeling off Key West includes offshore wreck sites and tours of **Cotrell Key, Sand Key** and the **Western Dry Marks**. Huge pelagic fish and graceful rays lure explorers to this area.

☆☆☆☆ **Sand Key**, marked by a lighthouse, lures snorkelers to explore its fields of staghorn coral. Depths range from the surface down to 45 ft.

Cosgrove Reef, noted for its large heads of boulder and brain coral, attracts hordes of large fish and rays.

☆☆☆☆ Seldom visited, though pristine, are the **Marquesa Islands**, 30 miles off Key West. Extreme shallows both enroute and surrounding the islands make the boat trip difficult in all but the calmest seas and docking impossible for all but shallow draft cats and trimarans. Check with local dive shops for trip possibilities.

☆☆☆☆ **The Dry Tortugas**, an uninhabited island group lying 70 miles off Key West, sit in the midst of a pristine shallow reef tract, ideal for snorkeling with vibrant staghorn thickets, hordes of fish and critters. On calm days, both high-speed ferry and seaplane tours depart for Garden Key, site of the Fort Jefferson Monument. Seaplane tours are half day, the ferry departs Key West 8am and returns 7pm. Bring a picnic lunch, cold drinks and snorkeling equipment.

Spanish explorer Ponce de Leon discovered these island in 1513 and named them *Las Tortugas*, meaning the Turtles, for the throngs of turtles around the islands. The latter day name, Dry Tortugas, came about as a way to warn sea travelers that the islands have no fresh water.

In any case, the great numbers of loggerhead turtles are gone, but not all, most snorkelers spot at least one or two.

You reach the Dry Tortugas by high-speed ferry ☎ 305-294-7009 or 800-926-5332, or seaplane ☎ 305-294-0709, and should carry in all of your gear. Check with Key West dive shops for the availability of trips (see also Aerial Tours chapter). For the very adventurous, overnight camping trips can be arranged. Seaplane-snorkel tours to the Dry Tortugas can be booked at Key West Airport 305-294-0709. Or try the **Yankee Freedom**, a 100-ft, high-speed ferry with an air-conditioned cabin, spacious sun deck, complete galley, complimentary breakfast and full bar. ☎ 305-294-7009 or 800-634-0939.

☆☆☆☆ **The Marquesas**, equally magnificent in reef life, are approachable only in periods of exceptionally calm seas by private boat. Navigation information is available though the US. Coast Guard.

On the 30-mile crossing to the Marquesas you can spot sharks and rays as they dart under the boat along the sandy bottom. Armies of tulip shells with resident hermit crabs guard the remote island beaches.

Key West and Lower Keys Tours

Key West offers a unique variety snorkeling excursions. Sail-snorkel cruises visit secluded islands surrounded with beautiful coral reefs, often including lunch and refreshments.

Dolphin Watch. Join Capt. Alma Join Capt. Alma Armendariz and Capt. John Baltzell to observe wild Bottlenose dolphins and play in the beautiful warm waters of the Florida Keys. Daily journeys allow six passengers per trip aboard a spacious 31' catamaran.

Dolphin Watch was started in 1986 by Capt. Ron Canning to provide people with an alternative to captive dolphin encounters in the Keys and to help people connect with nature and themselves. Through patience and respect they have been able to establish a trusting relationship with a pod of dolphins and share this with people from all over the world. Dolphin Watch is the original Key West dolphin tour and has been bringing people and dolphins together for over 18 years. ☎ 305.294.6306 Fax 305.292.1676. Website: www.dolphinwatchusa.com. Board at Key West's Historic Seaport.

On neighboring Stock Island, personalized charters can be arranged aboard the six-passenger trimaran, **Fanta Sea**. ☎ 305-296-0362.

History buffs will want to book a snorkel trip on Key West's largest tall ship, the 86-ft, wooden windjammer **Appledore** ☎ 305-296-9992. Half-day reef trips depart at 10:30 am and 3:30 pm wsinter through spring.

The 65-ft schooner, **Reef Chief** ☎ 305-292-1345 offers splendid snorkeling charters to uncrowded sections of the ecological reserve only. Call for schedule. Daily snorkel trips. Website: www.reefchief.com.

Sail-racing fans will delight in touring the out-islands aboard the **Stars & Stripes**, a huge 54-ft., 49-passenger replica of the racing catamaran famed by Dennis Conner. This ninth version was designed especially for cruising the shallow channels and reefs of Key West. For maximum comfort and enjoyment, this sailing yacht features a 29-ft. beam, glass bottom viewing, and a fully shaded lounge. The ultra shallow draft (25") allows the captain to pull up to sandy beaches at Woman Key and other spots which are off limits to many charter boats. Board at Lands End Marina ☎ 305-294-7877 or 800-634-MEOW. Website: www.adventureskeywest.com.

Sunny Days, a large sailing catamaran departs the dock at the end of William St. Three-and-one-half hour trips depart at 9 am and 1 pm. Includes gear, instruction and cold sodas. Beer and wine after snorkeling.

Reef Raiders Dive Inc. offers snorkeling trips aboard the 53-ft catamaran, *El Gato* departing 9:30 and 1:30. Beer, wine and soda included on all tours.

ECO South Tours feature back country, snorkeling and dolphin watch morning trips on one- or two-person, lightweight kayaks. Before setting out, you will receive basic paddling and snorkeling instructions from expert guides. Refreshments. ☎ 305-797-9346. Website: www.eco-south.com

Holiday Watersports, at Holiday Inn Beachside, Key West, Fl 33040, offers snorkeling and dolphin watch boat tours. ☎ 305-295-8200, fax: 305-292-7252. Email: keywest-tours@msn.com

Safari Charters, located at the Banana Bay Resort,, offers sailing, kayaking and snorkeling and ecological-tours to the Great White Heron Wildlife Refuge. ☎ 296-4691 or 888-6SAFARI. Email: eric@safari charters.com. Write to: 2319 N. Roosevelt Blvd, Key West, FL 33040.

Sea-Clusive Charters books all-inclusive, overnight trips along the Keys or to the secluded Dry Tortugas. Day trips to Looe Key or remote locations in the Marquesas Keys. ☎ 305-872-3940. Email: seaclusiveKW@aol.com. Write to: Oceanside Marina, Key West, FL 33040

Seaplanes Of Key West fly you 70 miles west off Key West to the Dry Tortugas National Park for snorkeling, bird watching and historic sights. ☎ 305-294-0709 or 800-950-2FLY. Email: info@seaplanesofkeywest.com.

Snuba Of Key West offers a cross between scuba diving and snorkeling. Guests sail on luxurious catamarans. It's safe and easy to learn. Located at 201 Front Street, Key West, Fl 33040. ☎305-292-4616 or 305-923-4320. Email: ljcdive@keysinet.com

Sunny Day Catamarans runs half-day, sail-snorkeling trips to the Dry Tortugas aboard high-speed catamarans ☎ 305-296-5556. Email: cattours@aol.com. Board at Key West Historic Seaport.

Froggie's Glassbottom Adventures features reef snorkeling, wild dolphin watching and champagne, sunset tours—four trips in one. ☎ 305.747.0342. Email: info@froggieskeywest.com. Write to: 711 Eisenhower Drive, Key West, FL 33040

Captain Seaweed Charters offers swim and snorkel encounters with dolphins in their natural habitat. Boat trips include lunch, beverages and snorkel gear. Six person maximum. ☎ 305-872-7588, boat ☎ 305 509-1145, fax 305-872-7587. Email: captseaweed6@aol.com. Write to: Oceanside Marina, Key West, FL 33040.

Captain Sheri Sullenger's **Wild about Dolphins Tours** combines dolphin watching and snorkeling tours. Snorkeling is over a reef. The four-hour trip aboard the *Amazing Grace* includes lunch, use of snorkeling gear and boat trip. Contact her at ☎ 305-294-5026 or by Email at: wildfin@aol.com.

Danger Charters offer back country sail, kayak, and snorkel trips aboard traditional schooners. Charters depart daily from the Hilton Marina. All gear, kayaks, wetsuits (in winter months), instruction, snacks and beverages are included. ☎ 305-296-3272. Email: wfoxdanger@aol.com. Located at the Hilton Resort, Key West, FL 33040

Yankee Freedom Ferry. Travel fast, comfortably, safely to the Dry Tortugas National Park and Fort Jefferson aboard the 100-ft Catamaran Yankee Freedom II. Your fare includes a continental breakfast, picnic lunch, guided tour of Fort Jefferson, and the use of the snorkel gear. ☎ 305-294-7009 or 877-327-8228. Email: ferry@yankee-fleet.com. Write to: 240 Margaret Street, Key West, FL 33040

Dream Catcher Charters supply everything including snorkeling gear, a light fruit lunch buffet, dolphin watching and extremely comfortable boats. Professional crew and top notch gear. Custom charters available. ☎ 305-745-2114 or 888-362-3474. Email: flakeys1@bellsouth.net. Board at Sunset Marina, Key West, FL 33040

Tips and Rules for Boaters

Be sure to display a divers flag if you are snorkeling from your own boat. Strong currents may be encountered on the outside reefs. Check before disembarking. One person should always remain on board.

Be aware of weather, sea conditions and your own limitations before going offshore. Sudden storms, waterspouts and weather-related, fast moving fronts are not uncommon. Nautical charts are available at marinas and boating supply outlets throughout the Keys.

Key Largo and Looe Key National Marine Sanctuaries provide mooring buoys to which you should attach your boat rather than anchor. If no buoys are available, you should drop anchor only in sandy areas. The bottom in sandy areas appears white.

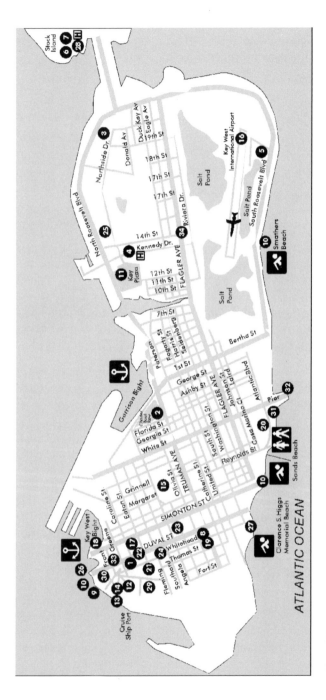

Key West Attractions and Points of Interest

1. Audubon House
2. Charter Fishing Boats
3. & 33. Conch Train Depots
4. De Poo Hospital
5. East Martello Museum and Gallery
6. Florida Keys Memorial Hospital
7. Golf Course
8. Hemingway House

8. Hospitality House
10. Key West Beaches
11. Key Plaza Shopping Center
12. Mel Fisher's Treasure Museum
13. Key West Aquarium
14. Key West Chamber of Commerce
15. Key West City Cemetery
16. Key West International Airport

17. Key West Women's Club
18. Land's End Village and Turtle Kraals
19. Lighthouse and Military Museum
20. Playground
21. & 34. Post Offices
22. Oldest House
23. Peggy Mills Garden
24. San Carlos Opera House

25. Searstown Shopping Center
26. Sightseeing Boat
27. Southernmost Point U.S.A.
28. Tennessee Williams Fine Arts Center
29. Truman's Little Whitehouse
30. Waterfront Playhouse
31. West Martello Tower
32. White Street Fishing Pier

ATLANTIC OCEAN

In protected areas of the Keys, destruction of coral formations through grounding or imprudent anchoring can lead to penalties and fines of up to $50,000. Minor damage to coral fines start at $150. Give yourself plenty of room to maneuver. For Key Largo National Marine Sanctuary use chart 11451 or 11462, and for Looe Key National Marine Sanctuary use chart 11442 or 11445.

Where to Stay in the Florida Keys

For a complete list of home rental agencies, resorts, motels and campgrounds call ☎ 800-FLA-KEYS or write to P.O Box 1147, Key West, Florida 33041. Website: www.fla-keys.com.

Following are a sampling of popular Florida Keys accommodations. All can book you a reef tour. Pets are not welcome unless otherwise noted. " MM" denotes Mile Marker number.

Key Largo

Amy Slates Amoray Lodge on Florida Bay offers 16 lovely, modern apartments. Snorkeling trips leave from the resort dock. Walking distance to several good restaurants. Sundeck, jacuzzi, fresh water swimming pool. ☎ 800-426-6729 or 305-451-3595. Email: amoray@aol.com.

Holiday Inn, Key Largo, MM 99.7, sits next to a large marina. Restaurant, pool. ☎ 800-THE-KEYS or 305-451-2121. www.holidayinnkeylargo.com.

Kellys Motel, MM 104.5 sits on Florida Bay. Boat dock and ramp. Reef trips. ☎ 305-451-1622 or 800-226-0415. Email: info@aqua-nuts.com.

Ocean Pointe, MM 92.5, oceanside, features modern, clean suites, heated pool, tennis, marina with rental slips. Suntan beach. ☎ 800-882-9464, fax 305-853-3007.

Marina Del Mar Resort and Marina offers guests two properties one on Florida Bay, the other on a canal. Rooms at both are nicely furnished with wicker furniture and sunny prints. Snorkeling tours daily. ☎ 800-451-3483, 305-451-4107, Email: marina-del-mar@msn.com. Bayside Resort Accommodations ☎ 305-451-4450.

Ramada Ltd., MM 99.7 oceanside, offers 88 rooms and five suites. Pool. Continental breakfast . No beach. ☎ 800-THE KEYS or 305-451-3939.

Westin Beach Resort Key Largo, MM 97, bayside, offers a luxurious rooms, a sandy beach on Florida Bay. Fine restaurants. ☎ 800-539-5274, fax 305-852-5553. Website: www.keylargoresort.com

Islamorada
Plantation Key to Long Key
Chesapeake Resort, MM 83.5 ocean side sprawls over six acres with 65 rooms, two heated pools, hot tub, tennis courts, laundry and outdoor gym. Long sandy beach. Boat ramp, kayak rentals, power boats to 33 ft. Snorkeling excursions from adjacent marina. ☎ 800-338-3395 or 305-664-4662. E-mail: info@chesapeake-resort.com.

Cheeca Lodge offers pampered seclusion, oceanside, at MM 82. The luxurious resort offers a wealth of activities and a staff of expert instructors. Dive shop on premises. Daily, afternoon snorkeling trips take off for Cheeca Rocks, a nearby shallow reef. ☎ 800-327-2888 or 305-664-4651.

Hampton Inn MM 80 ocean side has 59 suites, 16 rooms, four handicapped accessible rooms . Suites have two TVs with VCRs. Heated pool, spa, tiki bar, dock. Watersports center offers snorkel excursions and kayak rentals. Outback Steakhouse next door. ☎ 305-664-0073 or 800-426-7866. Website: www.keys-resort.com.

Holiday Isle Resorts MM84 encompasses an entire beach club community with every imaginable watersport and activity. Guests choose from rooms or suites. Rates for every budget ☎ 305-664-2321, 800-327-7070, fax 305-664-2703. Website: www.holidayisle.com.

Marathon
Marathon is mostly residential, appealing to those who seek a quiet vacation.

Holiday Inn, 13201 Overseas highway, offers 134 recently renovated rooms, a freshwater pool, AC, TV, phone, and daily reef trips with the adjacent Abyss Diver Center. ☎ 800-224-5053 or 305-743-5460.

Hawks Cay Resort and Marina offers 177rooms and suites. Heated pool, saltwater lagoon with sandy beach, 18-hole golf course nearby, marine mammal center featuring dolphin shows. Boat slips for large and small craft. ☎ 800-753-7000, FL 800-432-2242. Website: www.hawkscay.com.

Buccaneer Resort, MM48.5, bay side has 76 units, beach, cafe and boat dock. ☎ 800-237-3329 or 305-743-9071. Email: www.buccaneer@florida key.com. Dive shops nearby.

Big Pine Key
Looe Key Dive Resort, MM27.5, ocean side, is the close to Looe Key Marine Sanctuary. Simple canal-side suites with one or two bedrooms, kitchen and patio.

Snorkel and sunset cruises daily. Dive shops nearby. ☎ 800-942-5397.

Little Torch Key

Little Palm Island. Located on an out island, this deluxe resort offers all recreational facilities. Ultra luxurious suites include private balcony, fans, AC, refrigerator, wet bar and whirlpool. Launch transfers to the island are provided. No TV or phones. ☎ 800-GET LOST or 305-872-2524.

Key West

Key West has three main resort areas — Old Town, the center of activity and where you'll find posh, oceanfront resorts, South Roosevelt Blvd., which runs along the Atlantic Ocean, and North Roosevelt Blvd., the commercial strip packed with fast food joints that run along the islands northern, Gulf shores. For a complete list of Key West accommodations call ☎ 800-LAST-KEY.

Best Western Key Ambassador Resort, 3755 South Roosevelt Blvd., Key West. Offers 100 guest rooms with two queen-sized beds or one king.. All with tropical decor and views of the garden, ocean or pool. Short drive to Smathers Beach, two miles to Old Town attractions. ☎ 800-432-4315 or 305-296-3500.

Fairfield Inn by Marriot, 2400 N. Roosevelt Blvd., features100 rooms, a heated pool, cable TV, handicapped access. ☎ 800-228-2800 or 305-296-5700.

Hampton Inn, 2801 Roosevelt Blvd. Located on the Gulf, Hampton Inn features 157 units, island decor, freshwater pool, cable TV, Jacuzzi, sun deck. Handicapped accessible. ☎ 305-294-2917, US 800-HAMPTON.

Hyatt Key West Resort and Marina, 601 Front St. Oceanfront, this stunning 120-room landmark resort sits two short blocks from Duval and the heart of Old Town. Pool, three restaurants, private sandy beach and marina. ☎ 800-554-9288 or 305-296-9900.

Wyndhams Casa Marina Resort, 1500 Reynolds St. Billed as the islands largest oceanfront resort, featuring 314 rooms, tennis, water sports, private beach, two pools, whirlpool and sauna. Handicapped accessible. Expensive. ☎ 800-626-0777, in Florida 800-235-4837or 305-296-3535.

Wyndham Reach Resort, 1435 Simonton St. Elegant, Spanish style resort located on a natural sand beach. Features 149 luxurious rooms and suites with island or ocean view. Rooms have ceiling fans, balcony, wet bar, hair dryers. Handicapped accessible. Walk to attractions, restaurants. US ☎ 800-626-0777 or 305-296-5000.

Southernmost Motel in the USA, 1319 Duval. Features two pools, Jacuzzi, tiki bar poolside, walking distance to shops, night life, across from beach pier on ocean. ☎ 800-354-4455 or 305-296-6577.

Additional Information

Getting There: All major national and international airlines fly into Miami Airport. Connecting scheduled flights land in Marathon and Key West.

Driving: From the North, take Florida Turnpike to Exit 4-Homestead-Key West. From Tampa, take I-75 south to Naples, then east to Miami and the Turnpike Extension. Or take 41 South, then east to the Turnpike Extension, then south to US 1.

From Miami Airport: Take LeJeune Road south to 836 west. Then take the Turnpike Extension to US 1 south, which runs the length of the Florida Keys. Climate: Sub-tropical. In winter temperatures range from 75° to 85° F. Fall brings chance of a hurricane. Summer temperatures range from 85to 95F. Dress: Lightweight, casual. Wetskin or light wetsuit needed in winter.

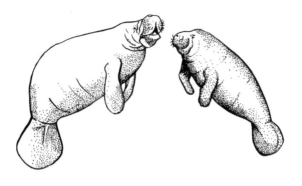

Florida Springs

Kings Bay, Crystal River and Homosassa River, on Florida's central west coast are the place to swim with manatees. In fact, its the only area that doesn't restrict snorkelers from getting close. These gentle giants inhabit the Crystal River Wildlife Refuge between mid October and May. Nearby Rainbow River is also an excellent manatee watching spot.

Visibility isn't always terrific as the manatees dig up the bottom eating mudgrasses, but every encounter is memorable. The clearest spot, and a favorite for photography, in the west coast spring area is Three Sisters Spring, which has a white-sand bottom. Three Sisters is not an official part of the sanctuary, but is on the list currently being considered.

Snorkeling in the chilly, 72° F springs water requires wearing at least a c th inch wet-suit. Dive shops offers rentals (see page 127).

About the West Indian Manatee

Florida's manatees are a highly endangered species. Population studies indicate that there may be as few as 800 manatees in Florida waters. Many are killed or severely injured by power boats. Habitat destruction puts these docile creatures in jeopardy.

It is illegal to harass, harm, pursue, hunt, shoot, would, kill, annoy or molest manatees. When you enter their areas, stay on top of the water and wait for them to come up to you. If they do not, you must settle for viewing them from a distance. There are seven sanctuaries in this area. Some prohibit touching or getting within 50 ft of the manatees. The one place where interaction is allowed is Crystal River.

Boat rentals are readily available, however, contributor and manatee rescue worker, Francois Fournier suggests joining a guided tour. The guides are trained professionals concerned with your safety and that of the manatee.

Plus, they will teach you the proper and legal way of interacting with manatees, thus making your experience very enjoyable.

Rescue and Rehabilitation Program

After the Marine Mammal Protection Act of 1972 and the Endangered species Act of 1973 were passed, marine specialists at Sea World, Orlando, were approached to aid in the rescue of beached or stranded marine mammals.In cooperation with the Department of the Interior, the National Marine fisheries Service, the Florida Department of Natural Resources and the Florida Marine patrol, Sea World developed the Beached Animal Rescue and Rehabilitation Program in 1973. Since that time, animal care specialists have responded to hundreds of calls to aid sick, injured or orphaned manatees, dolphins, whales, otters, sea turtles and a of birds. The marine life park bears all costs of the rescue program, including research, transportation and rehabilitation.

As a result of research conducted by Sea Worlds animal husbandry staff in, animal care and aquarium departments, valuable baseline data is being established and shared with scientists worldwide. Food preferences, responses to antibiotic therapy, the safest transportation equipment and the swiftest rescue techniques have been documented by the staff. Sea Word is the largest of two facilities in the state that are authorized to rescue, care for and release manatees. If your vacation includes a trip to Orlando, be sure to plan a stop at SeaWorld where you can view the recovering manatees.

Florida Springs' Snorkeling Tours

Birds Underwater features excellent guided snorkel tours in Crystal River and a Manatee Awareness Program. Owners Bill Bird and Diana are both licensed Coast Guard captains and scuba instructors. Diana has been working with manatee snorkel programs for eleven years and brings a wealth of delightful experiences to every tour. Early morning tours depart from the dive center dock. Accommodations available in two modern, riverside cottages at low cost. Kayaks. ☎ 352-563-2763. E-mail: bird@birdsunder water.com. Website: www.birdsunderwater.com. Write to: Bill & Diana Oestreich, 320 N.W. Highway 19, Crystal River, FL 34428.

American Pro Diving Center in Crystal River offers guided snorkel tours to Crystal River, Rainbow River and daily during the manatee season. Special packages combining two or more areas are offered as are discount hotel reservations. They also offer a Snorkeling Encounter with Manatee course. Accommodations in modern, riverside cottages with on-site boat and kayak. ☎ 800-291-DIVE or 352-563-0041. Write to: 821 South East Highway 19, Crystal River, Florida 34429. Website: www.americanprodiving.com.

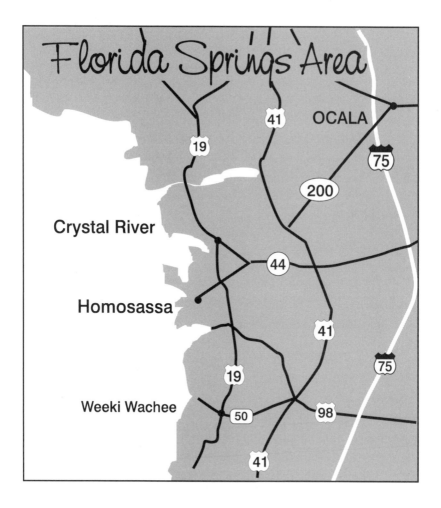

Crystal Lodge Dive Center takes snorkelers on their 8:30 am trip to first swim with manatees, then to explore the springs. ☎ 352-795-6798. The dive center is adjacent to the EconoLodge motel property at 614 N.W. US Highway 19, Crystal River, FL 34428.

Sunshine River Tours is an eco-tourism guide service in Homosassa, Florida. In addition to Manatee swim and snorkel tours, they offer Scalloping Trips and River-to-Gulf-of-Mexico Tours. Sunshine's Captain Mike will not book more than 10 persons per Manatee Encounter. And, if manatee snorkel encounters are not as good as expected, he will add a complimentary nature river tour to your manatee tour package.

Crystal River has a larger concentration of manatees, but Homosassa offers a quieter, more personal experience with these wonderful mammals. Email: captmike@sunshinerivertours.com. ☎ 866-645-5727 or 352-628-3450.

A good spot to view manatees without getting wet is the **Springs Wildlife Park**, where you can go below the waters surface in their floating observatory. The park is located at 4150 South Boulevard, Homosassa, FL 34446.

Where to Stay in Florida Springs

Econo Lodge Crystal Resort, adjacent to the Crystal Lodge Dive Center features guest rooms and studios with kitchenettes. Located at 2575 US Hwy 19, Crystal River, FL. Private dock, launching ramp, tours, fresh water pool. ☎ 352-795-9447.

Plantation Inn & Golf Resort sits 400 yards from the main spring at Crystal River. Lovely grounds and accommodations. Dive shop on premises. ☎ 800-632-6262 or 352-795-4211. Write to: 9301 W Ft. Island Trail, Crystal River, FL 34423. Website: www.plantationinn.com.

Comfort Inn features guests rooms and standard amenities. The hotel is two miles from Kings Bay in Crystal River at 4486 N. Suncoast Blvd. ☎ 352-563-1500.

The Crown Hotel features lovely victorian style accommodations in a refurbished, 100-year-old hotel. Located at 109 North Seminole Avenue, Inverness, Florida. ☎ 354-344-5555. Website: www.thecrownhotel.com. Email info@thecrownhotel.com.

Days Inn rents comfortable guest rooms, café, pool. ☎ 800-329-7466 or 352-795-2111.

For additional information on campgrounds, boat rentals, fishing, marinas and accommodations, contact the **Citrus County Chamber of Commerce** ☎ 352-795-3149. Website: www.citruscountychamber.com. Write to 28 N. W. Highway 19, Crystal River, Florida 34428

Guadeloupe

Named for Our Lady of Guadeloupe by Christopher Columbus in 1493, this charming French island is blessed with miles of beautiful white-sand beaches and spectacular coral reefs.

Guadeloupe is actually two main islands connected by a bridge across the River Salee and several out-islands. From the air it resembles the wings of a butterfly. Basse-Terre, the western wing, is mountainous, highlighted by the still-active volcano, Mt. Soufriere. Travelers touring this portion of the islands will find rain forests, bamboo trees, hot springs, postcard waterfalls, and a profusion of tropical flowers, fruits, almond and palm trees. Grande-Terre, the eastern wing of Guadeloupe, is flat, dry, and home to modern resorts, beautiful beaches, sugar cane fields and unlimited topside tourist attractions.

English is NOT widely spoken. Non-French-speaking visitors to Guadeloupe should pick up a French phrase book and familiarize themselves with the language. Also, snorkelers should bring their own equipment.

Topless sunbathing, snorkeling, scuba and swimming are *de rigueur* on Guadeloupe.

Best Snorkeling Sites of Guadeloupe

Pigeon Island, a mountain in the sea off Basse-Terre's west coast is the prime snorkeling area. The area consists of two land masses, North Pigeon and South Pigeon. The waters surrounding it come under French Government protection as an underwater natural park—The Cousteau Marine Sanctuary.

☆☆☆☆☆ **North Side Reef**. You'll find superb seascapes for photography on the north side of North Pigeon Island. Huge clusters of tube sponges, some six feet tall, and enormous green and purple sea fans grow on the ledges and outcrops of the wall. The reef begins in the shallows and drops off small canyons and outcrops. Divers are befriended by large gray snappers, which are tame and may be handfed. Seas are calm, visibility excellent.

☆☆☆☆☆ Pigeon Island's **West Side Reef** is the best snorkeling area in the Cousteau Marine Sanctuary. Its shallow walls ruffle with enormous feather dusters, sea plumes, sea rods, huge sea fans and sponges. Barrel sponges (large enough to camp in) thrive among clumps of elkhorn and enormous brain corals.Several puffer fish and unusual golden moray eels frequent this reef. Expect calm seas and exceptional visibility.

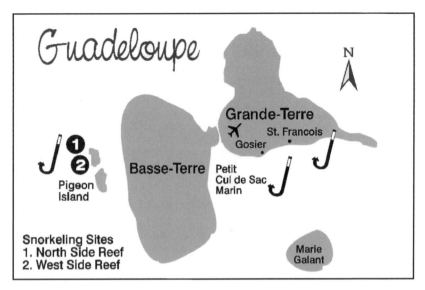

Additional snorkeling sites are found among the lagoons and bays of **Les Saintes**, the east coast of BasseTerre, and off-shore **Gosier** (the south coast of Grande Terre). Check out **Mouton Vert, Mouchoir Carr**, and **Cay Ismini.** They are close by the hotels in the bay of Petit Cul de Sac Marin, near Rivire Sale, the river separating the two halves of Guadeloupe. North of Sale is another bay, **Grand Cul de Sac Marin**, where the small islets of **Fajou** and **Caret** also offer decent snorkeling. St. Francois Reef on the eastern end of the south shore of Grande-Terre is a good, shallow, patch reef area as is **Ilet de Gosier**, off Gosier.

Snorkel Tours & Rentals

Plaisir Plonge is directly opposite Pigeon Island on Malendure Beach in Bouillante on Basse-Terre (☎ 011-590-98-8243). Plaisir runs fast, comfortable boats for daily scuba and snorkeling excursions to Pigeon Island. The boats have wide hydroplanes that double as diving platforms. Les Heures Saines (☎ 011-590-98-8643) and Aux Aquanautes Antillais (☎ 011- 590-98-8730) offer a variety of programs for divers and snorkelers. Glass-bottom/snorkeling boats depart from Malendure Beach daily.

Where to Stay on Guadeloupe

If your tongue doesn't curl comfortably around conversational French, head for the bigger hotels where English is spoken. Or if getting to know people is one of the reasons you travel, stay at a *Relais Crole,* a small family-owned inn. Most of the hotels are situated on Grande-Terre (one-hour drive to Malendure).

Among the small hotels close to Pigeon Island on Basse-Terre are Raphael Legrands charming 12-room **Auberge De La Distillerie** at Tabanon near Petit-Bourg. This fully air-conditioned inn is a short ride from Pigeon Island dive operators. ☎ (011) 590-94-2591, fax 590-94-1191. The adjacent restaurant, Le Bitaco, is noted for tasty Creole dishes. Freshwater pool. Website: www.frenchcaribbean.com.

Le Domaine de Malendure, on Basse-Terre overlooking Cousteau's Reserve, offers 44 deluxe, air-conditioned, hillside cottages with TV, telephone and bath. Restaurant, pool and swim-up bar. Snorkeling tours to Pigeon Island. ☎ 800-322-2223 or 800-742-4276. Website: ddm@french caribbean.com.

Hotel Paradis Creole, at Pigeon, is a small dive lodge operated by local divers. Bungalow studios or rooms can be packaged with boat tours and meals. ☎ 011-590-98-7162 or 590-98-8663.

La Creole Beach Resort, located on the beach at Gosier, offers 156 large, well appointed rooms. Dive Shop on premises offers tours to the coral reef surrounding Gosier Island and to Pigeon Island. ☎ (011) 590-90-4646, fax 590-90-1666. In the US ☎ 800-322-2223 or 800-742-4276. Website: www.frenchcaribbean.com.

La Sucrerie du Comte offers 26 bungalow rooms on the site of an old rum distillery. By the sea at Sainte Rose in the north of the western wing of Basse-Terre ☎ 011-590-28-6017. Website: prime-invest-hotels.com.

Meridien Guadeloupe, just east of Gosier at St. Francois, features 265 deluxe, beachfront rooms. Nearby dive shops offer tours to the reefs around Gosier Island and to Pigeon Island. ☎ 212-805-5000, direct 011-590-88-5100, fax 011-590-88-4071. Website: www.meridien-gpe.com.

Canella Beach Hotel in Gosier sits in walking distance of restaurants, shops and entertainment. This lovely three -star hotel offers 146 spacious rooms with TV, AC and kitchens. White sand beach, watersports shack, pool and beach side restaurant. Multilingual staff. Website: frenchcaribbean.com. ☎ 800-322-2223.

Auberge de la Vieille Tour, Gosier, sits in a seven-acre tropical park with great sea views, an 18th-century windmill and 104 deluxe rooms with balconies. Features include TV, phones, radios, AC, safes and mini-bars. Two fine restaurants, tennis, sand beach and fresh water pool ☎ 800-322-2223. Website: frenchcaribbean.com or www.sofitel.com. Email: H1345@accor-hotels.com.

Sailboats, crewed or bareboat, are plentiful. For rentals or tours try **Marina Bas-du-Fort,** Pointe-A-Pitre. ☎ 90-82-95. Full-day picnic sails on the trimaran, La Grande Voile ☎ 84-4642, or catamaran, Papyrus, can be arranged through your hotel. ☎ 90-9298.

Additional Information

Additional Information: At press time all Guadeloupe tourist boards in the U.S. and Canada were closed. For up-to-date information on resorts, airlines, documents, language, customs, climate and religious services, you can email the Guadeloupe office or log onto one of their websites: www.frenchcaribbean.com or www.guadeloupe-fr.com. E-mail: office. tourisme.Guadeloupe@wanadoo.Fr

Hawaii

Hawaii, one of the world's best vacation spots, offers snorkelers a lush, tropical paradise splashed with wild orchids, fields of sugar cane and pineapple. Green mountains pierce the horizon before sloping down to endless, white sand beaches.

Underwater Hawaii brings coral encrusted lava tubes, tunnels, archways, cathedrals, and caves. sunken volcano craters brimming with creatures, carpeted with vibrant corals and sponges.

Giant sea turtles, eagle rays, squid, Hawaiian turkeyfish, dolphins, whales, crustaceans, octopus, tiger cowries and tame morays abound in the islands' crystal waters. In fact, thirty percent of it's marine life exists nowhere else in the world. Sunken tanks and Jeeps, abandoned after World War II, lie motionless on the ocean floor, camouflaged now with layers of coral and barnacles.

Oahu

Oahu is the gathering place for vacationers, and Waikiki Beach, with miles of high rise hotels creating a luminescent skyline, is the undisputed capital. Honolulu, the cultural center, vibrates with concerts, dance performances, and live theater. Outside Honolulu, small countryside communities dot a vast expanse of open country. The Nuuanu Pali Lookout provides a panoramic view of the windward side of the island. Expert body surfers test their skills at the uncrowded beaches. At Makapuu Point daring hang-gliders soar from towering cliffs. On the leeward side of Waianae Range, small towns and wide beaches line the coastline. North shore snorkeling is excellent during summer when the seas are calm.

Best Snorkeling Sites of Oahu

☆☆☆☆ **Hanauma Bay Marine Life Conservation District,** on the southeast shore of Oahu, is the most popular snorkeling site in all of Hawaii. This state marine preserve hosts more than one million visitors each year. Formed from an ancient volcanic crater, the bay is lined with a shallow inner reef that starts at 10 ft and slopes down to an outer reef. To get there, take H-1 east from Waikiki, which becomes 72. You won't miss it. Beach access.

☆☆☆ **Rainbow Reef,** just west of Waikiki Beach, is a favorite dive site for beginners. The reef begins at 10 ft and slopes to 30 ft. Also known as Magic

Island, Rainbow Reef shelters hundreds of tame tropicals, including fantail file fish, parrotfish, triggerfish, surgeon fish, and porcupine puffers. All demand hand feeding. Beach access.

☆☆☆ **Three Tables and Shark's Cove**, part of the **Pupukea Marine Life Conservation District** north of Waimea Bay, takes is name from a trio of flat rocks which break the surface close to the beach. Starting at a depth of 15 ft, snorkelers can explore large rock formations, caverns, and ledges. Beach access is easy, however, this spot is diveable only during summer months. Extremely rough surf and strong currents exist from October through April. Check sea conditions with local dive shops.

☆☆ **Sans Souci Hotel**, just east of Waikiki has good snorkeling out front.

Oahu Snorkeling Tours

Snorkel Bob's Oahu rents snorkel gear from basic to the very best. In addition, they have prescription masks available. Snorkel Bob's shops are located on Hawaii, Kauai, Maui, and Oahu. Gear rented on one island may be

Diamond Head, Oahu
Photo courtesy Hawaii Visitors Bureau

returned on another. ☎ 808-735-7944. Located at 700 Kapahuli Ave., Honolulu, HI 96816. E-mail: Snorkel bob@snorkelbob.com. Website: www. snorkelbob.com.

Where to Stay on Oahu

For a complete list of accommodations contact the Oahu Visitors Association at 800-GO-HAWAII. Website: www.gohawaii.com. Waikiki accommodations are nearest the beach-snorkeling sites. Money saving travel packages that include hotel and airfare are offered by most travel agents or your chosen airline and big travel companies such as Liberty Travel/GoGo Tours, American Express Travel Store. Compare prices before you book.

Nahua Condominium Suites offer low-cost units with parking. pool, TV, phone, TV, kitchens. ☎ 800-446-6248, fax 310-544-1643.

The Outrigger Waikiki, on the beach in Honolulu, features 530 air-conditioned guest suites, a beauty salon, health club, spa, lounge, parking, phone, pool and TV. ☎ 800-688-7444 or 808-923-0711 Website: www.outrigger.com. E-mail: reservations @outrigger.com.

The Royal Hawaiian Hotel, has luxurious, air-conditioned guest rooms, beauty salon, lounge, parking, parking, phone, pool, restaurant, TV. ☎ 866-500-8313 or 808-923-7311. Website: www.royal-hawaiian.com.

Maui, The Valley Isle

Two mountain ranges, the West Maui mountains and Haleakala, cover most of Maui. Haleakala rises to 10,000 ft. Hiking here, especially at sunrise, is more of an "encounter" than a sport. Visitors enjoy wandering along the "road to Hana," a remote town on the windward side of Haleakala, which passes bamboo forests, waterfalls and gardens of wild fruits and flowers. On the northwest side of Maui you can explore Lahaina, an old whaling village. Lahaina Harbor is a bustling sailing port where you can see yachts from all over the world.

Maui County offers snorkelers an endless variety of sites. It is also a jumping-off point for snorkeling tours to the islands of Lanai, Molokai, Molokini and Kahoolawe. At these out-island dive sites, you'll see strange creatures rarely seen elsewhere, docile 50-foot whale sharks and during the winter months humpback whales. Snorkel-tour operations are located in the main resort areas of Wailea/Kihei and Lahaina. Trips to Molokini and other nearby sites take 15 to 30 minutes; trips across the channel to Lanai and Molokai can take 1½ hours.

Best Snorkeling Sites of Maui

☆☆☆☆☆ **Molokini Crater**, a crescent-shaped island two miles from Maui, is by far this island's most popular dive and snorkel site. Expect to see as many as 30 to 40 dive boats anchored here at one time.

Formed by the top of an old volcanic crater, this area is unique because it combines many ecosystems within a small area—deep water, shallow reef, flowing and still waters, with their natural complements of marine animals. Good visibility.

Marine life and sub-seascapes fascinate photographers and explorers alike. You can snorkel inside or outside the crater in the shallows or along the walls. Whales, porpoises and unusual marine animals are common at Molokini Crater. Plan a morning trip to the crater. Stronger currents are encountered in the afternoon.

☆☆☆**Grand Canyon**, off the southern end of Lanai, is an enormous underwater canyon with walls of lava where huge turtles and rays glide along the bottom and parrotfish of all colors, triggerfish and surgeonfish hover near the ledges. Shrimp and squirrel fish hide in the crevices. Depths start at 20ft. Boat access.

☆☆☆ **First and Second Cathedrals**, also off Lanai, has coral encrusted pinnacles rising from 60 ft to just below the surface. Snorkel trips tour this area only during morning hours, since afternoon currents can be treacherous. Visibility is excellent during periods of calm water and weather. Boat access.

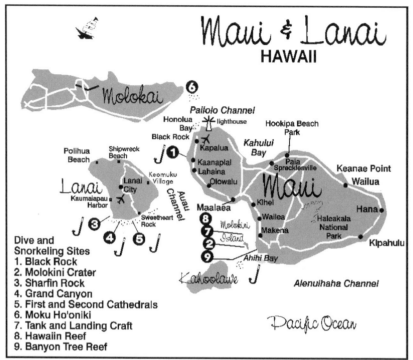

Maui & Lanai
HAWAII

Molokai

Pailolo Channel

Honolua Bay — lighthouse
Black Rock
Kapalua
Kaanaplai
Lahaina
Olowalu

Polihua Beach
Shipwreck Beach
Keomuku Village

Lanai
Lanai City
Kaumaiapau Harbor
Sweetheart Rock

Auau Channel

Maalaea
Kihel

Hookipa Beach Park
Kahului Bay
Paia
Sprecklesville
Keanae Point
Wailua

Maui

Hana

Wailea
Makena
Haleakala National Park
Kipahulu

Molokini Island

Ahihi Bay

Kahoolawe

Alenuihaha Channel

Pacific Ocean

Dive and Snorkeling Sites
1. Black Rock
2. Molokini Crater
3. Sharfin Rock
4. Grand Canyon
5. First and Second Cathedrals
6. Moku Ho'oniki
7. Tank and Landing Craft
8. Hawaiin Reef
9. Banyon Tree Reef

☆☆☆ **Black Rock** sits on the northwest shore of Maui off Beach. Snorkelers enjoy exploring the cove created by a peninsula. The bottom is sandy and the lava walls of the peninsula are inhabited by a wide variety of fish. Visibility is good. Depths shallow. Maximum 20 ft.

☆☆☆ **Sharkfin Rock**, off the south shore of Lanai, is a large rock formation that protrudes from the water like a shark's fin. The rocks top a vertical wall that drops to 90 ft. This is a popular site for feeding lemon butterfly fish. Around the ledges you'll find orange stonycup coral and, nearby, moray eels and nudibranches.

Maui Snorkeling Tours & Rentals

Book morning tours for the calmest seas.

Maui Diving offers Molokini Crater and Lanai snorkel cruises. Tours depart at 7 am. Lunch included. Returns about 12:30. Equipment rentals. ☎ 800-959-7319; in Maui (808)667-0633. E-mail: bia@mauidiving.com. Website: www.mauidiving.com

Dive Maui/Offshore Adventures arms snorkelers with detailed, local snorkeling maps to terrific dive spots right off the beach where you'll join huge turtles and hundreds of different reef fish. Depths range from 10 ft. to 60 ft. Weather and sea conditions determine site selection. 900 Front St., Lahaina, HI 96761. E-mail: info@divemauiscuba.com. ☎ 866-821-7450 or 808-667-2080.

Kelii's Kayak Tours. Trips lasting from two and one-half to five hours leave from the north, south and west shore of Maui. Write to: P.O. Box 959-420, Kihei, HI 96753. ☎ (888) 874-7652. Website: www.keliiskayak.com. E-mail: info@keliiskayak.com.

Mauibound Adventures runs five gorgeous Catamarans to all the best spots. Tours and prices vary. Some are snack cruises, others offer champagne and buffet fare. All provide snorkel gear, flotation devices and instruction. ☎ 877-464-6284. Website: www.mauibound.com. Credit cards accepted.

Maui Eco Tours features kayak-snorkel trips through Maui's top marine reserve where turtles and dolphins are frequent companions. Single and double ocean kayaks. complimentary meals and drinks. ☎ 808-891-2223.

Snorkel Bob's Lahaina, 1217 Front Street, Lahaina, HI 96761. ☎ 808-661-4421 and Snorkel Bob's Napili, 5425 C Lower Honoapiilani Hwy., Lahaina, HI 96761. ☎ 808-669-9603 offer gear rentals, maps and tips. (See Snorkel Bob's Kona for complete description).

Where to Stay on Maui

For a complete list of resorts contact the Maui Visitor Bureau ☎ 800-GO-HAWAII. Website: www.gohawaii.com or www.visitmaui.com. Write to P.O. Box 580, 1727 Wili Pa Loop, Wailuku, Maui, Hawaii 96793.

Royal Lahaina Resort at 2780 Kekaa Drive, offers 592 guest rooms, cottages and suites on a beautiful half-mile stretch of beach, three restaurants, pool, tennis, salon, resort shuttle, snorkeling gear, scuba lessons. The 12 story, beachfront complex sits near Lahaina Town, 26 miles from Kahului airport. Moderate rates. ☎ 800-222-5642 or 805-497-7934.

Sheraton Maui Hotel on Kaanapali Beach in Lahaina is near Black Rock, a favorite reef and wall dive for snorkelers and divers. The hotel features a lovely garden, restaurants, and Polynesian entertainment in the lounge. ☎ 866-500-8313 or 808-661-0031, fax 808-661-0458. Check with your travel agent for packages or online. Moderate to Expensive.

Kaanapali Beach Resort, 2525 Kaanapali Parkway, Lahaina, Maui, encompasses 10 resort hotels and condominiums, golf, tennis, shopping, all on a three-mile long beach adjacent to Lahaina's sites and attractions. ☎ 800-262-8450 or 808-661-0011. Website: www.kbhmaui.com.

Hawaii, The Big Island

Located 120 miles southeast of Oahu (40 minutes by air), Hawaii is the largest island of the Hawaiian archipelago. The birthplace of King Kamehameha, the best known ruler of the islands, it is also the location of the islands' only active volcanoes. Molten lava still flows to the sea. More than 20,000 varieties of orchids grow here.

The entire west coast of Hawaii is a diving and snorkeling paradise. Over 50 miles of the shoreline are protected from high winds and swells, and many snorkeling areas can be reached easily from the beach. The most spectacular spots are just offshore. All sites are less than 30 minutes away by boat.

Best Snorkeling Sites of Hawaii

☆☆☆☆☆ **Red Hill**, located 10 miles off South Kailua, has four different dive sites that range from 15 to 70 ft in depth. Expect visibility from 75 to 100 ft. The fish population is enormous with many varieties of eels, turtles, frogfish, porpoises, shell fish and lobsters. Boat access.

☆☆☆☆☆ **The Aquarium at Kealakekua Bay**, an underwater state park, is a beautiful reef inhabited by thousands of tame fish who enjoy following snorkelers. The shallows can be reached from the beach, but the deeper reefs and drop-offs require a boat. Seas are flat calm, making this a popular site for novices. Divers can spot parrotfish, rudderfish, sergeant majors, bird wrasse, bronze tangs trumpet fish, raccoon butterfly fish, tame moray eels and many more. The bottom is hard coral—lobe, finger, plate, cauliflower, octocorals—and patches of sand. Visibility is best on the outer reef. This is where Captain Cook was killed.

☆☆☆☆ **Kaiwi** lies two miles from Kailua Bay, a five minute boat ride. Depths range from 15 to 50 ft. Snorkelers will see caves, pinnacles and coral encrusted lava arches. Video and still photographers can capture graceful manta and eagle rays or large turtles here. Triton and conch shells are found on the bottom as well as 7-11 crabs. Swarms of all types fish abound. Visibility is almost always 75 to 100 ft here and the seas are calm with a small south surge during the summer.

☆☆☆☆☆ **Anaeho'omalu Bay Beach Park**, north of Kealakekua Bay, just past Mile Marker 77, features a lovely sand beach, pretty corals and a lot of fish. Visibility decreases with high winds and heavy surf. Beach access.

☆☆☆☆ **Palemano Point**, off the southern end of Kealakekua Bay is known for vibrant corals. Snorkelers enjoy photographing rudderfish, yellow

Hawaii

KONA COAST

HAWAII

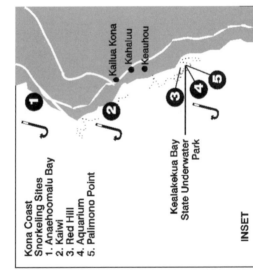

Kona Coast
Snorkeling Sites
1. Anaehoomalu Bay
2. Kaiwi
3. Red Hill
4. Aquarium
5. Palimono Point

Kailua Kona
Kahaluu
Keauhou

Kealakekua Bay
State Underwater
Park

INSET

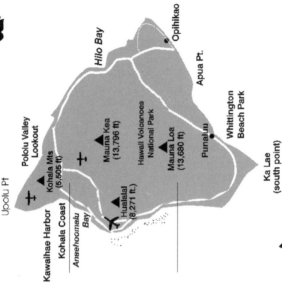

Upolu Pt

Kawaihae Harbor
Kohala Coast

Anaehoomalu
Bay

Kohala Mts
(5,505 ft)

Pololu Valley
Lookout

Hilo Bay

Hualalai
(8,271 ft.)

Mauna Kea
(13,796 ft)

Hawaii Volcanoes
National Park

Mauna Loa
(13,680 ft)

Opihikao

Apua Pt.

Punaluu

Whittington
Beach Park

Ka Lae
(south point)

tangs, and trumpetfish. Visibility is good, water usually calm. No facilities. Rocky shoreline. Beach access.

Hawaii Snorkeling Tours & Rentals

Eco-Adventures offers dedicated snorkeling trips to 66 sites with depths of 15-30 ft. Sign up for as trip at the lighthouse building, 745614 Palani Road, Kailua-Kona, HI, 96740. Kona Coast ☎ 800-949-3483, fax: 808-329-7091. Websites: www.ecodive.com or www.eco adventurestravel.com. Email : info@ecodive.com.

Kona Coast Divers offers complete vacation packages. Snorkeler rates include mask, fins and snorkel. Their superb night, manta ray trip includes a chemlite stick. Owner Julie Cunningham has been diving and snorkeling Kona Coast for several years and knows all the best places. Fast , safe boats. 74-381 Kealakehe Parkway, Kailua-Kona HI, 96740. ☎ 808-329-8802 or 800-562-3483. The only dive shop on the water on at Honokohau Marina. E-mail: divekona@kona.net. Website: www.konacoast divers.com.

Jack's Diving Locker charters boats for the day for snorkeling or swimming with dolphins. Individual snorkelers join scuba divers for reef tours. Snorkel gear is supplied. The shop is located at 75-5813 Alii Dr., Kailua-Kona, HI 96740. ☎ 800-345-4807. E-mail: divejdl@gte.net. Website: jacksdiving locker.com.

Manta Ray Dives of Hawaii offers dedicated snorkeling trips on glass bottom boats. Non-snorkeling companions or "ride alongs" are welcome. Night snorkeling with manta rays and day trips to the "Amphitheater" are favorites. ☎ (800)-982-6747. Website: www. mantaraydiveshawaii.com. E-mail: mantaraydivshawaii.com. Located at 75-217 Nani-Kailua Drive, #166, Kailua-Kona.

Red Sail Sports whisks snorkelers to the best spots aboard their luxurious, 50-ft sailing catamaran, *Noa Noa*. The morning snorkel cruise includes a continental breakfast, buffet luncheon, snorkel gear, towels and expert guides. *Noa Noa* also carries a fully-stocked bar. Red Sail is children friendly with a good variety of sizes in masks, snorkels and other gear. Children one-to three-years old sail free, ages four to 12, half price. Whale watching and dinner cruises are also offered.

Contact Red Sail Sports, 425 Waikoloa Beach Drive, Waikola, HI 96738. ☎ 877-RED-SAIL or 808-886-2876. E-mail: info@redsail.com. Website: www.redsail. com.

Snorkel Bob's Kona rents snorkel gear from basic to the very best. In addition, they have prescription masks available. Snorkel Bob's shops are on Hawaii, Kauai, Maui, and Oahu. Gear rented on one island may be returned on another. 75-5831 Kahakai St., Kailua-Kona, HI 96740. 808-329-0770. E-mail: SnorkelBob@snorkelbob.com. Website: www. snorkel bob.com.

Where to Stay on Hawaii

For a complete list of accommodations contact the Hawaii Visitor sand Convention Bureau toll free ☎800-GO-HAWAII or on the internet at www.gohawaii.com or www.bigisland.gohawaii.com. Resorts listed are near beach entry snorkeling areas.

Hilton Waikoloa Village in Kamuela features a Dolphin Quest program for guests. Participants learn about the world's oceans and its inhabitants. Dockside encounters are offered for children 5- to 12 and 13- 19 years old. Dolphin Doubles for 16 years and older allow in-water encounters. This huge resort offers every amenity including golf, hair salon, tennis courts, freshwater pools, cable TV. Book at ☎ 800 HILTONS. Website: www.hiltonwaikoloa village.com.

Royal Kona Resort, Kailua-Kona, offers 441 guest rooms, health club, movies, phones, pool, fridges, tennis, TV, AC, lounge, ☎800-222-5642 or ☎ 808-329-3111, fax 808-329-9532. Websites: www.royalkona.com or www.hawaiihotels.com.

Kona Village Resort, Kailua-Kona rents 125 units. Nice beach, beach bar, fitness center, pool, tennis. Quiet–No phones, no TV. ☎ 800-367-5290. Website: www.konavillage.com.

Kona Seaside Hotel offers air-conditioned rooms, cable TV, refrigerators, balcony or patio, two fresh-water swimming pools. ☎ 800-560-5558, local 808-320-6157. Email: info@konaseaside hotel.com.

Website: www.sand-seaside.com.

Kauai, The Garden Isle

Kauai, a tropical oasis famed for its relaxed, rural atmosphere, features postcard waterfalls, beautiful beaches, swimming lagoons (featured in the classic movie *Bali H'ai* and the former TV series *Fantasy Island*), exotic birds, rain forests, botanic gardens, deep canyons, and lush valleys. It is also the oldest Hawaiian island and the richest in folklore and history.

Because Kauai is so old, its marine life is more unusual and varied than the marine life anywhere else in the state. South shore sites are accessible year-round and offer snorkelers an underwater fantasy land teeming with

Rainbow Diver II

every kind of fish and coral imaginable. On the north shore, huge surf pounds the beaches during winter months, but summer offers opportunities to explore networks of lava tubes.

Best Snorkeling Sites of Kauai

☆☆☆☆☆ **Niihau** (the Forbidden Island), located 18 miles from Kauai, is privately owned and populated almost entirely by native Hawaiians. It is a cultural preserve dedicated to the traditions and culture of old Hawaii. Residents lead a primitive life style without benefit of electricity, medical facilities or paved roads.

Dive boats regularly tour the magnificent coral reefs surrounding the island. Besides spectacular drop offs and arches, large, open-ocean game fish such as rays and sharks are often sighted here. For advanced, open-water snorkelers only.

☆☆☆ **Tunnels at Ha'ena Beach State Park** sits approximately nine miles west of Princeville on Route 56, across from the Dry Cave. Walk east along the shore and enter from the sandy beach. An outer reef protects this area, providing calm water.

☆☆☆☆ **Oasis Reef**, on the south shore, is protected and diveable all year. A lone pinnacle surrounded by sand rises from 35 ft to just below the

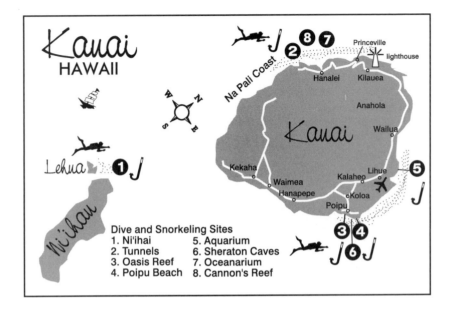

Dive and Snorkeling Sites
1. Ni'ihai
2. Tunnels
3. Oasis Reef
4. Poipu Beach
5. Aquarium
6. Sheraton Caves
7. Oceanarium
8. Cannon's Reef

ocean surface. This is a gathering place for thousands of fish including false moorish idols, triggerfish, butterfly fish and porcupine puffers. Octopus are found in the flats, lobsters and moray eels reside along the ledges. Depths run from four to 35 ft. Boat access.

☆☆ **Poipu Beach** offers ideal conditions for beginners. No current, depths from three to 20 ft and plenty of fish. Go south on Poipu Rd. from Koala town to Hoowili Rd. Turn right on Hoowili Rd. Parking and full facilities available. Beach access.

☆☆☆☆ **Aquarium**, on the southeast side of Kauai, takes its name from the variety of colorful tropicals in residence. This shallow reef stretches into an expanse of lava ledges and small coral valleys. You'll see several cannons from an 18th-century wreck. Depths from 25 ft.

Kauai Snorkeling Tours & Rentals

Bubbles Below offers advanced snorkelers adventurous summer trips to Niihau. This is great snorkeling for seaworthy, open-water swimmers in good physical condition. Snorkelers join the scuba dive boats. Board at the Port Allen small boat harbor. ☎ 866-524-6268 or 808-332-7333. E-mail: kaimanu@aloha.net. Website: http:www.bubblesbelowkauai.com.

Sea Turtle

Courtesy Sea Fun Kauai

Snorkel Bob's has two locations on Kauai. **Snorkel Bob's Kapaa,** 4-734 Kuhio Hwy., Kapaa, HI. ☎ 808-823-9433. And **Snorkel Bob's Koloa,** 3236 Poipu Rd., Koala, HI. 808-742-2206. (See Snorkel Bob's Kona)

Seafun's staff includes a marine biologist who accompanies snorkelers to shore-entry sites. Passenger vans pick you up at your hotel and transport you to the sites. Ages 5 and up welcome. E-mail: tours@gte.net. ☎ 800-452-1113 or 808-245-4888. Web: http:www.alohakauaitours.com/seafun/tours@gte.net.

Where to Stay on Kauai

For Kauai resorts,condos and other accommodations ☎ 800-245-2824. Websites: www.kauaivisitorsbureau.com or www.gohawaii.com

Sheraton Kauai features 413 rooms and suites, all no taller than four stories high. The resort offers a children's program, spa, fitness center, beach activities center and all amenities. ☎ 866-500-8313 or 808-742-1661. Located at 2440 Hoonani Road, Poipu Beach.

Poipu Kai Resort features 350 condo units, health club, spa, tennis, tv. One-, two-, three- and four-bedroom rates are available by the week, month or season. Low to moderate. ☎ 800-688-2254

Poipu Shores rents oceanfront studios, one- and two-bedroom units. Near restaurants and shopping. Moderate. ☎ 800-367-5004

Hyatt Regency Kauai Resort & Spa offers 600 deluxe oceanfront rooms, shops, restaurants, golf, beach, lagoon, play ground,river pools and spa. ☎ 808-742-1234, fax 808-742-1557. E-mail: info@kauai-hyatt.com.

Additional Information

All-expense packages including airfare can simplify planning your trip to Hawaii and save you quite a bit of money. Several major airlines fly into Honolulu International Airport from all mainland cities in the United States. **Note:** Snorkelers should use a water-resistant sun screen with a high sun protection factor (SAF) rating to prevent painful sunburn. Opaque shirts will protect your back.

See your travel agent or call 800-GO-HAWAII. Write to Hawaii Visitors Bureau, 2270 Kalakaua Avenue, Honolulu, Hawaii 96815. Website: www.gohawaii.com.

Honduras
The Bay Islands

Located between 12 and 40 miles off the coast of Honduras, the Bay Islands (*Las Islas de la Bahia*) serve as a remote outpost set in the middle of the world's second largest barrier reef.

Roatan, the largest of the 70-island chain, is the most populated, with 30,000 residents, and the most developed. It is where you'll find the most dive resorts and creature comforts. Guanaja, next in size, is surrounded by its own barrier reef. Third in size, and a newcomer to this resort-island group, is Utila. The Cayos Cochinos, a mini-cluster of small fishing-village islands boasts one resort on their biggest island, Cochino Grande.

The smaller islands are uninhabited or sparsely populated. Most do not have roads. Phones, faxes and e-mail are newcomers. Surrounding reefs are impressive with brilliantly-colored sponges and corals, towering pinnacles, walls, tunnels, wrecks and caves. Visibility and water clarity are superb. Big turtles, grouper, rays, eels, and pelagics proliferate despite an active fishing

Pictured Above: *The Bay Islands*
Photo Courtesy Honduras Institute of Tourism

industry. And novice snorkelers discover their own special paradise in the small patch reefs that dot the shallow bays throughout the area.

Plan on an entire day to reach the Bay Islands from the U.S. The islands are close to Honduras' coastline, but the mainland airport at San Pedro Sula is 160 miles away. Some flights depart La Ceiba, which is closer. Connections are often erratic. Luggage sometimes arrives late. Sand fleas and no-see-ums are a nuisance. Apply repellent beforehand.

Best Snorkeling Sites of The Bay Islands

The Bay Islands have a number of calm, sheltered areas, but the ordeal of getting to and around the islands makes it a poor choice for small children.

Roatan

☆☆☆☆☆ The reef at **West End Wall,** which encompasses **Peter's Place** and **Herbie's Place**, starts at the shore and extends out 20 yards where the wall drops off sharply from a ledge at 15 feet. Visibility often exceeds 100 ft. Fishlife is superb, with schools of horse-eye jacks, permits, and schoolmaster. Seas are calm, with an occasional light current. No spear fishing.

Guanaja

☆☆☆☆☆ **The Bayman Drop**, a wall dive off the north shore, has some shallow spots good for snorkeling. Check the current before entering the water. The top of the wall is between 10 and 40 ft. Lots of fish. No collecting or spear fishing.

☆☆☆☆ **Pavilions**, a series of pillar corals and out croppings with soft corals and sponges has hordes of fish and invertebrates. Beware of the fire coral which seems hotter here than other parts of the Caribbean. The site is off Michael's Rock around the point next to the Bayman Bay Club.

Cayo Cochinos

☆☆☆☆ **Cayos Cochinos** are a group of 13 small islands deemed a Biological Reserve and managed, in part, by the Smithsonian Institution to conduct a scientific study of the reef. The park is patrolled by park rangers. Snorkeling from the shore or by boat is outstanding.

Utila

☆☆☆☆☆ **Utila**, fringed by yet-unnamed virgin reefs and canyons, offers some of the best shore diving in the Caribbean. Wildlife is exceptional with turtles, eagle rays, southern sting rays and tropicals. Offshore sites are a 15-to-45 minute boat ride. Shore dive areas sit about 150 yards out.

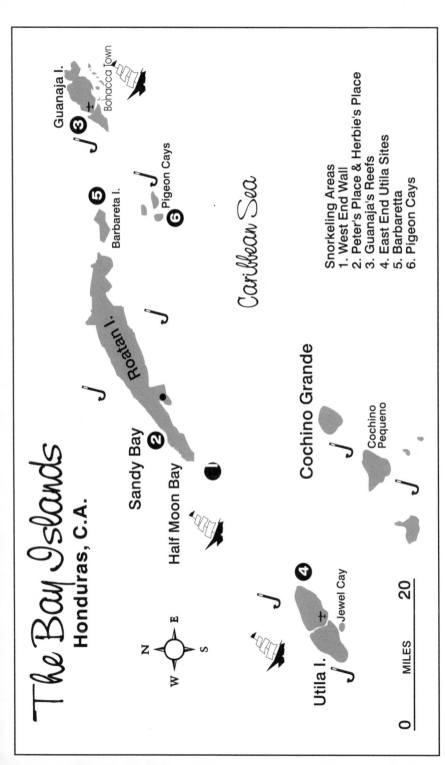

The Bay Islands
Honduras, C.A.

Guanaja I.
Bonacca Town
Barbareta I.
Pigeon Cays
Roatan I.
Sandy Bay
Half Moon Bay

Cochino Grande
Cochino Pequeno
Jewel Cay
Utila I.

Caribbean Sea

N
E
S
W

0   MILES   20

Snorkeling Areas
1. West End Wall
2. Peter's Place & Herbie's Place
3. Guanaja's Reefs
4. East End Utila Sites
5. Barbaretta
6. Pigeon Cays

Barbaretta

✰✰✰ **Barbaretta Wall** off Barbaretta island, a favorite snorkeling- picnic spot between Guanaja and Roatan, features a wonderland of barrel sponges and soft corals. The wall stretches for a mile.

Pigeon Cays

✰✰✰✰ **Pigeon Cays** are a small cluster of islands surrounded by shallow, protected reefs, all perfect for snorkeling.

Where to Stay on the Bay Islands

Bay Island Resorts cater specifically to scuba divers and snorkelers. Most offer boat trips to surrounding reefs. Some resorts offer water-taxi service or have kayaks for getting around the bays. The main après-dive activities are fishing, bird watching and hiking. Additional accommodations are online at www. letsgohonduras.com.

Roatan

Anthony's Key Resort features rustic cabins. No beach, but the Institute for Marine Sciences is on the grounds and features dolphin swims. Snorkelers join scuba divers on reef trips. ☎ 800-227-3483, or 954-929-0090. E-mail: akr@gate.net Website: www.anthonyskey.com.

Bay Islands Beach Resort on Sandy Bay, offers a snorkel package for everyone from a beginning swimmer to the most advanced diver. Courses include reef ecology, fish identification and dive boat tours. Or explore on your own. Shallow reefs and lagoons are a short swim from shore. Outlying Spooky Channel has a new marked snorkeling trail maintained by the resort.

Guest rooms vary from an estate house to villas or a lodge along six acres of beachfront property on the northwest shore of Roatan. Dive shop, bar and grill. All rooms are air conditioned with private bath. Some rooms offer disabled guests roll-in showers and grab bars. Chair-friendly ramps and boardwalks connect the dive shop, rooms and bar, and café. ☎ 800-4 ROATAN or 610-399-1884, fax 610-399-5265. Website: www.bibr. com/resort.htm E-mail: bibrusa@aol.com.

Coco View Resort, on the south side, is a group of ocean side bungalows, two-story cottages and cabanas that are built over the water. Standard rooms each have one double and one twin bed. Bungalows have two rooms, each with a king size bed.

Great wall dives lie a stone's throw from the beach bar. Nearby is a 140-ft tanker wreck, Prince Albert in 25 ft of water that can be seen from the surface. Disabled access. ☎ 800- 282-8932, 800-525-3833 or 352-588-4132, fax

352-588-4158. Website: www.cocoviewresort.com, Email: ccv@roatan.com

Fantasy Island Beach Resort sprawls across its own 15-acre island off the south coast. A small bridge connects the resort to the main island. Built in 1989 by local entrepreneur, Albert Jackson, the resort's 73 air-conditioned guest rooms have phones, refrigerators, full baths and cable TV. Good shore snorkeling off the beach. ☎ 800-676-2826 or hotel direct 813-353-9511. www.honduras.com/fantasyisland. Email: fantasyisland@honduras.com.

Inn of Last Resort, features 30 large guest rooms decorated with tropical accents. All rooms are air-conditioned. Restaurant. Good shore diving off the resort's beach. ☎ 800-374-8181. Website: www.lastresort.com. Email: info@lastresort.com

The Reef House Resort touts 11 lovely cottages in two wings. All are furnished in tropical decor. Two are air-conditioned, the rest have ceiling fans and the trade winds for cooling. Decent shore diving exists off the jetty in front of the resort. ☎ 800-328-8897, hotel direct 504-45-2142. Website: www.reef houseresort.com. Email: reefdiving@aol.com.

Playa Miguel Beach House Rentals comprise seven private, oceanfront homes—all relatively inexpensive. None are air conditioned, but all are quite comfortable during winter months. The reef, two walls and a shipwreck sits 100 yards offshore. Top of the reef averages 25-ft depths. ☎ 800-282-8932, direct 352-588-4132. Web: www.roatan.com. Email: info@roatan.com.

Guanaja
Posada Del Sol is a luxurious Spanish villa resort on 72 acres of oceanfront greenery and, except for two small villages, is the only developed area on the southeast shore. Handicapped access. ☎ 800-282-8932 or 352-588-4132; E-mail: res@roatan.com. Website: www.roatan.com.

Utila
Laguna Beach Resort offers rustic, air-conditioned bungalows perched at the water's edge. An impressive fringing coral reef lies about 150 yards off shore. The dock takes you half-way there. Kayaks. ☎ 800-282-8932 1800-66-UTILA, Direct (011) 504-445-3239. E-mail: res@utila.com. Web: http://www.utila.com.

Cayos Cochinos
Plantation Beach Resort, formerly a pineapple plantation, on Cochinos Grand is a 10-room beachfront inn. Rooms are clean and simple. Great snorkeling is a giant stride off the beach. ☎ 800-282-8932, Write to 8582 Katy Freeway, Suite 118, Houston TX 77024. E-mail:res@roatan.com. If

your flight in arrives after 4:00 pm or departs before 8:00 am on departure, an overnight on the mainland will be necessary.

Travel Tips

Getting There: The best days to travel are Friday and Saturday. From Miami—American Airlines (☎800-433-7300) has daily flights to San Pedro Sula, Honduras. From Houston: Continental Airlines to San Pedro Sula with a stop in Tegucigalpa. Isleña Airlines flies to the Bay Islands every day but

Moray Eel
Copyright © 2004 Jon Huber

Sunday from Tegucigalpa, San Pedro Sula and La Ceiba to Guanaja. Direct flights to Roatan from Miami, Houston and New Orleans are provided by TACA weekly. Water taxis are sent by the one-island resorts to pick you up.

Precautions: Register your cameras and electronic gear with customs before visiting Honduras. Do not bring drugs, plants or flowers into or out of the country.

Clothing: Shorts and tee shirts, jeans and sneakersLong-sleeve shirts and long pants are good for mountain hikes and protection from bugs or sunburn.

Snorkelers should wear protective clothing from the hot sun.

Electricity: Most resorts have 110 volts, but some have 220. Carry an adaptor.

For Additional Information: Contact the resorts direct, the tour operators listed under "Dive Resorts," or the Honduras Institute of Tourism, ☎ 800-410-9608. Website: letsgohonduras.com. Also www.roatan.com, hondurastips.honduras.com (click on the map to navigate this site) and bayislandsdirectory.com.

Puerto Rico

Beautiful beaches, first-class hotels and easy access from the US make Puerto Rico a favorite all-around vacation spot.

Underwater terrain is diverse, with shallow reefs off Humacao on the east coast, caves and wrecks off Aguadilla on the west coast, and dramatic walls at The Great Trench which starts in the Virgin Islands, stretches the entire length of Puerto Rico's south coast and winds up at Cabo Rojo on the west coast. Marine life is exciting, with manatees in the brackish mangrove areas, pelagics at Mona Island (50 miles southwest), and all species of sea turtles at Culebra. In winter, migrating humpback whales travel the Mona Passage off the west coast. Dolphins frequent the eastern shores. Towering soft corals grow to 20 ft. Snorkeling is best around the out islands and off the east coast.

Puerto Rico's Best Snorkeling Sights
EAST COAST

Snorkeling off Puerto Rico's east coast centers around Fajardo, Humacao, and the offshore islands of Icacos, Palominos, Palminitos, Monkey Island, Vieques, and Culebra. Outstanding features include towering soft corals and abundance of fish. Many of the mainland dive sights are close to shore, but the visibility is dramatically better offshore. Shore diving is possible off Fajardo,

Pictured Above: *Flamenco Beach, Culebra*
Photo by Bob Krist, Puerto Rico Tourism Co.

but freshwater runoff near the shore clouds the water and lowers visibility. Spearfishing and coral collecting are prohibited.

Culebra and Vieques

Trips to out islands—Culebra and Vieques—take off from Humacao or Puerto del Rey Marina at Fajardo, north of Humacao. Puerto del Rey (☎ 787-860-1000) is the largest marina in the Caribbean, with 700 deepwater slips and service facilities. For ferry schedules: ☎ 787-863-4560 (Fajardo terminal), 787-741-4761 (Vieques terminal), www.travelandsports.com. If you wish to ferry an automobile you must reserve space a week in advance.

Culebra, a mini-archipelago with 23 offshore islands, sits mid-point between Puerto Rico and St. Thomas. Shallow coral reefs surround the entire area. Nearby Culebrita is a good spot for snorkeling and photos.

The main five-mile-long island, home to 2,000 people, is a National Wildlife Refuge known for its lovely white sand beaches, sea bird colonies—boobies, frigates, and gulls—and as a nesting ground for all species of Caribbean sea turtles—leatherback, green, hawksbill and loggerhead. The turtles nest from April through July. Refuge, ☎ 787-742-0115. Write: Refuge Manager, General Delivery, Lower Camp, Culebra, PR 00645.

Vieques is a popular camping island for locals and day trip for east coast divers and snorkelers. Known for its beautiful beaches, two thirds of the island is owned by the US Navy. The rest is rural.

Shallow reefs and drop offs lie within one mile of the shoreline. Many with some very shallow areas. Sea conditions, sometimes rough, vary with the wind. Swells on the leeward side average two to three ft. Vieques subsea highlights are walls, giant barrel sponges, large fish populations, and a magnificent phosphorescent bay. Beach dives are possible off the West end at Green Beach with reef depths starting at 10 ft.

Two towns, Esperanza and Isabel Segunda, serve Vieques' 8,000 residents.

Vieques is a one-hour boat trip from Fajardo or Humacao. Or by air from San Juan's international airport.

Puerto Rico's East Coast Dive Operators

The Dive Center at the Westin Río Mar Beach Resort, Rio Grande, features a Catamaran Sailing & Snorkeling Adventure Trip, with snorkeling lessons. A relaxing 45-minute sail to one of the small deserted islands off the northeast corner of Puerto Rico is followed by two hours of beach combing, swimming, and snorkeling instruction. After an extensive lunch buffet, the boat sails a short distance and anchors over the reef for about two hours of snorkeling. ☎

787-888-6000. E-mail: info@westinriomar.com. Web: www.westinriomar.com/recreation/scuba.html

La Casa del Mar Dive Center, Fajardo, at the El Conquistador Resort. Offers half-day snorkeling tours to some of the best spots. Also offers dive/sailing trips, underwater vehicle trips, and trips to Bioluminescent Bay. Through the Resort, ☎ 800-468-8365, 787-863-1000 x7919; dive shop. E-mail: lacasadelmar@hotmail.com. Website: www.lacasadelmar.net.

Culebra Dive Shop, Culebra, offers snorkeling and dive trips specifically around the Island of Culebra. ☎ 787-742-0566, 787-501-4656. E-mail: divecul@coqui.net. Website: www.culebradive shop.com

Sailing & Snorkeling Operators

Most of the sailing is from Fajardo, typically on a catamaran, with snorkeling and lunch. Destination is the cays just to the northeast of Fajardo, with the favorite being Cayo Icacos.

Caribbean School of Aquatics, San Juan, sails from Fajardo. Snorkel tours on the Fun Cat Catamaran, and dive party boat Innovation. On Fun Cat tours, non-swimmers are supplied with floats to enjoy the coral and fish with everyone. On the Innovation tour, new swimmers enjoy snorkeling with the instructors. Snorkeling equipment, lessons, and refreshments included. ☎ 787-728-6606, fax 787-383-5700. E-mail: info@saildiveparty.com. Web: www.saildiveparty.com

Castillo Tours & Watersports, Fajardo features transportation from major hotels for sailing and snorkeling trips on the *Barefoot III* and *Stampede* catamarans to uninhabited Icacos Island. Swimmers as well as non-swimmers take advantage of professional instruction in snorkeling. The catamaran anchors 200 ft offshore over a living coral reef where you can view the underwater wonders with the help of a guide. Equipment, instruction, refreshments. ☎ 787-791-6195. E-mail: reservations @castillotours.com. Website: www.castillotours.com.

Chamonix Catamaran, Fajardo. offers three- ,four- and five-hour sail/snorkel trips, all with buffet or snacks) aboard three catamarans: *Harbor Cat*, a 65ft Corinthian double-decker power catamaran; *Chamonix*, a 53ft Gold Coast catamaran; and *Wave Dancer*, a 32-ft Sea Runner. ☎ 787-885-1880, 787-885-6826. E-mail:connally@coqui.net. Website: www.snorkelparty.com.

East Wind Excursions, Fajardo has three boats sailing from Puerto Del Rey Marina: a 62-ft sailing catamaran with glass-bottom windows and water slide that visits nearby deserted islands for beach combing and snorkeling; 30-

and 90-passenger power catamarans that take snorkelers to Culebra, Bioluminescent Bay and Vieques. ☎ 787-937-4386, 787-860-3434, fax 787-860-1656. E-mail: Jayanne@eastwindscat. com. Website: www. eastwindcats.com.

Erin Go Bragh Charters, Fajardo features a 50-ft Ketch for snorkeling tours, day trips, short-term charters and overnights to *Bioluminescent Bay*. Owner operated. ☎ 787-860-4401, 787-409-2511, fax 787-863-5253. E-mail: captbill@egbc.net. Website: www.egbc.net.

Where to Stay on Puerto Rico's East Coast

NOTE: Accommodations in Puerto Rico range from large resort complexes to small Paradores—family owned and operated country inns that offer quality lodging near places of great natural beauty, historical monuments and points of interest. These inns range from centuries-old haciendas to small properties in local fishing villages, and must meet the Tourism Industry Standards to use the Paradores name and symbol. For a list of all types of accommodations contact the Puerto Rico Tourism Company, *New York* ☎ 800-223-6530, *California* 800-874-1230, Florida 800-815-7391, Canada 800-443-0266, Puerto Rico 800-866-7827, 800-443-0266 .

Accommodations listed in the sections below are near to snorkeling beaches and/or dive operators offering reef trips.

Westin Río Mar Beach Resort, Rio Grande, is a 500-acre tropical resort 45 minutes from San Juan on a lovely palm-lined stretch of Río Mar Beach, and adjacent to the lush El Yunque Caribbean National Forest. It features 600 luxurious guest rooms and suites (all with balconies), 12 restaurants, spa, fitness center, casino, two golf courses, tennis center, endless watersports, Kid's Club, and Dive Center on premises. ☎ 800-4-RIOMAR; hotel direct, 787-888-6000. E-mail: info@westin riomar. com. Website: www.westin riomar.com.

Wyndham El Conquistador Resort, Fajardo, located atop a 300-ft cliff over- looking the Atlantic Ocean and Caribbean Sea. Each of the resort's four unique environments offers delightful touches and amenities of its own: The Grand Hotel features panoramic views, luxurious bathrooms and spacious walk-in closets; the ultra-luxurious Las Casitas Village offers a Spanish-style atmosphere with private check-in, pool and personal butler; the villas of Las Olas Village are built into the side of a cliff and offer breathtaking ocean views; and the balconies of La Marina Village overlook the sea—just steps from the marina and quaint shops. 16 restaurants and lounges, casino, golf course, six pools, spa, fitness center. Scuba diving, sail and snorkeling tours, wave

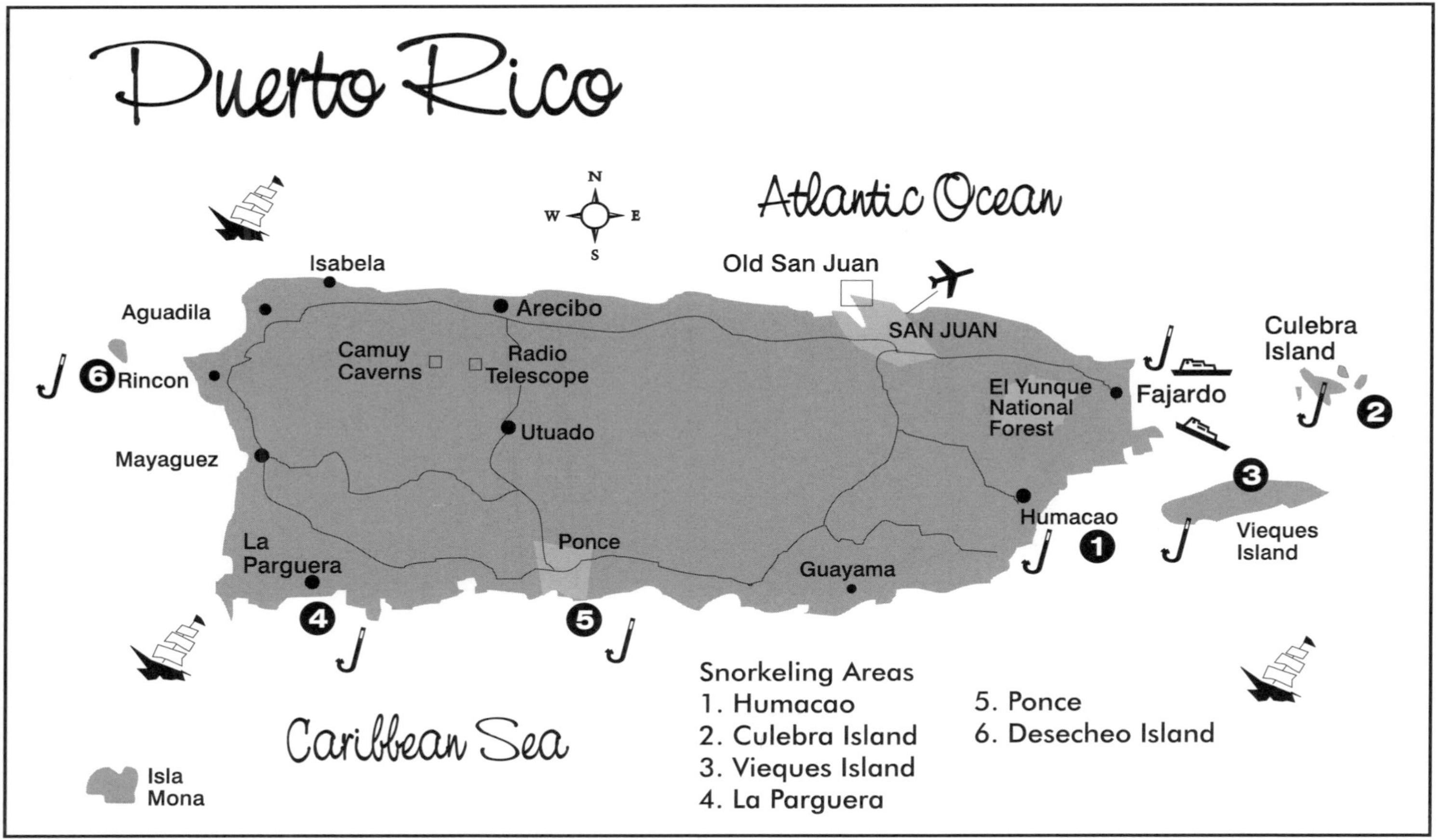

Puerto Rico

Atlantic Ocean

Old San Juan

SAN JUAN

El Yunque National Forest

Fajardo

Culebra Island

Vieques Island

Humacao

Isabela

Arecibo

Radio Telescope

Camuy Caverns

Utuado

Ponce

Guayama

La Parguera

Mayaguez

Aguadila

Rincon

Isla Mona

Caribbean Sea

N
W — E
S

Snorkeling Areas
1. Humacao
2. Culebra Island
3. Vieques Island
4. La Parguera
5. Ponce
6. Desecheo Island

running, horseback riding, board surfing. Private Palomino Island. ☎ 877-999-3223; hotel direct: 787-863-1000. E-mail through e-mail form on Wyndham website. Website: www.wyndham.com.

SOUTH COAST

Dive trips off the south coast originate in Ponce, Puerto Rico's second largest city or La Parguera, a sleepy fishing village known for its famed *Phosphorescent Bay*—one of four bio-luminescent bodies of water in the world. It is also home to the University of Puerto Rico's Marine Science Facility.

A two-and-one-half hour drive from San Juan airport, La Parguera is not yet heavily populated by tourists. Accommodations are modest, local attractions and other activities are limited. No beaches.

Best Snorkeling Sites Of Puerto Rico's South Coast

✰✰ **Ponce Caja de Muertos** (Coffin Island), Cayo Ratones, Cayo Caribe, and Cayo Cardon form a crescent barrier reef from Ponce west to Tallaboa. All are a 20-minute boat ride from Ponce. Shore dives are possible off Coffin Island—a park administered by the Department of Natural Resources. Depths are from 15 ft.

Puerto Rico's South Coast Dive Operators

Parguera Divers, located at the Hotel Parador Posada Porlamar, is a PADI and NAUI instruction facility. A three-hour guided snorkeling tour visits two protected reefs. Trips include refreshments. Mask, snorkel, and fins can be rented. ☎ 787-899-4171, fax 787-899-6023. Write: Parguera Divers, P.O. Box 3097, Lajas, Puerto Rico 00667-3097. Web: www.pargueradivers.com. E-mail: dive@pargueradivers.com.

Dive Copamarina, at Copamarina Beach Resort, in Guánica. Offers snorkeling tours off Gilligan's Island (less than a mile away). ☎ 800-468-4553; hotel direct 787-821-0505,.Web: www.copamarina.com. E-mail: info@copmarina. com.

Marine Sports & Dive Shop, in Ponce, visits Coffin Island. ☎ **787-844-6175.**

Where to Stay on Puerto Rico's South Coast

Copamarina Beach Resort, in Guánica, sits halfway between Ponce and La Parguera. A 20-acre beachfront resort on a 3/4-mile beach, it offers 70 deluxe, air-conditioned rooms, tennis court, cable TV, direct dial telephone, restaurant and pools. Newly refurbished villas. Snorkeling tours are off Gilligan's Island, less than a mile away. ☎ 800-468-4553; hotel direct,

El Morro Fort

Photo by Bob Krist for The Puerto Rico Tourism Co.

787-821-0505, fax 787-821-0070. E-mail: info@copmarina.com. Website: www.copamarina.com

Hotel Parador Posada Porlamar, in La Parguera, has 27 quiet and cozy air-conditioned rooms with TV, pool, and charming gardens. Near Phosphorescent Bay. The dive dock for Parguera Divers is directly in front of the hotel. No beach. Low rates. ☎ 787-899-4015.

Parador Villa Parguera, in La Parguera, faces Phosphorescent Bay and is next door to the dive dock. Features waterfront rooms, saltwater swimming pool, and restaurant. No beach. Low rates. ☎ 787-899-3975, 787-7777. E-mail: pvparguera@aol.com. Website: www.villa parguera.com.

WEST COAST

West coast waters are generally too rough for snorkeling, other than offshore Desecheo Island.

☆☆☆☆ **South Gardens**—Desecheo Island, 13 miles offshore, is being considered for a marine sanctuary. This popular west-coast dive features a huge fish population, immense barrel sponges, giant sea fans (six ft across) and shallow depths. Sting rays and turtles are frequently sighted. Dives are off the protected southwest tip of the island. Snorkelers will be encircled by curious fish along the rocky shore. For experienced ocean swimmers only.

Puerto Rico's West Coast Dive Operator

Aquatica Dive and Bike Adventours, Aguadilla, offers a wide variety of adventures including beach and boat snorkeling, and coastline bike/snorkeling tours. A PADI/NAUI instruction center, it also offers courses, repairs, and rentals. Boats depart from Aguadilla or Joyuda Beach. ☎787-890-6071. Web: www.aquatica.cjb. net.

Paradise Scuba & Snorkeling Center, La Parguera. Offers a full range of snorkeling tours and bioluminescent-bay trips. Instruction, certification, equipment. 787-899-7611 Idoitteau@yahoo.com

Parguera Divers, located at the Hotel Parador Posada Porlamar in La Parguera (in the southwest corner of the Island), is a PADI and NAUI instruction facility. A three-hour guided snorkeling tour visits two beautiful, protected reefs. Refreshments. Mask, snorkel, and fins can be rented. ☎ 787-899-4171, fax 787-899-6023. Write: Parguera Divers, P.O. Box 3097, Lajas, Puerto Rico 00667-3097. E-mail: dive@paragueradivers.com. Website: www.pargueradivers. com.

Dive Copamarina, at Copamarina Beach Resort in Guánica (in the southwest corner of the Island. Offers snorkeling tours off Gilligan's, as well as dive tours. ☎ 800-468-4553; hotel direct, 787-821-0505. E-mail: info@ copmarina.com. Website: www.copamarina. com

Sailing and Snorkeling Operators

Alelí Tours, Lajas; La Parguera. Catamaran sailing, snorkeling, guided tours to mangroves, coral reefs and Guánica Dry Forest. 787-390-6086.

Where to Stay on Puerto Rico's West Coast

Hotel Parador Joyuda Beach is a newly remodeled inn with 41 air-conditioned rooms with cable TV, internet, phone, private bath. Restaurant, pool, pool bar, and a nice beach. The dive-boat pier is a short walk away. Joyuda Beach on Cabo Rojo is a quaint fishing and resort community with more than 20 great seafood restaurants. ☎ 787-851-5650, 787-851-5643, fax 787-255-3750. Write to Box 18410 Cabo Rojo, P.R. 00623. E-mail: mail@joyudabeach.com. Website: www.joyudabeach.com.

Additional Information

For current information on documents, customs, airlines, condo rentals and sports operators, contact the Puerto Rico Tourism Company Offices: *In New York:* ☎ 800-223-6530; *In California:* ☎ 800-874-1230; *In Florida:* ☎ 800-815-7391; *In Canada:* 230 Richmond St. West, Suite 902, Toronto, Ontario M5V 1V6, Canada; Puerto Rico: ☎ 800-443-0266, 800-866-7827, 787-721-2400. Websites: www. GoToPuertoRico.com. ☎ 787-791-1014.

Saba

Located 30 miles off the coast of St. Maarten, this tiny, five-mile-square mountain is often visited as a day trip. The smallest of the Netherlands Antilles, Saba rises from the sea like the nose of a friendly dolphin breaking the waters surface. Its cliffs rise sharply from the blue Caribbean, culminating in mist-shrouded 2,855-foot Mount Scenery.

Tiny, white villages cling to the sides of the mountain—Hells Gate, Windwardside, St. Johns, The Bottom—linked by a road that dips and soars, curves and backtracks like a giant roller coaster. Visitors arrive at one end of the road or the other since it begins at the airport and ends at the pier.

Snorkeling is superb, though weather dependent. Most reefs and pinnacles are within 100 yards of shore—five or six minutes by boat. With little fishing, less than 1,000 divers per year and a government long-active in marine management, fish life is spectacular. Water clarity is too. The sea floor is a dense, heavy, black sand—not prone to silting or clouding the water. A constant wash of open-ocean currents supports a rich growth of soft and hard corals on submerged lava rocks and pinnacles. And, it is one of the few destinations left in the Caribbean where you can still find huge turtles and grouper.

When to Go

The best visibility is during winter, though seas can be rough outside the leeward side of the island. Summertime brings warmer 80° F water with plankton blooms and lowered visibility, but a tremendous amount of fish life. Water temperature varies from 76° in February to 82° F in October. Sea conditions vary. The island is round with no natural harbors and a very small leeward side. Seas are usually calm, but tropical storms can rule out many dive sites.

Saba National Marine Park

The Saba National Marine Park (SMP) was established in 1987 to preserve Saba's marine resources for the benefit and enjoyment of the people, in perpetuity. The project was funded by World Wildlife Fund-Netherlands, the Prince Bernhard Fund, and the Dutch and Saban Governments.

The park encompasses the entire island and includes the waters and the seabed from the highwater mark down to 200 ft and two offshore seamounts. It was set up by Dutch marine biologist, Tom vant Hof, who also established successful marine parks in Bonaire and Curacao.

Park officials maintain a system of mooring buoys and administer the Saba Marine Park Hyperbaric Facility, a four-person recompression chamber operated by a staff of trained volunteers.

Visitors to the marine park are charged a dollar-a-dive to help maintain the park and facilities. Spearfishing and collect- ing of any marine animals are prohibited. Snorkelers must not sit or stand on the corals. Anchoring on corals is prohibited. Vessels entering the park are advised to contact the marine park office on VHF channel 16 for directions on anchoring. Write: Saba Marine Park, Fort Bay, P.O. Box 18, The Bottom, Saba, N A. ☎ (011) 599-416-3295, E-mail: info@sabapark.org. Web: www.sabapark. org.

Best Snorkeling Sites of Saba

Saba's entire coastline is excellent for snorkeling. There are three locations for easily entering the water: the Fort Bay Harbor area, Wells Bay/Torrens Point area and Cove Bay near the airport. Snorkeling trips to the outer reefs can be arranged at the dive shops.

☆☆☆ **Torrens Point** off the islands northwest corner is the start of the Edward S. Arnold marked Snorkeling Trail. An outstanding shallow dive spot, depths range from five to 30 ft as you swim from marker one through 11. Black volcanic rocks, small caves and ledges swarm with fish and invertebrates. Pink sponges and lace corals grow in the crevices. Light pouring through the tunnels creates dramatic photo opportunities.

This spot is weather-dependent. Ocean swells from the north, usually during winter months, make exploring the open caves hazardous, especially the areas known as #10, The Rocks, and #9, Into The Alley. Check with a local divemaster before entering the water.

☆☆☆ **Ladder Labyrinth** is an erratic maze of coral-covered mounds off Saba's western, leeward coast. Depths are from 30 ft. The reef is vibrant with enormous lavender sea fans, swaying sea plumes and a carpet of star corals. Hundreds of crevices within the labyrinth teem with banded coral shrimp and lobsters. Schools of curious barracuda circle the area. Seas are usually calm. Good for experienced snorkelers. Boat access.

Additional boat-access, snorkeling spots include: **Hot Springs, Hole in the Corner, Core Gut** and **Tent Reef**.

Saba Snorkeling Tours & Rentals

Snorkelers join the scuba boats or go in off the shore. Sites are five to 15 minutes from the pier. Expect to sign a waiver before joining a boat trip.

Sea Saba Advanced Dive Center, a PADI training facility with two 38-ft custom dive boats tailors trips to visitors requests. Snorkelers join scuba divers

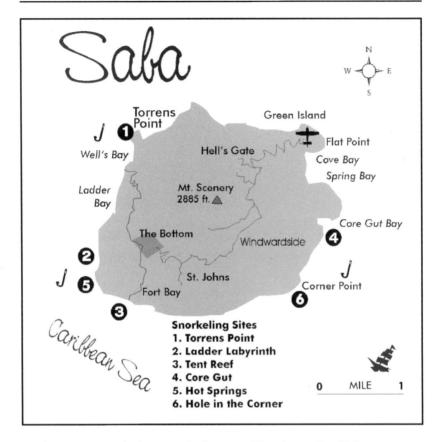

Saba

Snorkeling Sites
1. Torrens Point
2. Ladder Labyrinth
3. Tent Reef
4. Core Gut
5. Hot Springs
6. Hole in the Corner

0   MILE   1

on the noon trip which is to a shallow site. The shop offers E-6 processing, equipment sales and rentals. ☎ (011) 599-416-2246 or fax (011) 599-416-2362. Write: P.O. Box 598, Windwardside, Saba, NA. E-mail: divemaster@ seasaba.com. Website: www.seasaba.com.

Saba Deep Dive Center at Fort Bay Harbor, on the southwest side of the island, offers guided snorkeling tours. The shop is part of a dive complex in the restored old harbor masters building with a restaurant, sundeck and dive boutique upstairs. Vacation packages. ☎ (011) 599- 416-3347, fax (011) 599-416-3397. Write: Saba Deep Dive Center, P.O. Box 22, Fort Bay, Saba, NA, or E-mail: diving@sabadeep.com or sabadeep@unspoiledqueen.com. Web: www. sabadeep.com.

Saba Divers & Scouts Place "Dive Hotel" offers gear rentals, boat tours to the best snorkeling sites. Snorkelers join scuba groups on the afternoon reef trips. Hotel packages. ☎ (011) 599-416-2740, fax (011) 599-416-2741.

Write: Barbara and Wolfgang Tooten, P.O. Box 543, Windwardside, Saba, NA. E-mail: sabadivers@unspoiledqueen.com.

Where to Stay on Saba

Accommodations may be reserved through your travel agent, direct or packaged through the dive shops listed above.

Juliana's Hotel offers nine bright, spacious, and airy ocean- and garden-view one-bedroom units, one apartment, and two separate traditional Saban cottages (two-bedroom), all with full amenities. Terrace dining in Tropic's - The Natural Café. Saba residents, Franklin and Juliana Johnson, own and maintain the property. ☎ 800-223-9815, 800-365-8484, or hotel direct (011) 599-416-2269, fax (011) 599-416-2389. Write: Juliana/Es, Windwardside, Saba NA. E-mail: info@julianas-hotel.com. Website: www.julianas-hotel.com.

The Cottage Club, a quaint group of 10 Saban cottages with full kitchens, bath, cable TV, phone, fax, and two beds, is a favorite spot for snorkelers. Newly added natural stone swimming pool. Book through your travel agent or direct. ☎ (011) 599-416-2486/2386, fax (011) 599-416-2476. Write: The Cottage Club, Windwardside, Saba, NA. E-mail: cottageclub@unspoiled queen.com. Website: www.cottage-club.com.

Scouts Place Hotel, Bar, Restaurant ("The Dive Hotel") offers 10 units with bath, fridge, cable TV, and balcony, and three cottages. Tropical patio, pool, two gazebo-styled terraces for dining. Restaurant and bar, frequented by Saba locals. Dive shop. ☎ (011) 599-416-2740, fax (011) 599-416-2741. E-mail: sabadivers@unspoiledqueen.com. Web: www.sabadivers.com.

Willards of Saba is a deluxe resort set on a dramatic cliff 2,000 feet above sea level. Great if you are mixing hiking with snorkeling. The views take in the summit of Mount Scenery at 2,864 ft, the Caribbean and Atlantic Oceans and five neighboring islands. The 7 elegant rooms are spacious with private balconies. Property has a solar-heated pool, restaurant with fireplace, Jacuzzi. ☎ 800-504-9861, (011) 599-416-2482, fax (011) 599-416-2482. E-mail: willards@unspoiledqueen.com. Website: www.willardsofsaba.com.

Additional Information:

For up to date information on hotels, dive operators, customs, documents, driving, tours and airlines contact the Saba Tourist Office (011) 599-416-2231, E-mail: iluvsaba@unspoiledqueen.com. Website: www.sabatourism.com.

Caradonna Caribbean Tours offers travel services to Saba. ☎ 800-328-2288, 1-407-774-9000, fax 407-682-6000. E-mail: sales@caradonna.com.

St. Eustatius (Statia)

St. Eustatius, a tiny island about 38 miles south of St. Maarten and 17 miles southeast of Saba, has the distinction of being home to the first museum you snorkel through. As one of the lesser-known islands in the eastern Caribbean—so small and with a name so long, it is often deleted from maps. Like, Saba, Statia is often toured as a day trip via ferry from St. Maarten.

Statia's topside profile is marked by The Quill, a 2,000-ft extinct volcano, that covers most of the south end. Steep limestone cliffs interspersed with a few stretches of black-sand beach dominate the island's western coast. There are few roads, and donkeys are still used for exploring rocky inland trails. Offshore, lie the ballast stones and rubble of more than 200 sunken 17th-century, wooden trading ships, highlighted by giant golden sea fans and lush, soft corals. Most are close to shore, a few minutes by boat.

Overall, the island is perfect for snorkelers seeking a quiet haven. There is virtually no crime. Doors are rarely locked and the people are extremely friendly.

When to Go
Visibility is best in winter, though seas occasionally get rough. Summer brings calm seas, warmer water and more fish. Water temperature varies from 76° in February to 82°F in October.

Sunken Treasure Hunting
The remains and treasures of 17th- and 18th-century sailing ships are played up in many Statia dive articles, but the island's real treasures are her lovely shallow reefs. The ship's wooden hulls rotted away centuries ago. What's left are some wonderful old anchors and piles of stone ballast where small fish play hide and peek.

A few sites have, in fact, given up treasures of jewels and exotic pottery, but any charted wrecks not yet salvaged are buried in the sand and would require extensive excavation work to uncover. Plus, if a diver happens upon an intact artifact, it must go to the St. Eustatius Historical Foundation. Treasure hunting is discouraged—metal detectors are prohibited, as is "fanning" of the bottom to find artifacts. Exceptions which divers may keep are fragments of clay pipe stems or bowls and blue beads (slave beads), Uninhabited shells and broken pieces of dead coral may also be taken.

Best Snorkeling Sites of Statia
There are several snorkeling sites around Statia with depths from 3 ft. Visibility often exceeds 100 ft with water temperatures averaging 80°F.

☆☆ **The Snorkeling Museum** is an underwater cannon display established for the St. Eustatius Historical foundation at Oranje Bay in Lower Town through the Golden Rock Dive Center (see Dive Operators).

☆☆☆ **False Shoal,** outside of Kay Bay off the southwest shores, is an unusual formation of huge boulders that rise from the bottom at 25-30 ft to within a foot of the surface. Coral cover is minimal, but fish life is superb, with big congregations of tiger groupers, French and queen angels, several species of parrot fish and swarms of reef fish.

☆☆☆☆ **Outer Crooks Reef** is a pretty, shallow reef, five minutes by boat south of the city pier. The reef's ledges form a Vee shape, which might stand for variety as every imaginable hard and soft coral thrives within its bounds. Fish life, too, is diverse, with schools of smallmouth and striped grunts, black durgons, blue head wrasse, coneys, rock hinds, banded and four-eyed butterflyfish, rock beauties, blue tang, bar jacks, damsels, fairy basslets, princess parrots, queen parrots, stoplight parrots, Spanish hogfish, sharknose gobies, spotted drum, honeycomb cowfish, burrfish, and huge porcupine fish—some over three ft long.

There are also secretary blennies. It takes a sharp eye to spot these tiny fish, but if you can, try watching them for a few minutes. You'll see them dart out for food that's drifting by, then quickly shoot tail first back into their holes. They are unafraid of divers and make great subjects for close-up photography.

At night, divers have spotted copper lobsters and orange-ball anemones.

☆☆☆☆ **Outer Crooks** is a best pick for getting reacquainted with the water and your gear after a long dry spell. Maximum depth, 40 ft.

☆☆ **City Wall** is 40 yards out from shore in front of Dive Statia and the hotels in Lower Town. The rock wall parallels the shore from 75 yards south of the Golden Era Hotel to the pavilion at Smoke Alley. This was the old sea wall for Lower Town back in the days of sailing ships. Storms, erosion, a freak earthquake and wave action have since repositioned the shoreline and the wall underwater. The top is at six ft, the bottom at seven to 13 ft. In many areas the wall is folded or crumpled, forming deep crevices where fish and creatures stand guard. Reef fish are plentiful. The deepest point of the wall is 12 ft.

☆☆☆ **North Point** is an outstanding site at the north point of the island. The area is strewn with huge boulders, some up to 40-ft tall. The boulders are covered with corals, sea fans and gigantic barrel sponges—up to five ft across. Fish life is extraordinary. Huge two-ft French angels swim by. Spotted eagle rays and reef sharks cruise the area. Good for experienced snorkelers..

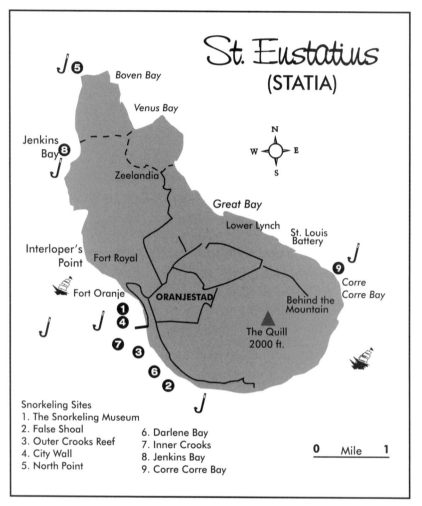

St. Eustatius
(STATIA)

Boven Bay

Venus Bay

Jenkins
Bay

Zeelandia

Great Bay

Lower Lynch
St. Louis
Battery

Interloper's
Point   Fort Royal

Corre
Corre Bay

Fort Oranje   **ORANJESTAD**

Behind the
Mountain

The Quill
2000 ft.

Snorkeling Sites
1. The Snorkeling Museum
2. False Shoal
3. Outer Crooks Reef
4. City Wall
5. North Point

6. Darlene Bay
7. Inner Crooks
8. Jenkins Bay
9. Corre Corre Bay

0   Mile   1

☆☆ **Darlene Bay** is excellent for snorkeling when the seas are calm. The dive (or snorkel) boat anchors in a sandy area offshore of the shallow reefs or will drift with you as you swim among lava outcrops and fingers. Maximum depth is 20 ft. The lava and corals come up to the surface at the bay's south end. Good fish life—turtles, sea fans, sea whips and branching corals.

It is easiest to reach this site by a five-minute boat ride. It is a most difficult hike for a shore entry, with large rocks and loose gravel to negotiate, but if you are very rugged, you can reach it by heading south along the coast for half an hour after passing the ruins of Crooks Castle.

Additional good snorkeling is found at Inner Crooks, just north of Crooks Castle (max. depth 18 ft); Jenkins Bay (max. depth 25 ft) on the northwest corner of the island; and Corre Corre Bay (max. depth 40 ft), opposite town on the Eastern shores.

Snorkeling Tours & Rentals

Dive Statia is a full-service facility offering guided reef and wreck trips. Their boats range from inflatables to a 31-ft cabin boat. Hotel vacation packages. ☎ 866-614-3491; local ,011-599-3-182435. Website: www.divestatia.com. Write P.O. Box 158, St. Eustatius, NA. E-mail: info@divestatia.com.

Golden Rock Dive Center, Oranjestad, features snorkeling trips and rentals. ☎ 800-311-6658 or (011) 599-3-82946. Website: www.goldenrock dive.com E-mail:grdivers@goldenrockdive.com

Scubaqua at the Golden Era Hotel, Orange Bay, Lowertown, Oranjestad offers boat trips. ☎ 599-3-182160. Website: www.scubaqua.com.

Where to Stay on Statia

Statia hotels add a 5%-10%service charge and 7% government room tax. Room rates range from $80 to $150 per night.

The Golden Era Hotel, Lower Town, offers 20 contemporary, air-conditioned rooms with wall-to-wall carpeting, room phones and hot and cold showers. Surfside restaurant features Caribbean cuisine. Scubaqua dive center on premises-a full service PADI facility. ☎ 800-223-9815 or 011-599-3-182345, fax 011-599-3-182445. Canada, 800-344-0023. Low rates. E-mail: goldera@goldenrock.net

King's Well offers eight lovely rooms on Orange Bay, each with a fridge and cable TV. Great views! Walk to the beach and Dive Statia. The hotel pub, a favorite après-dive meeting place, serves steaks, jaeger and wiener schnitzels. ☎ 011-599-3-182538. Low rates. Book through Caribbean Connections: ☎ 800-692-4106 or 203-261-0295. Website: www.turq.com/kingswell/

The Old Gin House is the faithful reconstruction of an 18th century building that housed a cotton gin. Constructed from old brick used by sailing ships for ballast, the hotel features a library, ocean view terrace and is within walking distance of Statia's historic district and Fort Oranje. Guest rooms have queen size beds, private baths, cable TV, air-conditioning and direct dial telephones. Website: www. oldginhouse.com. E-mail: reservations @oldgin house.com ☎ 011-599-3-182319, fax:011-599-3-182135

Additional Information

St. Eustatius Tourist Office, Oranjestad, St. Eustatius, Netherland Antilles. ☎ 011-599-3-182433, Website: www.statiatourism.com.

St. Lucia

Saint Lucia, (pronounced loó sha), the second largest of the Windward Islands, sits 1,300 miles southeast of Florida and 21 miles from Martinique.

Excellent snorkeling reefs lie off the islands sheltered southwest corner at Anse Chastanet (pronounced *ants-shas-tan-ay*) and Soufriere Bay. Within 150 ft of their shorelines lies a 30-mile-long coral reef on a shelf at 10- to 30-ft depths. Outside the coves strong currents rule out snorkeling tours. The entire area is protected as a marine park.

When to Go

Visit St Lucia from January to April, the dry season. The rainiest months are from June through November; August-September are the worst. Annual rainfall varies from 55 inches on the south coast to 140 inches in the interior. Air temperatures average 80F.

Best Snorkeling Sites of St. Lucia

☆☆☆☆ **Anse Chastanet Reef**, which lies off the Anse Chastanet Hotel, has a nice shallow area with a small cavern, sponges, large brain and boulder corals at depths of five to 25 ft. A resident school of squid are joined by goat fish, a frog fish, parrot fish, chromis and wrasse.

☆☆☆☆☆ **Pinnacles** are four spectacular seamounts that rise from the depths to within a few feet of the surface. These coral-covered subsea cliffs are a macro photographers dream, alive with octopi, feather dusters, arrow crabs, seahorses, squid, and shrimp. Cleansing currents nurture big barrel and vase sponges and a lattice of soft corals—sea plumes, sea whips and sea fans. Lots of fish. Black corals at depth.

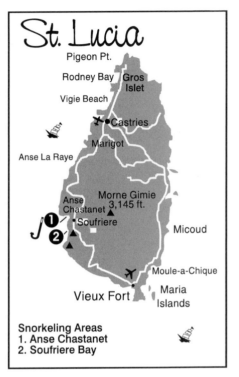

Snorkeling Tours & Rentals

Scuba St. Lucia is a PADI five-star training facility located at Anse Chastanet. The seven instructor shop offers introductory and advanced open-water and rescue courses plus specialty courses in marine life identification, scuba diving and UW photography. E6 processing and photo rentals are available. Five custom dive boats. Hotel-dive packages with Anse Chastanet Hotel. ☎ 888-GO LUCIA, (011) 758-459-7755, fax (011) 758-459-7128. Write: P.O. Box 7000, Soufriere, St. Lucia. W.I. E-mail: scubastlucia@candw.lc. Website: www.scubastlucia.com

Where to Stay on St. Lucia

St. Lucia accommodations for all budgets, some as low as US $40 per night. For a complete list of inns and hotels call ☎ 800-4-STLUCIA (800-456-3984) or 212-867-2950. E-mail: stluciatourism@aol.com. Website: stlucia.org

Marigot Beach Club Hotel and Dive Center offers 30 units from simple guest rooms to luxury villas. All with balconies, mobile phones, private bath. Resort features a gym, pool, private sundeck, water sports center, dive shop, Low to moderate rates. ☎ 800-2ST-LUCIA, (011) 758-451-4974. E-mail: mbc@candw.lc. Website: www.marigotdiveresort.com.

Anse Chastanet Beach Hotel is the island's premier dive resort and a favorite of snorkelers—the reef is right off the hotel beach. It's named for a French aristocratic families who settled on the island during the 18th century—the Chastanet family who originated in the Bordeaux region. *Anse* is antique French for Bay.

The resort is set amidst a lush 400-acre plantation, and edged by a secluded, quarter-mile-long, soft-sand beach. Some of the 49 rooms are scattered on a steep hillside, others beach side. ☎ 800-223-1108, 1-888-GO-LUCIA (465-8242). Website: www.ansechastanet.com. E-mail: ansechastanet@candw.lc. Write: P.O. Box 7000, Soufriere, St. Lucia, W.I.

St. James Club Morgan Bay Resort's 238 guest rooms sprawl across 22 green acres on secluded *Choc Bay*, a short trip from the airport. Luxury rooms have satellite TV, large balconies, high ceilings, tropical decor, direct-dial phones. Beach, freshwater pool, fitness center, restaurants. A self-contained, one-price-includes-(almost)-all resort ideal for singles, couples, and families. Supervised children's activities. Full-service diving and snorkeling excursions additional charge. ☎ 800-330-8272, hotel direct: (011) 758-450-2511, fax (011) 758-450-1050. Write: Box 2167, Choc Bay, Gros Islet, St. Lucia, W.I. E-mail: sjrmb@candw.lc. Website: www.wyndhamstlucia.com. Book yacht charter online at www.oasismarigot.com.

Additional Information:

Contact the St. Lucia Tourist Board. *In New York*, 800 Second Ave., Suite 400, N.Y., N.Y., 10017, ☎ 800-456-3984), 212-867-2950, E-mail: stluciatourism@aol.com.

In Canada, 8 King Street East, Suite 700, Toronto, Ontario M5C 1B5, Canada, ☎ 800-869-0377, 416-362-4242, fax 416-362-7832, E-mail: sltbcanada@aol.com.

In London, 421a Finchley Road, London NW3 6HJ, England, ☎ 0870-900-7697, fax 020-7431-7920, E-mail: stlucia@axissm.com. Website: www.stlucia.org.

The Turks & Caicos

Uncrowded beaches, outstanding visibility and exotic marine life beckon snorkelers to the Turks and Caicos. Eight main islands and countless uninhabited cays comprise this archipelago located 575 miles southeast of Miami, off the southern tip of the Bahamas.

The chain caps two major limestone plateaus that step down onto a wide shelf then plunge to sheer coral walls—a backdrop for passing manta rays in spring, humpback whales in winter, dolphins and sea turtles year round. Pristine patch reefs along this shallow shelf begin right offshore.

Most vacationers head for the two main resort islands, Providenciales (Provo) or Grand Turk, the seat of government, though a growing number of travelers are snorkeling Salt Cay and South Caicos.

When to Go

Mid November through April brings the driest weather. Calm seas and the best rates for hotels arrive with summer. Some resorts close down during hurricane season, July through November.

THE CAICOS

The six principal islands of the Caicos, West Caicos, Providenciales, North Caicos, Middle Caicos, East Caicos and South Caicos, and their numerous small cays offer superb snorkeling. Providenciales (Provo) is the most developed island of the Turks and Caicos.

Best Snorkeling Spots of Providenciales

Provo's snorkeling spots are weather dependent. On calm days, the north-west side offers terrific snorkeling conditions. When high winds churn up rough seas, the southern coast becomes diveable. Rent a 4-wheel drive vehicle to explore that area.

There are numerous patch reefs scattered along Grace Bay that are good snorkel sites. Most aren't very large, but all are well populated by fish.

☆☆☆ **Smith's Reef**, located north of Turtle Cove off Bridge Road at the beginning of Grace Bay, has a snorkel trail that is maintained by the National Trust. The reef trail runs along a shallow shelf through flourishing elk horn and staghorn corals, vase sponges and pink-tipped anemones. Depths run from eight to 25 ft, with the majority eight to 10 ft. Residents include turtles, parrot fish, yellow and blue-headed wrasses, queen angels and lots of juvenile fish. There is also a HUGE green moray who pops his head out from the coral now

Photos this page—Courtesy Turks & Caicos Tourism

and then, as well as stingrays, small eagle rays and nurse sharks. A large barracuda hangs out and adores getting close to snorkelers.

Beach access. If you can't find the entry point, stop in at Provo Turtle Divers in Turtle Cove for directions.

☆☆☆☆ **The Bight Reef** off Provo's beautiful North shore in the Bight area of Grace Bay lies within walking distance of Beaches Resort and Treasure Beach Villas. To find it, turn off the main road onto Penns Road. This reef, smaller than Smiths and not quite as deep—maximum depth averages 12 ft, drops down to shallow gardens of teal seafans, iridescent sponges and

corals splashed across winding rows of shallow canyons. A marked snorkeling trail maintained by the National Trust, provides haven for Nassau grouper, moray eels, sea turtles, snapper, sergeant majors, basslets, and schooling grunts. Exceptional visibility. This area is usually calm though sea conditions will vary with the wind. Beach access.

☆☆ **North West Point** at Malcom Roadstead Beach is a good spot to see squid, queen triggerfish and silversides. Strong

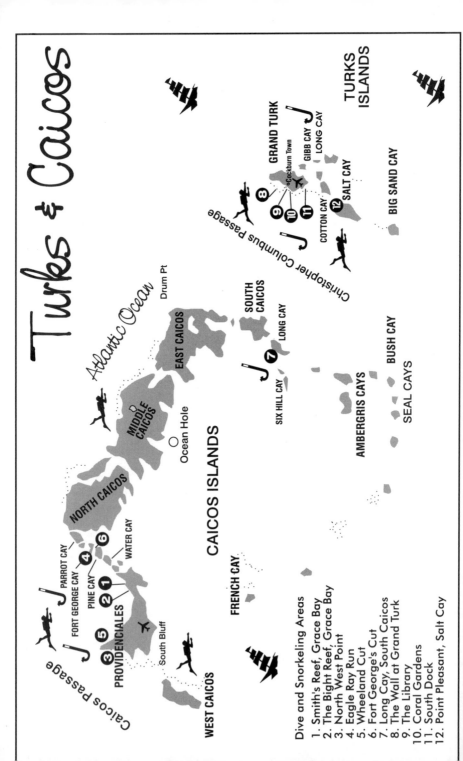

Turks & Caicos

Dive and Snorkeling Areas

1. Smith's Reef, Grace Bay
2. The Bight Reef, Grace Bay
3. North West Point
4. Eagle Ray Run
5. Wheeland Cut
6. Fort George's Cut
7. Long Cay, South Caicos
8. The Wall at Grand Turk
9. The Library
10. Coral Gardens
11. South Dock
12. Point Pleasant, Salt Cay

✰✰ **North West Point** at Malcom Roadstead Beach is a good spot to see squid, queen triggerfish and silversides. Strong swimmers can swim out to a nice patch reef about 200 yds off the north end of the beach. Thickets of elk horn coral swarm with juveniles, stingrays and a few nurse sharks. Beware of boat traffic if you venture out from the shoreline—carry a floating dive flag. This area can get big breakers during the winter months. Beach access.

✰✰✰ French and queen angels, eagle rays, turtles, spotted groupers and lobster congregate at **Eagle Ray Run**, off Fort George Cay. Reef depths range from the surface to about 20 ft. Super. Good Visibility. Boat access.

✰✰✰ **Wheeland Cut,** off Provo's northwest point near Navigation Light, provides a glimpse of small sharks, turtles, lobster, and a host of critters in a garden of dense elkhorn corals. Vase sponges and gorgonians thrive in the light current. Boat access.

✰ **Fort George's Cut** on Provo's northeast end off Fort George Cay, is perfect for beginners. Small cannons manned by small barracuda lie on the bottom. Beach access.

Provo Snorkeling Tours & Rentals

Art Pickering's **Provo Turtle Divers** offers reef trips from their Ocean Club location. Use of gear included. Friendly and helpful service. ☎ 800-833-1341 or 649- 946-4232, fax 649-941-5296. Write to Box 219,

Nassau Grouper
Photo Courtesy of Turks & Caicos Tourism

Providenciales, Turks & Caicos, B.W.I. Website: www.ProvoTurtleDivers .com. E-mail: Provo TurtleDivers@provo.net.

Flamingo Divers offers snorkelers guided reef trips aboard two 29-ft. custom Delta dive boats, NAUI and YMCA instruction, resort courses and rental gear. ☎ 649-946-4193, fax 649-946-4193. Write to P.O. Box 322, Providenciales, Turks & Caicos, B.W.I. Website: www. flamingodivers.com.

Dive Provo at the Ports of Call Village and Allegro Resort offers boat tours of Grace Bay, hotel pick up, snorkel shuttle. Photo and video. ☎ 800-234-7768. E-mail: diving @diveprovo.com. Website: www. diveprovo.com.

Where to Stay on Providenciales

Note: A few Turks and Caicos' hotels close during summer months. For additional information contact the tourist board. ☎ 800-241-0824 or 649-946-2321/2, fax 649-946-2733. Website: www.provo.net

Allegro Resort & Casino, a luxury, all inclusive 230-room hotel, features three restaurants, a health club, conference, tennis courts and Dive Provo, a full-service dive and snorkeling center. ☎ 800-858-2258 or 649-946-5555, fax 649-946-5522. Website: allegroturksandcaicos.com; email:allegro @tciway.tc.

Comfort Suites, across the way from Grace Bay offers 98 junior suites each with a sleep sofa, refrigerator, cable TV, air conditioning, safe,phone with data port. Large pool, tiki bar. Not beachfront, but near to everything. Snorkeling trips arranged at the excursion desk. ☎ 800-228-5150 or 649-946-8888, fax 649-946-5444. Website: comfortsuitestci.com.

Miramar Inn sits on a hill overlooking Turtle Cove, a small resort community where you'll find restaurants, shops, dive shops and beaches. The inn features two pools, tennis courts, miniature golf, a bar, restaurant, and sun deck. Air-conditioned guest rooms have cable TV, and phone. ☎ 649-946-4240, fax 649-946-4704. Website: www.erebus.tc; E-mail: www.miramar resort@tciway.tc

Ocean Club Resort on Grace Bay sits beachfront with luxurious air-conditioned guest rooms, restaurant, bar, TV, laundry service. Snorkeling and scuba trips. Pool. ☎ 800-457-8787 or 649-946-5880, fax 946-5845. E-mail: res@oceanclubresorts.com. Website: www.ocean clubresorts.com.

Treasure Beach Villas offers 18 deluxe beachfront suites. Near beach snorkeling sites. ☎ 649-464-4325, fax 649-946-4108. E-mail: treasure beach@tciway.tc, Website: www.provo.net/treasurebeach/.

Coral Gardens, an all-suite resort on Grace Bay, rents one- and two-bedroom, fully-equipped, oceanfront units with every creature comfort. Snorkeling is directly in front of the resort beach. 800-532-8536. 649-941-3713, fax 649-941-5171. Website: www.coralgardens.com. Email: coralgardens@telus.net.

Beaches Turks & Caicos, an all-inclusive, 380-room, beach front, luxury resort, features a water sports center and all amenities. Snorkeling trips. ☎ 800-BEACHES (2322437) or 649-946-8000. Website: www.beaches.com. Email: beaches.tci@tciway.tc.

Grace Bay Club, a posh, all-suite resort features an 18-hole golf course, sail boats, board sails and snorkeling/picnic excursions. All suites have air conditioning, ceiling fans, direct dial phones, 33 channel cable TV with VCR, a safe, and kitchens. Beautiful beach. ☎ 800-946-5757, fax 800-946-5758. E-mail: info@gracebayclub.com, Website: www.gracebayclub.com

SOUTH CAICOS

South Caicos, a true beachcomber's paradise, offers a quiet escape from telephones, television and newspapers. About the closest thing to rush-hour traffic you'll find is a herd of wild horses that roam the island's Eastern Ridge. Snorkeling on the outlying reefs and uninhabited cays is magnificent, especially off the western shores where countless coves shelter thick growths of elkhorn and staghorn corals, throngs of fish and crustaceans. Reef trips are through the Harbour Beach Resort, which has three 24-ft skiffs.

Nearby snorkeling islands, Long Cay and Dove Cay are great for picnic excursions.

Where to Stay on South Caicos

South Caicos Ocean Haven offers 24 air-conditioned rooms, restaurant, bar and terrific snorkeling nearby. No phones, no TV. ☎ 649-946-3444. E-mail: dive@southcaicosoceanhaven.com. Website: www.clubcarib.com

GRAND TURK

About 3,700 permanent residents populate Grand Turk, capital of the Turks and Caicos Islands. Cockburn Town is its principal municipality. Divers and snorkelers form the tourist population.

This tiny, seven-square-mile island is separated from the Caicos by a 22-mile-wide channel known as the Turks Island Passage. Like the Caicos, Grand Turk is synonymous with superb snorkeling. Its best spots lie along the reef fringing the west coast.

Turtle Cove Yacht Club
Photo Courtesy Turks & Caicos Tourism

Best Snorkeling Sites of Grand Turk

Good beach snorkeling is found off the The Osprey Beach Hotel, the Arawak Hotel and the Salt Raker Inn where juvenile reef fish (angels, barracudas) shells, and small turtles blast by shallow coral heads.

☆☆☆☆ **The Grand Turk Wall**, with depths starting at 20 ft, is the place to spot huge Nassau grouper, big barracuda, oversized parrot fish, rock beauties, and Spanish hogfish. Yellow and lavender vase sponges envelope broad platforms of pastel gorgonians and colonies of hard corals.

Visibility excels except during the plankton blooms. This springtime "bloom" creates a soupy cloud over parts of the reef, but also acts as a dinner invitation for a circus of manta rays to somersault in. Mini-critters such as cleaner shrimp and octopi work the crevices of the reef. A superb area for video and still photography. For advanced ocean snorkelers only. Boat access.

☆☆☆ **The Library,** (buoy 10) off Cockburn Town, rates as a favorite snorkeling spot along the wall. Huge schools of gray snapper, creole wrasse, sergeant majors, turtles, crabs and scorpion rove around mountains of beautiful red and orange corals and sponges. Depths start at 18 ft. Seas in summer are dependable flat. Winter brings swells.

☆☆ **South Dock** at the south end of Grand Turk is a virtual junkyard of lost cargo from ships inhabited by a flirty community of frog fish, sea horses, batfish, eels, and shrimp and crabs. Sponges cover the pilings. Check with the dockmaster before entering the water.

☆☆☆☆ Snorkeling trips take off to **Round Cay** and **Gibbs Cay**, two out islands surrounded by elkhorn reefs. Bright sponges and gorgonians color abound. At Gibbs, friendly stingrays greet you in the shallows off the beach. They will pose for your pictures while you pet and handfeed them.

Grand Turk Snorkeling Tours & Rentals

Cecil Ingham's **Sea Eye Diving** features boat and beach dives. Cecil has been operating on Grand Turk for several years and is known for quality service. He is also an accomplished underwater photographer. The shop offers E-6 processing and a full assortment of Nikonos cameras and lenses and excursions to nearby Gibbs Cay. Hotel packages. ☎ 800-768-0669, 649-946-1407, fax 649-946-1407. Website: wwwseaeyediving.com. Email: ci@tciway.tc.

Oasis Divers also takes snorkelers to Gibbs Cay, where they provide a beachside picnic. On the way to the island, they dive for conch which is served in a salad while burgers are cooking for lunch. Whale watching trips are offered during January, February and March when the Humpback whales pass by Grand Turk on their way to the Silver Banks to breed. Manta ray watch tours are offered in springtime. ☎ 800-892-3995, local 649-946-1128. E-mail: oasisdiv@tciway.tc. Website: www.oasis divers.com.

Where to Stay on Grand Turk

For a list of resorts and other accommodations contact the Turks & Caicos Reservation Center at ☎ 800-548-8462 or 305-667-0966. Write to: Franklin International Plaza, 255 Alhambra Circle, Suite 312, Coral Gables, FL 33134. Please note that a few small hotels close during the summer months. Room rates average $100 to $150 in summer; $105 to $225 in winter. Villas and posh resorts are higher. Check with individual resorts for current prices.

The newly renovated **Turks Head Hotel** overlooks the sea from seven guest rooms—all with phone, air conditioning and TV. Restaurant. ☎ 649-946-2466, E-mail: turkshead@tciway.tc Website: www.grand-turk.com.

The Salt Raker Inn, a 150-year-old Bermudian shipwright's home, features guest suites that open onto the sea or gardens. Air-conditioning and ceiling fans. ☎800-548-8462 or 649-946-2260, fax 649-946-2432. E-mail: sraker@tciway.tc. Website: microplan.com.

Osprey Beach Hotel (formerly the Sitting Pretty) has been totally reno-vated with modern spacious suites, restaurant, beach bar, sand beach and pool. ☎ 800-548-8462 or 649-946-2260, fax 649-946-2432. E-mail: sraker @tciway.tc.

SALT CAY
Salt Cay lies seven miles southeast of Grand Turk. This sparsely-populated island offers beach combing and snorkeling as the mainstay of activity.

Salt Cay Snorkeling
Point Pleasant, The Turks and Caicos' best snorkeling spot off the northern tip of Salt Cay, will leave you in awe with massive vertical brain corals, giant elkhorn and staghorn gardens all in 15 ft of water. You can swim side by side with big turtles, stoplight parrot fish, pompano, and eagle rays. This fabulous spot is always calm with no currents. Visibility exceeds 100 ft. Beach or boat access.

Where to Stay on Salt Cay

Castaways Beach House offers six simple, beachfront rooms for moderate rates. ☎ 649-946-6921, fax 649-946-6922. Email: castaways@tciway.tc.

Mount Pleasant Guest House has eight, recently renovated, comfortable, beachfront rooms with TV. ☎ 649-946-6927 for voice and fax Website: www.turksand caicos.tc/mtpleasant.

For Additional Information
Find up-to-date information on airlines, hotels, customs, documents, religious services, driving and more from the Turks & Caicos Tourist Board, P.O. Box 128, Grand Turk, Turks and Caicos Islands, 800-241-0824, 649-946-2321. Websites: www.turksandcaicos.tc, www.provo.net or www.caicosadventures.tc.

United States Virgin Islands

The USVI's three main islands—St. Croix, St. Thomas, and St. John—offer the snorkeling vacationer an enormous variety of reefs and dropoffs—all in gin-clear water, protected from strong winds and waves.

ST. CROIX

The largest of the USVI, St. Croix plays host to over 50,000 visiting snorkelers per year, the main attraction being Buck Island National Park—the most famous snorkeling spot in the world. Many other terrific sites are accessible by beach entry.

Best Snorkeling Sites of St. Croix

☆☆☆ **Buck Island Reef** continues to capture the hearts of Caribbean tourists despite noticeable wear from recent hurricanes and a daily blitz of snorkelers. Established by President John F. Kennedy as a national monument, this 850-acre sanctuary houses the world's first underwater national park.

The Buck Island welcoming committee includes green parrotfish, sergeant majors, grouper, rainbow-striped angel fish, and the silvery Bermuda chub. Beginners and experienced snorkelers alike can experience this underwater fantasy in an unusually safe atmosphere. The reefs of Buck Island lie only 100 yds off the coast and no trail is more than 15 ft deep. As snorkelers enter the

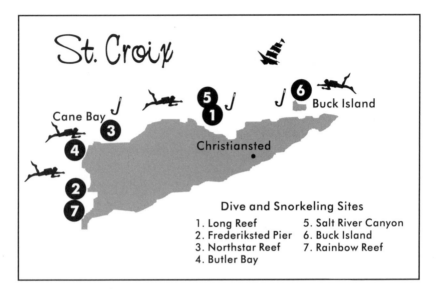

St. Croix

Cane Bay

Buck Island

Christiansted

Dive and Snorkeling Sites
1. Long Reef   5. Salt River Canyon
2. Frederiksted Pier   6. Buck Island
3. Northstar Reef   7. Rainbow Reef
4. Butler Bay

park, they are welcomed by a blue and white plaque shimmering below the surface. One marker (number 8) next to an unusual round coral full of veins inquires, "What would you name this coral?" The next marker says "You are right. Brain Coral." Arrows and signs guide the swimmer along the underwater trail and give the names of coral and other growths below the surface.

Since the reef park is strictly non-commercial, you are advised to rent gear before heading out. Whether you're coming from St. Thomas, St. Croix, or St. John, you can obtain equipment readily on all three islands. Charter boats of every description are widely available at low cost.

☆☆☆ **Long Reef,** a six-mile wide shallow area on the outskirts of Christiansted Harbor, offers a variety of reef dives. The bottom terraces gently from the shallows to 80 ft. Hundreds of caves and crevices along the reef shelter French angels, parrotfish, rays, turtles, morays, octopi, lobsters, and goatfish. A docile nurse shark makes frequent appearances. Huge brain and elkhorn coral formations prevail. Visibility varies. Boat access.

☆☆☆ **Cane Bay Dropoff** is the favorite beach dive. The reef lies about 140 yards off the beach, with depths ranging from the surface to great depths. Inside the reef, calm waters and a decent fish population make this spot a favorite of snorkelers. Light surf along the shore. Light current at the dropoff. Park along the road at Cane Bay Beach.

Additional shore entry dives are best at **Davis Bay** and **Butler Bay**. Visibility close to shore is weather-dependent and decreases when rain and wind churn the bottom. Equipment may be rented at any of the dive shops.

St. Croix Snorkeling Tours & Rentals

Cane Bay Dive Shop offers three locations—the original Cane Bay Dive Shop on the North shore, Cane Bay West in Fredericksted, and Cane Bay East in Christiansted. The North shore location offers walk-in dives to the Cane Bay drop-off. North shore: 340-773-9913. West shore: 340-772-0715; East shore: 340-773-4663. Website: www.canebayscuba.com.

Big Beard's Adventure Tours, in the Pan Am Pavilion, offers half-day and full-day sail-snorkel tours to Buck Island. ☎ 866-773-4482, 773-4482. E-mail: info@bigbeards.com. Website: www.bigbeards.com.

Mile Mark Watersports, Christiansted, offers full- and half-day snorkeling trips to Buck Island. Includes snorkel gear, instruction and a guided tour. ☎ 773-2628. Website: www.milemark watersports.com.

Captain Heinz and Captain Carl's Buck Island Tours offers guided tours of Bucks Island aboard 40-ft trimarans. Snorkeling equipment included. ☎ 773-3161. Website: www.visitstcroix.com.

N2 The Blue Scuba Diving, Christansted, offers afternoon snorkel trips aboard a custom dive boat. Includes equipment. Leaves from Frederiksted Pier and visits several snorkel spots on the west side of the Island. ☎ 1-866-712-BLUE, 713-1475. Website: www.n2blue.com.

Where to Stay on St. Croix

For a list of all types of accommodations available in the USVI, ☎ 800-372-USVI (800-372-8784), www.usvitourism.vi. In New York: ☎ 1-212-332-2222. In Canada: ☎ 1-416-622-7600, fax 1-416-622-3431.

Also, like the neighboring British Virgin Islands, the waters around the USVI are excellent for sailing, and many visitors combine a week of bare boating or live-aboard sailing with sub-sea exploring.

The Buccaneer Hotel, in Christiansted, is a luxurious, full-service 340-acre resort with 138 rooms and suites—all with patio or balcony, TV, AC. Snorkeling trips leave from the resort dock for Buck Island. ☎ 800-255-3881, 340-712-2100. E-mail: mango@thebuccaneer.com. Website: www.the buccaneer.com.

The Waves at Cane Bay offers 12 spacious seaside studios (8 with kitchenette, four with full kitchen), balconies, TV. Phone on premises. Snorkeling off the beach. Children 10 and under free. ☎ 800-545-0603, 340-778-1805. Web: www.canebaystcroix.com.

Cane Bay Reef Club, features nine spacious suites, each with full kitchen, bedroom, bath, living room (with futon), and balcony . Pool. Restaurant and bar. Children 18 and under stay free. ☎ 800-253-8534, 340-778-2966. Web: www.canebay.com.

ST. JOHN

St. John, the smallest and most verdant of the USVI, is the best for snorkeling and beach-front camping. Two-thirds of the 28-square-mile island and most of its stunning shoreline comprise the Virgin Islands National Park—part of the US National Park system.

Best Snorkeling Sites of St. John

☆☆☆ **Trunk Bay** on the islands north shore has a clearly marked underwater trail, with abundant soft and hard corals, yellowtail, damsel fish, and occasional turtles. The shallow reef sits just off beautiful Trunk Bay Beach, a great setting for vacation snapshots. Average depths: 10 to 15 ft.

☆☆☆ **Salt Pond Bay**, at the southeast end, is never crowded and is blessed with ample shade trees. Coral reefs stretch from both points of the Bay, offering snorkelers a full day's worth of adventure. Many fish and marine animals make their home here.

☆☆☆ **Chocolate Hole**, located at the east side of the mouth of Chocolate Bay, is distinguished by several rocks sticking up out of the water. The reef sits to the west of these. Depths run from four to 15 ft. Hordes of fish, including grunts, squirrelfish, blue chromis, parrot fish, rays, and turtles wander about. Seas are usually very calm unless the wind is from the south. Good for all levels.

☆☆ **Waterlemon Cay National Park** offers terrific fish watching for experienced swimmers. To get there, drive to Annaberg Sugarmill ruins, park and hike down the road to the beach (1/2 mile). Swim along the east side of the bay to Waterlemon Cay. There are loads of big Caribbean starfish in the sand and walls of fish all around the island, including big yellowtail snapper and jawfish. This spot is usually calm in summer, but choppy in winter when the wind is out of the northeast. Tidal currents may exist.

☆☆ **Caneel Bay Snorkeling Trail** is limited to guests of the Caneel Bay Resort or boaters who enter from the sea, but Caneel Bay's main beach is open to the public and offers some nice fish watching.

☆ **Francis Bay** is easiest to access by boat, but you can reach it by driving to the Annaberg Sugar Mill, then left to Francis Bay. The last stretch of road is gravel and dirt. Rocks, corals, and plenty of fish.

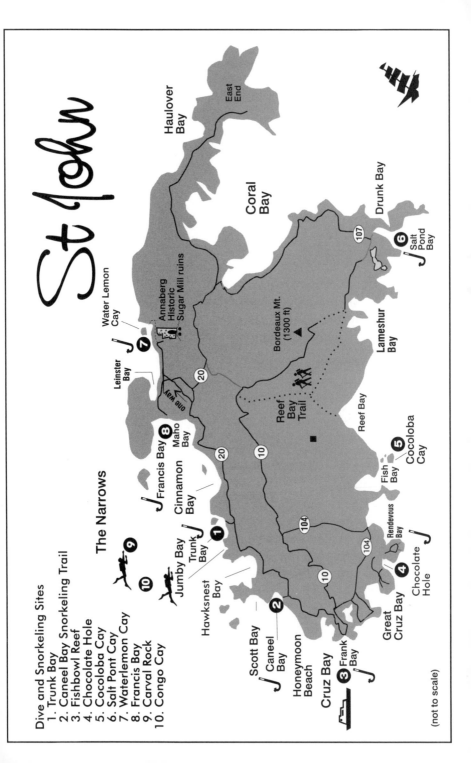

St John

Dive and Snorkeling Sites
1. Trunk Bay
2. Caneel Bay Snorkeling Trail
3. Fishbowl Reef
4. Chocolate Hole
5. Cocoloba Cay
6. Salt Pont Cay
7. Waterlemon Cay
8. Francis Bay
9. Carval Rock
10. Congo Cay

(not to scale)

Haulover Bay
East End
Coral Bay
Drunk Bay
Salt Pond Bay ⑥
Lameshur Bay
Bordeaux Mt. (1300 ft)
Water Lemon Cay
Annaberg Historic Sugar Mill ruins
⑦
Leinster Bay
one way
20
Reef Bay Trail
Reef Bay
Francis Bay ⑧
Maho Bay
The Narrows
⑨
⑩
Fish Bay
Cocoloba Cay ⑤
20
Cinnamon Bay
10
107
Jumby Bay
Trunk Bay ①
Hawksnest Bay
104
Rendevous Bay
Scott Bay
Caneel Bay ②
Honeymoon Beach
10
Great Cruz Bay
Chocolate Hole ④
Cruz Bay
Frank Bay ③
104

☆☆ **Cocoloba Cay**, a bare rocky site attached to St. John by rock, coral, and sand, requires boat access. The east side has huge coral formations, some 15-ft high, that died long ago, but now have new coral growing on top. Large coral patch reefs exist along the west side. Depths range from five to 30 ft. Highlights are angel fish, schools of blue tang, spadefish, jacks, pompano, and an occasional shark. This area is usually rough—good only on days with the wind from the north or northeast. Experienced ocean swimmers only. Boaters should anchor about 100 yards east of the cay.

☆☆ **Fishbowl Reef**, just south of Cruz Bay, is a nice shallow dive. Divers swim along ledges sparkling with beautiful elkhorn and staghorn coral. Soft corals undulate in the shallows. Many kinds of small reef fish are found hiding in the crevices. Boat access.

St. John Snorkeling Tours & Rentals

Low Key Watersports, in Wharfside Village, Cruz Bay, offers half/full-day snorkeling trips. ☎ 800-835-7718, 340-693-8999. P.O. Box 716, St. John, USVI 00831. E-mail: lowkey@viaccess.net. Web: www.divelowkey.com.

Cruz Bay Watersports, located in Cruz Bay and at the Westin St. John Resort and Villas, offers daily snorkel trips—from half-day trips to full-day excursions to the British Virgin Islands. ☎ 1-340-776-6234, fax 1-340-693-8720. Write: P.O. Box 252, St. John, USVI 00831. E-mail: info@divestjohn.com. Website: www.divestjohn.com.

Paradise Watersports, on the beach at Caneel Bay, offers an all-day snorkeling excursion to British Virgin Islands. (Proof of citizenship required to enter BVI.)☎and fax 1-340-779-4999, 1-340-774-5295 (evening). Write: P.O. Box 1554, St. John, USVI 00831. E-mail: paradiseh20@attglobal.net. Website: www.paradisevi.com.

Catamaran Adventure St. John, at the Westin Resort and Villas, offers snorkel/sails to Jost Van Dyke, Waterlemon Cay, National Park and Cays of St. John. ☎ 340-693-8000, ext. 1832. Website: www.adventurervi.com.

Rangers at the V.I. National Park conduct snorkeling trips at Trunk Bay on Tuesdays. Not for beginners. Provide your own gear. ☎1-340-776-6201 x238 (Visitor Center).

VI Snuba Excursions, in Trunk Bay, offers SNUBA, a cross between snorkeling and scuba diving. Air tanks float on rafts on the ocean and several 20-ft air hoses provide oxygen to the swimmers below the surface. Allows adults and children as young as 8 years old to safely descend to a depth of 20 feet with the aid of a SNUBA instructor. Personalized instruction, equipment, and guided underwater tours are all provided. ☎ 1-340-693-8063, fax 1-340-779-4519. Write: P.O. Box 831, St. John, USVI 00831. E-mail: info@visnuba.com. Website: www.visnuba.com.

Where to Stay on St. John

Caneel Bay Resort offers teriffic snorkeling off seven beaches surrounding the property. Features 166 guest rooms and cottages, three restaurants, seven beaches, seven tennis courts, fitness center. Children under 16 stay free. Guided snorkel tours on request. ☎ 800-928-8889 or 888-767-3966); hotel direct: 340-776-6111, E-mail: caneel@rosewoodhotels.com. Website: www.caneelbay.com.

The Westin St. John Resort and Villas offers 282 luxury guest rooms with all amenities. Children 17 and under stay free (2 max). Good snorkeling off the beach. Gigantic freshwater pool. Cruz Bay Watersports on premises offers snorkeling trips. Adventure Tours on premises offers catamaran-snorkeling trips that include equipment and lessons. ☎ 800-808-5020, 888-627-7206 or 1-340-693-8000. E-mail: concierge.01098@westin.com. Website: www.westinresortstjohn.com.

Gallows Point Resort, waterfront, features 50 suites with kitchens, AC, balconies, views. Pool, sundecks and restaurant. snorkeling from the beach. No children under 5 ☎ 800-323-7229, 340-776-6434, E-mail: information @gallowspointresort.com. Website: www.gallowspointresort.com.

Coconut Coast Villas offers studio suites and two-bedroom villas. Kitchen, TV, AC, private balconies. Freshwater pool. Under 15 stay free with parents. ☎ 800-858-7989, 340-693-9100, E-mail: info@coconutcoast.com. Web: www.coconutcoast.com.

Caribbean Villas and Resorts offers 80 villas/condos from one to six bedrooms. Children under five stay free with parents (two maximum). ☎

Annaberg Ruins

Courtesy USVI Tourism

Trunk Bay, St. John
Photo courtesy U.S. Virgin Islands Tourism

800-338-0987, 1-207-871-1129 E-mail: caribvilla@newton line.com. St. John office: 1-340-776-6152. Website: www.caribbeanvilla.com. E-mail: caribvillas@vipowernet.net. Campgrounds

Camping/snorkeling trips are popular on St. John. Take your own gear. Or stay at a luxury campground.

Cinnamon Bay Campground offers a combination of 126 cottages, campsites, and tents on Cinnamon Bay Beach in a national park. one-half-mile-long sandy, white beach. Watersports. Board surf and sailboat rentals. ☎ 800-539-9998, 340-776-6330, fax 340-776-6458. Website: www.cinnamonbay.com. Write: P.O. Box 720, Cruz Bay, St. John, USVI 00831-0720.

Maho Bay Camps. Offers 114-site luxury camping in the Virgin Islands National Park in roomy tent-cottages surrounded by lush foliage, providing privacy. Each tent-cottage has separate sleeping area with beds, linens, towels, eating and kitchen utensils, cooler, propane stove, electrical outlets, lights, fans. Private deck. Convenient bath-houses. White sand beach. Under 17 free. ☎ 800-392-9004, 340-776-6226, Box 310, St. John, USVI 00830. Email: mahobay@maho.org.

ST. THOMAS

St. Thomas is the second largest of the USVI and site of their capital, Charlotte Amalie.

Though some beach-entry diving exists here, the prettiest reefs and clearest waters are found around the outer cays. Some dive shops offer trips to the wreck of the *R.M.S. Rhone*. Cruise ship visitors will find an abundance of snorkeling opportunities.

Best Snorkeling Sites of St.Thomas

☆☆☆ **French Cap Cay** lies well south of St. Thomas, but worth the long boat ride for its lovely shallow areas that are filled with large sea fans, lavender, orange, and yellow vase and basket sponges. Expect a light current. Visibility is often unlimited. Good for photography. Experienced snorkelers.

☆☆☆ **Coki Beach** on St. Thomas' north shore sits adjacent to Coral World, an underwater viewing tower and a lovely reef that starts at 20 ft. You swim along a sand slope amid schools of snappers, French and queen angels. The reef is also a favorite hiding place for small fish, sea turtles, and stingrays. Star coral, sponges, crinoids, and rock are characteristic inhabitants.

☆☆☆ Additional good beach snorkeling exists at **Hull Bay** on the north coast and **Bolongo Bay**, plus the resort beaches at Sugar Bay Resort, Grand Bay Palace Resort, Secret Harbor Beach Resort, Sapphire Beach Resort,

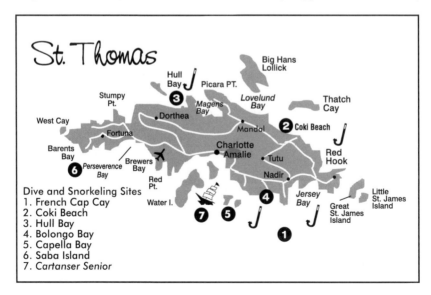

Christiansted Harbor, St. Croix
Courtesy USVI Tourism

Point Pleasant Resort, Marriott's Morning Star Resort, Grand Palazzo Resort, and Best Western Carib Beach Resort.

St. Thomas Snorkeling Tours & Rentals

Chris Sawyer Diving Center offers escorted, boat night snorkeling tours with instruction (for adults and children 10 years of age and up) from their Grand Bay Palace Resort location. Day snorkelers are welcome when accompanied by a certified diver. All gear, including photo equipment, is available for rental. ☎ 877-929-3483, 340-775-7320. E-mail: sawyerdive@ islands.vi. Website: www.sawyerdive.vi.

St. Thomas Diving Club, at the Bolongo Bay Beach Club, specializes in dive and snorkel excursions (beginner to advanced) to local and BVI sites. Equipment rentals. ☎ 877-538-8734, 340-776-2381. Write: 7147 Bolongo Bay, St. Thomas, USVI 00802. E-mail: bill2381@viaccess.net. Website: www.st-thomasdivingclub.com.

Virgin Island Ecotours offers a 2-1/2 hour guided kayak and snorkel tour through St. Thomas' Marine Sanctuary and Mangrove Lagoon—where participants can view snowy egrets, great barracudas, dwarf herrings, spotted eagle rays, jellyfish, mangrove crabs, and breeding nurse sharks—all in their natural habitat. Easy-to-maneuver, stable, sit-on-top kayaks. No experience necessary. ☎ 340-779-2155. Web: www.viecotours.com. E-mail: info@viecotours.com.

VI Snuba Excursions, at Coral World, offers SNUBA—a cross between scuba and snorkeling. Personalized instruction, equipment, and guided underwater tours are all provided. ☎ 340-693-8063, fax 340-779-4519. E-mail: info@visnuba.com. Website: www.visnuba.com.

Coral World, St. Thomas Marine Park and Underwater Observatory, offers Sea Trekkin' tours. Groups of up to seven adults and children (as young as 8) wear a helmet filled with oxygen, allowing them to walk underwater, as an expert guide leads them along an underwater trail 12-30 feet below the surface at an active coral reef. The unique helmet provides air and allows communication with the guide while keeping the head dry. No prior experience required. ☎ 888-695-2073, 340-1555, ext. 247. E-mail: rbutler@coralworldvi.com. Website: www.coralworldvi.com.

Dive World, on-site at Coral World Marine Park, offers SASY (Supplied-Air Snorkeling for Youth), for children ages six to 10. Used for snorkeling ONLY, SASY features tank regulators and non-deflatable flotation devices custom-fit for children, allowing them to swim with and observe fish and other marine life while on the surface. Children are shown how to use the equipment in shallow water and are then taken on a guided tour of a reef accompanied by an experienced PADI scuba instructor. ☎ 340-775-5971, E-mail: diveworld@islands.vi. Website: www.coralworldvi.com.

Where to Stay on St. Thomas

Bolongo Bay Beach Club offers 65 hotel rooms, 15 villa condos, and 5 inn rooms. Children under 12 free. Two restaurants, bar, tennis courts, fitness center. A Sunfish sailboat fleet, kayaks. Catamaran cruises, snorkeling, watersports, day sail to St. John. Equipment supplied. Good snorkeling off the resort's lovely beach. ☎ 800-524-4746; hotel 340-775-1800. E-mail: info@bolongobay.com. Website: www.bolongobay.com.

Grand Bay Palace Resort, an all-inclusive beachfront resort at Pineapple Beach, features 290 rooms (36 suites) with balconies. Two pools, three restaurants, fitness center, tennis courts, sauna, watersports. Guided beach snorkeling excursions with Chris Sawyer Dive Center on property. ☎ 800-635-1836 or direct 340-775-1510, E-mail: info@palaceresorts.com. Website: www.palaceresorts.com.

Marriott's Frenchman's Reef and Morning Star Beach Resorts is an award-winning, full-service beachfront complex with 504 guest rooms, including 96 at water's edge. All have TV, phones, and tropical décor. Three pools, tennis courts, seven restaurants, swim-up bars, coffee shop, health club with spa services, sauna. Under 19 with parents stay free (2 max). Snorkeling, sailing, jet skiing. Adventure Center Watersports on the resort's premises offers snorkeling tours. ☎ 800-223-6388; hotel: 340-776-8500. Website: www.marriottfrenchmansreef.com.

Sapphire Beach Resort and Marina offers 171 spacious suites with full kitchens, TV, phone, handicap access, private balconies. Two-tier freshwater pool, tennis courts, three restaurants, swim-up bar. Children under 18 free. A PADI dive shop on premises offers snorkeling tours. ☎ 800-524-2090 or 340-775-6100, fax 1-340-775-2403. E-mail: sbrsales@islands.vi. Website: www.sapphirebeachresort.com.

Best Western Carib Beach Resort on south coast Lindberg Bay, features 60 low-budget, ocean-view rooms with phones, TV, private balconies. Restaurant, pool. Children under 13 free (2 max). Watersports center on premises. ☎ 800-792-2742 or E-mail: info@caribbeachresort.com. Website: caribbeachresort.com.

Secret Harbour Beach Resort, on Nazareth Bay, the southeast Caribbean side, offers 58 beachfront suites with kitchens, TV, AC, balconies . Pool, tennis courts, café, bar. Children 12 and under stay free. Good snorkeling off the beach. Aqua Action Dive Shop on premises offers snorkeling boat trips. ☎ 800-524-2250 or 340-775-6550. E-mail: info@secretharbourvi.com. Website: www.secretharbourvi.com.

Villas

Blazing Villas, on Pineapple Beach offers 12 rooms situated in three villas, that feature patio gardens, full kitchens or kitchenettes, phones, TV, handicap access. Tennis courts, beach. Boat and shore snorkeling excursions with Chris Sawyer Diving. Guests use all of Grand Bay Palace Resort's facilities. ☎ 800-382-2002; direct: 340-776-0760, E-mail: blaze@islands.vi. Website: www.blazingvillas.com.

Cowpet Bay Villas faces Great St. James Island where good snorkeling via boat is found. White sandy beach. Kitchen, laundry room, AC/ceiling fans, cable TV, barbecue. Health club and tennis courts, snorkeling, scuba and sailing, parasailing. Gourmet restaurant on the beach. Maid service. ☎ 201-891-1450. Website: www.cvillas.com/stthomas/cowpet.

Live-Aboards Yachting Vacations

Virgin Islands Charteryacht League offers day sails (with snorkeling) and customized, extended, private, crewed yacht charters for two-200 passengers aboard sail or motorized yachts. ☎ 800-524-2061, 340-774-3944, fax 340-776-4468. E-mail: info@vicl.org. Website: www.vicl.org.

Regency Yacht Vacations, at Cabrita Point Resort, offers vacations aboard fully-crewed, live-aboard yachts from 40 to 100 ft. Charters customized to your preferences. ☎ 800-524-7676, 340-776-5950. Website: regencyvacations.com. E-mail: info@regencyvacations.com.

For Additional Information

For a complete list of airlines, extensive accommodation listings and travel information contact the United States Virgin Islands Division of Tourism ☎ 800-372-USVI (800-372-8784). Website: www.usvitourism.vi. *In New York:* 1270 Avenue of the Americas, Suite 2108, NY, NY 10020, ☎ 1-212-332-2222, fax 1-212-332-2223.

In Canada: 703 Evans Avenue Ste 106, Toronto, ON M9C 5E9, Canada, ☎ 1-416-622-7600, fax 1-416-622-3431.

In St. Thomas: P.O. Box 6400, Charlotte Amalie, USVI 00804, ☎ 340-774-8784, fax 340-774-4390.

For information about individual properties, call the St. Croix Hotel & Tourism Association (☎ 800-524-2026), the St. Croix Accommodations Council (☎ 1-340-713-9119), the St. Thomas-St. John Hotel & Tourism Association (☎ 340-77HOTEL, 340-774-6835), or the St. John Accommodations Council (☎ 800-416-1205).

Australia

The Great Barrier Reef

Visible from the moon with the naked eye, Australia's Great Barrier Reef stretches more than 1200 miles along Australia's Queensland coast, from Bundaberg in the south, to beyond Cape York in the tropical North Queensland Region. It encompasses 2900 different reefs and more than 918 rocks and islands, which drape across the Coral Sea for 350,000 square miles. Reef tourism concentrates in two areas, offshore from Cairns and the Whitsunday Islands, which cover five percent of the Marine park.

The reef was first documented by Explorer Matthew Flinders who named it The Great Barrier Reef during his 1800's survey of the Australian coast.

Sea life is impressive with 350 different types of corals, 4000 types of mollusks—including the giant clam, 1500 types of fish, 10,000 different sponges and 350 different echinoderms. Countless species depend on the reef's shelter for breeding. Humpback whales swim up from the Antarctic to have their young, six species of sea turtles breed on the shoals and manatees (dugong) make their home in the sheltered seagrass beds.

Photo above: *Deserted beach, Lady Elliott Island, Australia*

Tour boats tie up to tourist "pontoons," which are permanently anchored, man-made islands with changing areas, refreshments and a shaded place to relax between dives.

When to Go

Seasons are reversed from North America. Prime snorkeling months are July, August and September. Seas are at their calmest, with air temperature around 80° F and clear skies. The cyclone season runs from January through March.

Cost

Typical ten day to two week vacations cost less than $2000 (US) plus airfare. Of course, you can lower that by tent or RV camping in one the island parks or by staying in one of the lower cost hotels. Decent hotel rooms average $120 per night, dinner for two $68.

The Whitsunday Islands

The 150 Whitsundays make up the greatest density of islands off Australia's east coast. Some are uninhabited, some are privately owned, and 70 of them are National Parks. Many have their own protective reefs, eight of them house resorts. The other 850 islands peppered between the Great Barrier Reef and the mainland are made of sand, rock or coral.

The Coast

The mainland coast is a popular destination for bushwalks and bird watching. The Conway and Dryander National Parks shelter enormous hardwoods, massive strangler figs, and exotic wild orchids that hang in clusters from the trees. Terrain varies from deserted sandy beaches, unspoiled wetlands and national parks studded with rainforest to prosperous sugar plantations and cattle ranches. Saltwater crocodiles and manatees inhabit the marshes. Platypus inhabit the inland rivers.

Best Snorkeling Areas of the Whitsunday Islands

The best reef snorkeling lies on the outer fringes of the reef. Getting there requires taking a day or half-day cruise. Trips cost between $50(US) and $125 (US). Day trips by catamaran, motor yacht, helicopter and seaplane are offered all along the Queensland coast. If you prefer walk-in diving, head for Lizard Island, Heron Island or Lady Elliott Island, where you can swim straight off the beach over living coral. Heron and Lady Elliott also play host to nesting turtles and migrating seabirds.

☆☆☆☆ **Lizard Island**, at the northern tip of the reef lures those who can afford a higher price tag. Lizard features shore diving from several coves around the island and one of the world's finest resorts. Lizard is north of Cairns.

☆☆☆☆ **Heron Island** is our pick for the best well-rounded snorkeling vacation spot. This is one of a few areas where you can swim straight off the beach over living coral or arrange for cruises to the outer reefs. Between late November and April thousands of breeding turtles lay huge clutches of eggs on the beaches. Hatchlings can be seen scampering down the sands seeking the safety of the waters beyond the Reef. Heron is in the south end of The Great Barrier reef, north of the city of Gladstone.

☆☆☆ **Lady Elliot Island** sits on the Great Barrier Reef, 50 miles north east of Bundaberg. October to April, loggerhead and green turtles come up to lay their eggs on the beach directly in front of the resort. July to Mid October, humpback whales frolic around the coral fringe and are regularly sighted by reef walkers, snorkelers and divers in close proximity to the island. All year round, an enormous variety of fish life as well as turtles and manta rays are found in the turquoise waters.

Where to Stay

Heron Island Resort accommodates 250 guests with a choice of four types of accommodation—*Point Suites, Heron Suites, Reef Suites* and *Turtle Cabins*. All suites are serviced daily and feature tea and coffee facilities, refrigerator, ceiling fan, clock radio, hair dryer. Meals are included in the rates. Resort amenities include guest laundry, restaurant, coffee shop, pool over-looking the reef, tennis. Complimentary guided island walks introduce you to life on a coral cay. Snorkeling from the beach. Day trips to nearby Wilson Island feature a barbecue and more snorkeling sites. Hassle-free, vacations to Heron, including airfare and hotel from the US and UK , are offered by Swain Tours, an American company staffed by Australians. ☎ 800-22-SWAIN. Website: www.swainaustralia.com. E-mail: info@swaintours.com.

Combination reef and rainforest or reef and out-back vacations available. Hotel Direct: ☎ 800-225-9849. Website: www.poresorts. com.au.

Lizard Island Resort features cliff side villas overlooking Anchor Bay or Sunset Beach, two room suites with bay views or beachfront all with private balcony. Forty private rooms have king or twin beds, air-conditioning, ceiling fans, private bath, balcony, phone, fridge, mini-bar, bath robes and safes. Amenities include pool, boutique, lounge, library, laundry service, Royal Flying Doctor facilities, Daily activities. No children under six. Terrific vacations from the U.S. or U.K. are offered by Swain Australian Tours. ☎ 800-22-SWAIN, fax 610-896-9592. Website: www. SwainAustralia.com. www.poresorts.com.au.

Lady Elliot Island. Scenic flights from Hervey Bay and Bundaberg deliver guests to this island, which sports its own airstrip, at the southern most tip of the Great Barrier Reef. Lady Elliot, popular with locals, is more commercial than Lizard or Heron, but still a magnificent spot for snorkeling. The Great Barrier Reef sits just yards from the Resort with 75-ft visibility and several snorkeling sites that

Lizard Island
Photo Copyright © 2004 Maria Shaw

can be accessed directly from the beach. The resort offers suites and tents. No TV's or telephones. *The Island Suites* are beachfront apartments with private baths, spectacular views, tea/coffee making facilities, mini bar, fan and balcony. Families can opt for the Reef Units which contain one double and two bunk beds.

Tent Cabins have recently been refurbished and offer power and lighting, covered patio, bunk beds and close proximity to the beach and facilities.Resort amenities include pool, bar, cafe, a playground, souvenir and dive shop. ☎ 800-531-9222 Website: www.ladyelliot.com.au. Write to: Lady Elliot Island Resort, PO Box 3470 Tingalpa DC 4173 Queensland Australia. Direct ☎ 617-3390-8844, fax 617- 3348-8547. In Austrailia: 1800-072-200.

Cruising Vacations. Four and five day reef cruises aboard a luxurious mini-ship or a sailing yacht can be arranged through Swain Tours. ☎ 800-22-SWAIN, fax 610- 896-9592. Website: www. Swain australia. com.

Additional Information

 We found the most reliable, up to date information for trip planning from the United States or the United Kingdom from Swain Australia Tours, ☎ 800-227-9246, www.SwainAustralia.com.

The Australian Tourist Commission can be reached by mail at P.O. Box 954, Santa Clarita, CA 91380-9961, U.S.A. Website: www.australia.com. Queensland tourism at www.DestinationQueensland com.

Galapagos

The Galapagos, one of the world's most fascinating snorkeling and hiking destinations, encompasses a chain of mountainous, volcanic islands that straddle the equator 650 miles west of mainland Ecuador. Thirteen major islands, six smaller ones and countless rocks rise from the Pacific Ocean to sprawl over 30,000 square miles. More than 25% of the animals in Galapagos live nowhere else on earth. Accommodations are on small ships or live-aboard yachts that travel throughout the islands.

Inhabitants

Over millions of years the winds and ocean currents carried animals and plants to the Galapagos. These species adapted to Galapagos' rugged conditions and came to differ more and more from their continental ancestors. Today, many of the animals and plants that have evolved in the Galapagos never existed elsewhere. Different forms of the same species have evolved on different islands. Charles Darwin, observing the unique plant and animal life when he visited the archipelago in 1835 aboard the research ship *Beagle*, began to develop his theory of evolution. Darwin's visit to the Galapagos is regarded as a landmark in the history of science. He describes

Pictured Above: *Sealions on Rabida, an islet off James Island, Galapagos*

Sea Lion
Photo Copyright Marc Bernardi, Aquatic Encounters

the Galapagos as a "living laboratory of evolution" in his book *On the Origin of the Species.*

Adventurous snorkelers who explore the Galapagos experience an amazing community of sea life and birds. Fur seals, sea lions, penguins, bottle-nosed dolphin, colonies of huge moray eels, sea horses, marine iguana, red-lipped bat fish, Sally Lightfoot crabs, octopus, Moorish idols and king angelfish are abundant. Five convening ocean currents, predominated by the icy Humboldt, bring in huge schools of hammerheads, whale sharks, giant sea turtles, groupers and pelagic fish such as amber jack and barracuda. Plankton blooms attract manta and eagle rays. Orcas are occasionally spotted off shore.

Snorkelers joining the offshore expeditions should be in good physical condition and have some experience in open ocean swimming. Snorkeling from the beach areas is less taxing.

Water temperatures vary from 65°F to 75°F during August and September—the cooler months. An average water temperature of 70° F necessitates wearing a light wetsuit or lycra wetsuit for snorkeling.

Land Dwellers

Topside animals rival their marine peers in fascination. Thousands of seabird nests crowd the islands' rocky cliffs and shores. Albatross, frigate birds, blue-footed boobies and the infamous Galapagos tortoise provide endless film and video subjects. Because the islands were uninhabited when they were discovered in 1535, may of the animals had no instinctive fear of man, who they had never seen. Many are still extraordinarily fearless.

When to Go

The best time to explore the Galapagos is during December and January or between May and June. These four months bring the dol drums, calmer seas, less winds, milder currents.

Overall, the islands have two seasons. A hot, rainy season from January through May that brings the calmest seas with water temperatures hovering around 70 F. Marine life is excellent with manta rays and schooling pelagic fish sightings. The days are hot and sunny with average air temperatures in the

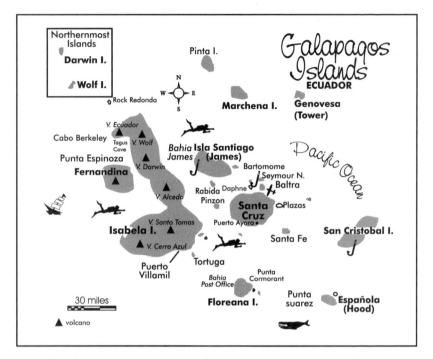

high 80s. Island tours are limited to 30 minutes, sometimes less. Sunburn is a major problem. The skies are often clear, but occasional heavy down pours are common. Many animals leave the trail areas. Some leave the islands until cooler weather returns.

June through December brings cooling winds and a light drizzle called *garua*. The thermometer hangs around the mid 70s during the day, lower at night. Island topside tours are extended. Between October and December seal pups are abundant, booby, frigate and albatross chicks can be seen. Underwater, marine life is good, but ray sightings are less frequent.

Getting to the islands

Visitors arrive by plane on Baltra Island where they are met by their guide and cruise ship or live-aboard yacht. Some of the islands have docks and some have "wet landings" that require wading through the shallows to land. Bring two pairs of sneakers and three times as much film as you originally planned.

Snorkeling

Both the snorkeling and land portions can get fairly rugged. Visibility averages 50 ft. Water temperatures range from 65° to 80° F. Visibility averages 50 ft.

Most week-long trips are to the central southernmost islands—Santa Cruz, San Salvador and Isla Santa Maria.

Sealions

Sealions are very mischievous, inherently playful and they make the rules, no exception. Expect them to charge straight at you, poke at your arm or leg, tug on your wetsuit, pull off your mask if you let them. If you don't want their full attention, try and keep some distance. During mating season the males may become aggressive. Give them space.

Park Rules

Be sure to pick up a copy of the Park Rules from your tour guide.

Note that no plant, animal, or remains of them (shells, bones, pieces of wood), or other natural objects should be removed or disturbed.

Be careful not to transport any live material to the islands, or from island to island. Check your clothing before landing on any of the islands for seeds or insects and destroy them or keep them on your vessel for disposal later on. Check your boot or shoe soles for dried mud before you leave your boat, this material will frequently contain seed and spores of plants and animals.

Exploring and Snorkeling the Islands

Both Spanish and English names are used for the islands.

SANTA CRUZ (*Indefatigable*), the hub of the Galapagos, offers the most creature comforts and tourist amenities. It is home to the Charles Darwin Research Station at Puerto Ayora where visitors can tour the Galapagos tortoise rearing pens. There is also the Tortoise Reserve where mammoth 200-year-old tortoises roam free. Small restaurants and shops offering post cards and tee shirts are at Puerto Ayora, a short walk from the research station.

Observe colonies of land iguanas and several different shallow-water birds at Dragon Hill on the northwest end of the island.

ISLA SANTIAGO (James), a five hour cruise north of Santa Cruz, is home to seals and flamingos at Puerto Egas. The flamingos feed at a salt extraction pit in a crater near the coast. Espumilla Beach on Santiago also shelters flocks of flamingos. Wet landings at Sullivan Bay. Good snorkeling among the lava formations. The fur seals will jump in to swim with you.

Land iguanas and flamingos reside on Dragon Hill. Darwin's finches, mocking birds and yellow warblers live in the highlands.

ISLA BARTOLOME is blessed with a dry landing site. Climb up a big staircase to the summit for a nice view of the area. Penguins and sea lions hang out around Pinnacle Rock. Sandy beach with good snorkeling.

Tortoise

Photo Copyright Marc Bernardi, Aquatic
Encounters

ISLA FLOREANA (Charles), one of the larger islands south of Santa Cruz and Isabela features The Barrel, a do-it-yourself postal service set up by 18th century whalers that still works! Be sure to bring a stamped postcard along to try it out. The island also has a sandy beach at Point Cormorant where sea turtles come ashore to lay eggs. An inland tidal pool shelters flamingos. Sea lions colonies haul out at nearby Loberla islet.

ISLA ESPANOLA (Hood), one of the southernmost islands, features a coral sand beach, sea lions, Sally Lightfoot crabs and several species of birds including the waved albatross, blue-footed boobies, masked booby birds, swallow-tailed gulls, mockingbirds and cactus finches. Nice snorkeling at the beach and nearby islets.

At Punta Suarez, you walk on lava rocks along a trail edged with blue-footed and masked booby-bird nests, colonies of marine iguanas and waved albatrosses. Sea lions, Darwin's finches and Galapagos doves are also on the island.

ISABELA (Albemarle) is the largest of the Galapagos Islands. It boasts a dry landing. Inland a steep, uphill climb takes you to Darwin's Saltwater Crater Lake. Penguins, flightless cormorants, boobies, pelicans and Sally Lightfoot Crabs patrol the beaches.

MOSQUERA, a tiny islet is home to a huge colony of sea lions who haul out in the sun. Give them a good deal of space during mating season and when pups are born.

NORTH SEYMOUR, a little island north of Sant Cruz and Baltra, is a good place to observe blue-footed boobies and frigate birds. Sea lions haul out on the windward side of the island.

SAN CRISTOBAL, capital of the archipelago, is rarely visited by tour boats.

TOWER (Genovesa) is noted for an incredible number of birds—frigate birds, red-footed boobies, lava gulls, doves, storm petrels, noddy terns and Darwin's finches. There is a wet landing at Darwin Bay, which was formed by a collapsed volcano and a dry landing at Prince Phillips' steps where you'll find great snorkeling.

Cruise Ships and Live-aboard Yachts

Call each operator for current rates. In addition to the cost of the cruise ship or live-aboard yacht (start at $1700) stay, expect to pay airfare from Ecuador to the islands (about $400 round trip), a $100 entrance fee to the National Park, which encompasses all the islands and a crew tip of about $100 (cash or travelers checks) per diver. A departure tax of $25 must be paid in cash.

Getting all your luggage and gear to Equador, then to the Galapagos can be laden with hazards. Visitors should buy cancellation insurance, and baggage insurance—available through most tour operators.

Land-based accommodations on the islands are limited. Snorkelers can join tours on the dive yachts, but will find less rugged snorkeling excursions offered by the government sponsored cruise ships. Airline and boat schedules always require an overnight stay on the mainland. Flights from the US arrive in either Guayaquil or Quito, the capital city.

For an enjoyable family vacation book a Galapagos vacation with **Metropolitan Touring**. They operate two ships that carry up to 90 passengers—The **Santa Cruz** and the **Isabela II**. Snorkelers combining an island to island tour will find plenty of snorkeling opportunities at the islands where snorkeling is allowed. Week long trips from Sunday to Sunday for a double costs from $3000 per person on the Isabela II, from $3,100 on the Santa Cruz. Low season—March 16 - June 14 and September 1 through Oct 31—costs less. Children under 12 with parents gets 50% off. Adventure Associates ☎ 800-527-2500 or 972-907-0414, fax 972-783-1286. E-mail: info@metropolitantouring.com. Website: www.metropolitan-touring.com.

The Oceanic Society offers naturalist-led expeditions aboard a comfortable yacht that accommodates 12 in six cabins. The tour offers ample opportunity for snorkeling. For dates and costs contact Oceanic Society Expeditions, Fort Mason Center, Building E, San Francisco, CA 94123. Trips depart Miami or Los Angeles airport. Website: www.oceanic-society.org. Email: reiremo@oceanicsociety.org. ☎ 800-326-7491 or 415-441-1106, fax 415-474-3395.

Aquatic Encounters. If extreme, rugged adventure is more your style, join a scuba diving group and venture offshore. The 90-ft motor yacht **Reina Silvia**, carries up to 16 divers and snorkelers in eight air-conditioned cabins with roomy, comfortable upper and lower bunks. Scuba divers are given priority, but snorkelers find extraordinary experiences at Wolf and Darwin

Islands, which this tour covers—like 50-ft whale sharks, and endless schools of dolphin.

Each stateroom has its own private shower and bath. The owner's cabin located on the upper deck with a king size bed is available upon request. The yacht has a swimming/diving platform aft and an extended bow pulpit for whale and dolphin watching. It also features a stereo system with semi-individual controls, cassette and compact disc players, TV and VCR. A desalinator provides all the fresh water needed. The nine-person crew includes three dive masters, a multilingual naturalist guide and a gourmet chef who bakes brownies, pizza, cookies and other treats after every dive. Meals are excellent varying from steak to fresh fish or lobster with plenty of fruits and snacks in a spacious dining room. This boat tours only when the doldrums occur—December, January, May and June—to assure divers and snorkelers a look at both the northern and southern islands. Book through Aquatic Encounters, owned by dive master and underwater photographer Marc Bernardi who is an expert on Galapagos diving The base price of $3190 per person includes four nights in a deluxe hotel in Quito, seven nights aboard the *Reina Silvia*, all meals on board, transfers to hotels and back in Quito. NOT included are airfare to Equador or the islands. ☎ 800-757-1365, pin code 1815 or 303-494-8384. Website: www. AquaticEncounters.com. E-mail: info@aquaticencounters.com. Write to Aquatic Encounters Inc. 1966 hardscrabble Place, Boulder, CO 80303. Free video available. Group snorkeling vacations can be arranged.

Additional Information:

Contact the tour operators listed—Adventure Associates ☎ 800-527-2500 or 214-907-0414, fax 214-783-1286; The Oceanic Society ☎ 800-326-7491 or 415-441-1106, fax 415-474-3395; Aquatic Encounters ☎ 303-494-8384, fax 303-494- 1202. Lindblad Expeditions also offers cruises with snorkeling. 800-425-2724. Website: www.expeditions.com.

Sharks

Sharks have generated more sensational publicity as a threat to snorkelers, divers and swimmers than any other animals, even though their bites are among the least frequent of any injuries divers sustain. Two opposing attitudes seem to predominate: either irrational fear or total fascination.

Paul Sieswerda, collection manager of the New York Aquarium, warns against taking either approach to this honored and feared species. Common sense and a realistic understanding of the animals should be used, he says, adding that "anything with teeth and the capability of biting should be treated with the same respect we give to any large animal having potential to inflict injury." The vast majority of sharks are inoffensive animals that threaten only small creatures; but some sharks will bite divers that molest them. Included are such common forms as nurse sharks and swell sharks. These animals appear docile largely because they are so sluggish, but large individuals can seriously injure a diver when provoked. Sieswerda cites an incident with a "harmless" nurse shark as the cause of 22 stitches in his hand—the result of aquarium handling.

Experience tells us that most sharks are timid animals. Fewer than 100 serious assaults by sharks are reported worldwide each year with the average being closer to 50. Less than 35% of these are fatal. More people are killed by pigs. A majority of those few fatal attacks on man are not cases of the infamous great white shark biting the swimmer in two; they involve four- or five-foot

---

Pictured Above: Hammerhead Sharks, Galapagos

sharks causing a major laceration in an arm or leg. Loss of blood due to lack of immediate medical attention is usually the cause of death. Overplaying the danger is equally unrealistic. Encounters with dangerous sharks by snorkelers on shallow reefs or shipwrecks are rare. When a shark encounters man, it tends to leave the area as suddenly as it appeared.

Sharks are largely pelagic animals found out in deep open water. Dangerous sharks are seldom found on shallow, clear water, snorkeling reefs. Most dive guides agree. They would change their line of work if they thought a huge set of jaws were awaiting them on each day's dive.

So use common sense. Avoid diving in areas known as shark breeding grounds. Don't join shark dives intended for scuba-equipped divers. Avoid spearfishing and carrying the bloody catch around on the end of the pole. If you do see a shark, leave the water. Above all do not corner or provoke the shark in any manner.

One crowd of fearful bathers in Miami clubbed a baby whale to death in the surf, thinking it was a shark. But, our favorite shark danger story comes from Florida divemaster, Bill Crawford. A young scuba diver begged to see a shark in the water. Finding one presented quite a problem. The area is largely shallow reefs and shark sightings are rare. Thinking hard, the divemaster remembered a big old nurse shark who could be found sleeping under a ledge on one of the outer reefs. She had been there for years totally ignoring the daily stampede of divers and snorkelers. So he took the young man to that spot and, as luck would have it, there was the shark. Upon seeing it sleeping under the ledge, the young diver became frozen with fear. In a wild panic he backed into a wall of coral, putting his hand deep into a hole where a big green moray eel lived. The nurse shark, true to its calm reputation, just kept sleeping. But the moray, incensed at the intrusion, defended its home by sinking its sharp teeth deep into the diver's hand.

Our favorite shark encounter, and one we highly recommend, is the "Jaws" exhibit at Universal Studios in Orlando, Florida, where people wait in long lines for the opportunity to be drenched, buffeted and threatened by a huge, relentless great white shark.

Jaws at Universal Studios, Orlando
Copyright © 2004 John Huber

First Aid for Sea Stings and Coral Cuts

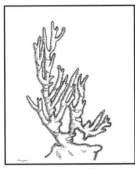

Firecoral

Art © Joyce Huber

Snorkelers and swimmers exploring coral reefs or coral-encrusted shipwrecks risk Mother Natures own version of chemical warfare stinging organisms, urchins and venomous fish.

Most stings caused by marine organisms such as fire corals, fire sponges, and jellyfish are not serious, but can become infected if not cared for immediately. Allergic reactions are also common.

On the other hand, some stings can bring excruciating pain and death within minutes. Extremely dangerous forms of venomous sea life are the Portuguese man-of-war, Pacific sea wasp (a jellyfish), stonefish, cone snail, which harpoons its prey by shooting out deadly teeth, and some species of pufferfish in the Pacific.

It is unlikely you will run into any lethal stinging sea animals while exploring, but it is a good idea to have a first-aid kit on hand for the ordinary varieties. Some household products that may help are meat tenderizer, ammonia, rubbing alcohol, antibiotic salve, and vinegar.

Coral Cuts

Coral leaves behind a hard skeleton, frequently razor sharp and capable of inflicting deep, painful wounds. Some living corals have stinging cells that make tiny punctures that rapidly disappear, but may leave itchy welts and reddening.

Fire corals, the most delicate in appearance, are often the most dangerous. All coral cuts, although usually superficial, can take a long time to heal.

The best strategy is to look, dont touch. Avoid exploring reefs or wrecks subject to heavy surges, wave action, or currents. It is easy for the unprepared diver or snorkeler to be swept or tumbled across a reef. And besides the chance of injury, you risk being fined. Many marine parks have out-lawed wearing gloves and touching coral.

If you do get cut, a tetanus shot is recommended, because live coral is covered with bacteria. Wash with a baking soda or weak ammonia solution, followed by soap and fresh water. When available, apply cortisone ointment or antihistamine cream. An application of meat tenderizer may speed the healing process, because the venom from stinging sea creatures is a protein, which the tenderizer destroys. Mix with water to make a paste and apply. The wound should be covered with a sterile dressing to prevent infection.

A commercial sea-sting kit is useful for minor coral scrapes. Follow up by seeing a doctor.

Jellyfish Stings

Jellyfish have thousands of minute stinging organs in their tentacles. Yet the stinging results only in painful skin irritation. The Portuguese man-of-war and Pacific sea wasp are exceptions: Their stings have, in rare cases, resulted in death.

Do not handle jellyfish. Even beached or apparently dead specimens may sting. Tentacles of some species may dangle as far as 165 feet. Avoid waters where jellyfish are abundant.

If youre stung, remove any tentacles and try to prevent untriggered nematocysts from discharging additional toxins by applying vinegar, sodium bicarbonate, boric acid, or xylocaine spray. Vinegar is the most effective in reducing additional nematocyst discharge.

Do not use fresh water or rub sand on the areayou may cause additional nematocyst discharge.

Antihistamines or analgesics are useful in relieving itching and redness. Meat tenderizer may help the pain. Sea sting kits also are recommended.

Sea Urchin Punctures

Sea urchins are radials with long spines. They are widespread in the Western Hemisphere. Penetration by the sea urchin spine can cause intense pain. The spines can go through wet suits, booties, or tennis shoes.

Large spine fragments can be removed, but be careful not to break them into smaller fragments that might remain in the wound. Alternately soaking the injured body part in hot, then cold water may help dissolve small fragments. Get medical attention for severe or deep punctures.

Clean the wound. Spines that have broken off flush with the skin are nearly impossible to remove, and probing with a needle will only break the spines into little pieces. Some spines have small, venomous pincers that should be removed, and the wound then should be treated as a poisonous sting. Small fragments may reabsorb. Drawing salve may be helpful.

Fish Stings

Venomous fishsuch as stonefish, zebra fish, and scorpion fishare often found in holes or crevices or lying camouflaged on rocky bottoms. Snorkelers should be alert for their presence and should take care to avoid them at all times. If you do get stung, get immediate medical assistance.